FRANCIS BORGIA

FRANCIS BORGIA
Grandee of Spain, Jesuit, Saint

by Cándido de Dalmases, S.J.
translated by Cornelius Michael Buckley, S.J.

St. Louis
THE INSTITUTE OF JESUIT SOURCES

This book is a translation of Cándido de Dalmases, *El Padre Francisco de Borja*, published by the Biblioteca de Autores Cristianos, Madrid, 1983. Chapter 7 of the present English edition ("The Ascetical Writer") was not included in the original Spanish edition.

First Edition

There is a second edition
authorized for sale only in Asia and Africa
by Gujarat Sahitya Prakash
Anand, 388 001, India

Number 11 in Series II: Modern Scholarly Studies about the Jesuits
in English Translation

© 1991 The Institute of Jesuit Sources
3700 West Pine Blvd.
St. Louis, MO 63108
Tel: 314-652-5737
Fax: 314-652-0810

Library of Congress Catalog Card Number 91-071124
ISBN 0-912422-60-2 clothbound
ISBN 0-912422-61-0 sewn paperbound

Contents

Preface

Why this new life of St. Francis Borgia? First of all because the timing seemed right. Having published my biography of St. Ignatius, *El Padre Maestro Ignacio,** in the Biblioteca de Autores Cristianos series, it seemed natural to follow up with that of his second successor at the head of the Society of Jesus. The present life of "Father Francis," as his contemporaries called him, is thus the sequel to my biography of St. Ignatius. With these two saints, so different in temperament but united by ties of mutual admiration and by the same ideal of working for the glory of God, an era in the history of the Society comes to an end. It is the age of the Society's foundation, consolidation, and expansion throughout the world.

But I also had another and more personal reason for writing this book. During my long career as a historian I had concentrated principally on the two great figures of Ignatius of Loyola and Francis Borgia. To Ignatius I had turned in my younger years as a source of personal direction for my life. Subsequently I was directed towards Francis Borgia by Joseph de Guibert, S.J., my professor of spirituality at the Gregorian University in Rome. While I was studying under him during his last year of teaching (1941-1942), which was cut short by his death, he suggested that I make a new critical edition of Borgia's *Meditations*, which he viewed as of the greatest importance because they seemed to be the first meditations to follow the course of the liturgical year and to be based on the Roman Missal. Since then, whenever I have had the spare time to do so, I have ferreted out Borgia's spiritual writings from various archives and libraries. In 1964 I published a selection of these writings as *Tratados espirituales* in the Espirituales Españoles series. (This volume omitted Borgia's meditations; apart from considerations of space, there was no place in this series of unpublished or hard-to-come-by manuscripts for materials already available in a satisfactory edition.)

But my chief reason for writing this book is my conviction that Francis

---

* Translated by Jerome Aixalá, S.J., as *Ignatius of Loyola, Founder of the Jesuits: His Life and Work* (St. Louis: The Institute of Jesuit Sources, 1985).

Borgia is a little-known and poorly understood saint. People know the story of his conversion: standing before the distorted corpse of Empress Isabel, wife of Charles V, he was supposed to have said—perhaps even did say—"Never more will I serve a master who can die." People also know that he was viceroy of Catalonia, duke of Gandía, grandee of Spain, and a key person in Charles V's court. During his life the emperor distinguished Francis with his trust; when dying he appointed him his executor. After renouncing the world Francis entered the Society of Jesus and became the order's third general. However, in all the stages of both his lay and religious life, there are many elements that warrant clarification. For example, there are still unexplored archival materials covering his tenure as viceroy in Catalonia. More ticklish problems arise concerning his policies as a superior in the Society, commissary general in Spain, and general of the order. Even during his lifetime it was whispered that, because his character had been molded in so different a milieu, Borgia had never succeeded in assimilating the Society's spirit. His first defender against these insinuations was Ignatius himself, who always displayed the greatest confidence in his noble subject, employed him in rectifying deviations within the Society, and never called him to task. Nevertheless, there is need for a study of Borgia's actual behavior as a Jesuit and as general.

My plan has been to deal with problems by going to the sources. I have had access to all the biographies of Borgia ever written, but confess to having made slight use of them—not because I underestimate their value but because I wanted to come to my own conclusions. I have no wish to deal in either panegyrics or polemics. My aim has been merely to set forth the facts concisely and clearly, so that the reader can find the information that interests him. Any judgment on Borgia I leave to the reader's discretion. I have not exhausted the resources; much remains to be done by future biographers and historians.

As an important figure in the histories of both Spain and the Society of Jesus, Borgia is well worth the long hours I have spent coming to know him. Please God I have succeeded in presenting him adequately to my readers.

Cándido de Dalmases, S.J.
Rome, January 1983

1. Family and Youth (1510-1539)

Ancestry

The saint's name was Francisco de Borja y de Aragón. At the baptismal ceremony in the collegiate church of Gandía, he was given the Christian name of Francis, in fulfillment of a promise made by his mother as she endured the pangs of a difficult childbirth. The surnames Borja and Aragón tell us that his origin was from two illustrious families: the popes Calixtus III and Alexander VI belonged to the one, the kings of the crown of Aragón descended from the other.

Borja was a place-name, attached to an Aragonese city. In all probability the family originally came from Aragón, moving from there to Valencia during the *reconquista* of that kingdom during the reign of James I ("the Conqueror") (1208-76). We find Borjas in the cities of Valencia and Játiva. The latter was the native city of the two popes who immortalized the name of Borgia.[1]

Alfonso de Borja, Pope Calixtus III, was the son of Domingo de Borja and of a certain Francina who, it seems, was a member of the Llançol family. A lawyer in the court of Alfonso V ("the Magnanimous"), Alfonso Borja had been appointed bishop of Valencia by Pope Martin V in 1429; later, on May 2, 1444, thanks to the influence of the king of Aragón, he was created cardinal. It was said that St. Vincent Ferrer had prophesied that one day he would be elected pope and would summon a crusade against the Turks. Whether this legend is true or false, we know that on April 3, 1455, two years after Constantinople fell to the Turks' might, Alfonso de Borja was elevated to the papacy and took the name Calixtus III, succeeding Nicholas V. His short pontificate (1455-58) was noted for a campaign against the Turks that halted their thrust in the Balkans.

Rodrigo Borgia, who on August 11, 1492, would be elected pope and choose the name Alexander VI, was the son of Jofré de Borja y Escrivá and Isabel de Borja, sister of Calixtus III. He was, therefore, the nephew of his predecessor. Moving to Italy, Rodrigo took a doctorate in canon law at the

University of Bologna; then, on September 17, 1456, his uncle created him cardinal. In 1457 he was appointed vice-chancellor of the Roman church; from this key post he exerted great influence on the affairs of the Roman curia. In 1468 Cardinal Rodrigo Borgia had a liaison with an unknown woman who bore him a son, Pedro Luis (1468-88); and Vannozza Catanei presented him with four more children during his cardinalate: Cesare (1476-1515), Juan (1478-97), Lucrezia (1480-1519), and Jofré (1481/82-1506).

By December 3, 1485, negotiations for the purchase of the duchy of Gandía had been settled; so on this date Fernando II of Aragón, known in history as Ferdinand the Catholic, granted the lands of the dukedom to Pedro Luis de Borja and shortly afterwards bestowed upon him the title and privileges of a duke. Prior to this date the title Duke of Gandía belonged to the royal house of Aragón. So Alexander VI's son Pedro Luis was the first Borja to become duke of Gandía. In his will, drawn up on August 14, 1487, he named his brother Juan heir to the dukedom and to his houses in Valencia and Gandía, so it was Juan who succeeded him after his untimely death on September 3, 1488.

Juan de Borja, Francis's grandfather, agreed to marry his brother Pedro Luis's betrothed, María Enríquez de Luna. The marriage agreements were signed in Valladolid December 13, 1488; but the ceremony was postponed until the month of August 1493, when the two were wed in Barcelona during the visitation of their Catholic Majesties to the city of the counts. Juan purchased a number of baronies in the kingdom of Valencia, among which was that of Llombai. In 1496 his father called him to Rome and named him captain general of the church. He then went off and engaged in battle against barons allied with the French king Charles VII, but fortune was not with him on the field. When he returned to Rome he was assassinated during the night of July 14/15, 1497. The motives behind this crime and its perpetrators remain to this day shrouded in mystery.

The second duke of Gandía left as survivors a son, also named Juan, and a daughter, Isabel. His wife, María Enríquez, was at that time only twenty-three years old. The tragedy of her husband's death caused a change in her life which can be described only as a genuine conversion. After seeing her son married in 1511, she entered the Poor Clares' convent at Gandía, the first of a number of young ladies from the Borgia family who entered that convent, including her daughter Isabel. In religion María Enríquez took the name María Gabriela; Isabel was henceforth known as Francisca.

Juan de Borja y Enríquez's first wife was Juana de Aragón y Gurrea, whom he married January 31, 1509. She was the daughter of Alfonso de Aragón, archbishop of Zaragoza, who in turn was the offspring of an amour between King Ferdinand II of Aragón and a Catalonian woman named Aldonza Roig.

Juana de Aragón died February 23, 1520, after bearing seven children during her marriage with the third duke of Gandía. That same year the duke was appointed grandee of Spain by Charles V, a distinction bestowed on only twenty-five representatives of the nobility. On this occasion five honorees belonged to the Aragonese crown, whereas the duke of Cardona was the only representative of the principality of Catalonia receiving this title.

Three of Juan de Borja's children were boys and four were girls. The firstborn, Francis, is the subject of this biography. Alfonso, the commendatory abbot of Valldigna, died before 1538. Enrique, named *comendador mayor* of Montesa in 1537, became a cardinal December 19, 1539, when he was only eleven years old. At the same time he was appointed bishop of the Italian diocese of Squillace. He died prematurely at Viterbo in 1540.

St. Francis's four sisters were María, Ana, Isabel, and Luisa, the oldest three of whom became Poor Clares at a very young age. In 1551 Ana (Sister Juana Evangelista) and her aunt, Sister Francisca, had gone to found the convent of Casa de la Reina near Valladolid; it was there she died in 1568. On January 1, 1541, Luisa married Martin de Aragón y de Gurrea, the fourth count of Ribagorza, who later became the fourth duke of Villahermosa. She lived a life of such virtue in the Villahermosa's palace at Pedrola that people began referring to her as the saintly duchess, just as they called her brother the saintly duke of Gandía. So it was that with this worthy designation she passes into history.

Francisco de Borja y de Aragón

The firstborn son of the third duke of Gandía and his wife Juana de Aragón came into the world on October 28, 1518, feast of the apostles Sts. Simon and Jude. The room in the ducal palace where he was born has since been transformed into a chapel. It is not difficult to imagine the rousing cheers from the ducal household that greeted this birth, for it assured the house of an heir. The people of the city and the towns within the duchy also participated in the jubilation; particularly happy were the Poor Clares of Gandía, who had prayed so fervently for the duchess during her labor and who had sent her a cord of St. Francis Assisi to wear about her waist during the protracted delivery.

Our information about Francis's childhood is sparse, because witnesses interviewed at the beatification process had little to say about the details of his early life, and his first biographers did not adequately fill in the missing pieces. Our best witness to his earliest years is his half brother, Tomás de Borja y de Castro-Pinós.

At the time he was summoned to give testimony at the beatification process for his brother, Tomás was archbishop of Zaragoza.[2] He testified that from a very early age Francis had shown a clear indication of the man he would one day become. Even by the time he was four, thanks to the lessons his teacher Doctor Ferrán had given him, he said his prayers with fervor and had learned the elements of the catechism. When he reached the age of reason he was given as his confessor Alonso de Avila, an exemplary canon from the collegiate church, to whom he confessed several times a year. Not much more can be added to these scanty details of his early formation. But this much is certain: from the time he was a young child, Francis's development took place in an authentically religious setting where he was given the finest education possible. The pious practice he later promoted in the Society of drawing lots for an annual patron saint had been a family custom. On one occasion during this family lottery, Francis drew the apostle James as his special patron for the year, and this was enough for him to foster a special devotion to that saint.

He had not yet reached his tenth birthday when he began to develop a liking for sermons, and these had a way of remaining vividly engraved in his memory. His brother Tomás recounted that once his grandmother and his aunt, both Poor Clares, told him to climb up into the pulpit; from there he delivered a fervent sermon on the Passion of Christ.

Very soon, even before he was ten, God tested him with the death of his mother on February 23, 1520. Then on March 13, 1523, his father signed a marriage agreement in Fréscano, Aragón, making Francisca Castro de So y de Pinós his second wife.

Twelve children were born to the duke of Gandía from this union. Among these we should single out Rodrigo, baron of Navarrés, whom Pope Paul III created cardinal December 20, 1536, and who died prematurely on August 6 the following year. The barony of Navarrés reverted to his father, who in his last will and testament granted it to another son, Pedro Luis Galcerán. Two years later, in 1540, this son was named *comendador mayor* of the Montesa military order; and in 1554, after the death of Francisco Llançol de Romaní, he became the order's grand master. Although he was only seventeen at the time, he was given this important distinction thanks to the influence of Charles V and of Pope Paul II. Some time later he became governor of Oran and, in 1590, deputy general of Catalonia, a post held by his half brother Francis some forty years earlier. As a professed knight in the Order of Calatrava, one of the three great military orders of Spain, on which the Order of Montesa was dependent, he was bound to perpetual chastity; nonetheless, he took advantage of the dispensation Paul III had granted in 1530 and married Doña Leonor Manuel, a Portuguese lady who was mistress of Princess Doña Juana of Austria's wardrobe. On the occasion of this happy event, which took place in 1558, Philip II elevated the barony of Navarrés to a marquisate. Pedro Luis died in Barcelona in 1592 during his tenure as viceroy.

The fate of two of Francis's half brothers was tragic. On February 27, 1554, while Diego was provost of the cathedral chapter of Valencia, he murdered Diego de Aragón, the bastard son of the duke of Segorbe, aided by his brother Felipe. The brothers were imprisoned in the castle of Játiva. Diego was executed by order of Philip II in 1562. Felipe, after serving some time in prison, was exiled from Spain. He went to Africa, succeeding his brother Pedro Luis Galcerán as governor of Oran. He died in 1587 while serving as governor of Messina in Sicily.

Two sisters, María and Ana, entered the Poor Clares in Gandía, where they were known as María Gabriela and Juana de la Cruz respectively. The latter went off to found the famous convent of the Descalzas Reales in Madrid; she became the first abbess of this convent in 1559 and continued to rule for forty years. Francis kept in contact with these two sisters of his, and between 1554 and 1559 he wrote one of his most beautiful spiritual tracts for the nuns of this convent, his *Meditation on the Three Powers of Christ our Redeemer*.[3]

Francis's other sisters married into the most distinguished families of Aragón and Valencia.

In addition to the Poor Clares, Tomás (1541-1610), his youngest half brother, maintained a really warm relationship with Francis. When Francis, at that time general of the Society of Jesus, made his painful return trip to Rome in 1572, it was Tomás who went along with him; and it was Tomás who assisted him at his death, as we will describe in full detail in chapter thirteen. We have already mentioned the deposition which Tomás gave as a witness at his brother's beatification process. A canon of Toledo, between 1594 and 1596 Tomás administered that diocese in the name of Albert, archduke of Austria. In 1599 he was appointed bishop of Málaga, and it was from there that he was transferred to the metropolitan see of Zaragoza in 1603. After 1606 until his death he served alternately as the diocesan administrator and viceroy of Aragón, thereby duplicating the career of St. John of Ribera, archbishop of Valencia and viceroy of the realm.

All of Francis's half brothers and sisters were minors in 1543 when their father, the third duke of Gandía, died. This event multiplied Francis's responsibilities and concerns.

The revolt of the Germanías

Twenty-three years earlier another hard blow had fallen on the house of Gandía. Called the *Germanías* uprising, this occurred after the death of the duchess in 1520. Possessing all the features of an anti-noble revolt, this movement was fanned by the bourgeoisie intent on taking over power first in the cities and then in the countryside. To some extent it coincided with the revolt of the Comuneros in Castile, but there was never any solidarity between these two separate popular movements. The revolt broke out in the city of Valencia in 1519, and in Vicente Peris it found its principal leader. When the viceroy, Diego Hurtado de Mendoza, tried to enter the city, he was challenged by a thirteen-man junta. Eventually a confrontation forced the viceroy to retreat to Játiva on June 21. Eight days later the first battle of the revolt was fought when the insurgents laid siege to the duke of Gandía's castle of Corbera. But the primary objective of the rebels was not Corbera, but rather the castle of Játiva, where Fernando de Aragón, duke of Calabria, was held in custody. On July 14, 1521, Játiva and its distinguished prisoner were captured. The rebels now moved to Gandía and in July, between the monastery of San Jerónimo de Cotalba and the city itself, fought a battle. Their ranks more than eight thousand men strong, the insurgents carried off the victory. After occupying the ducal palace and seizing between four and five thousand ducats, the rebel leader proclaimed himself lord and master of the territory. On July 26 the viceroy, the duke of Gandía, and other knights sailed from Denia, arriving in Peñíscola the following day. With them was Francis, then a boy of eleven. The viceroy sent the duke of Gandía ahead to negotiate with Castilian authorities for reinforcements. Meanwhile, the rebels did not know how to follow up on their victories. They suffered a severe setback, first at Orihuela, which was occupied and sacked on August 30, and then at Alicante, Jijona, and elsewhere, as those cities fell one after the other. On September 8 Peris made a triumphant entrance into Valencia, but the situation was really becoming more and more desperate for him and his men. After several victories the viceroy at last entered Valencia on February 19, 1522. Peris had determined to hold out to the bitter end; after his headquarters was surrounded, however, he soon died in combat. On March 4 his corpse was quartered; the cause of the *agermanados* was practically lost.

Once the storm was past, the duke of Gandía was able to go back to administering his holdings, but Francis did not return at that time to the ducal palace. His father took him to Zaragoza with his young sister Luisa and entrusted them to the care of the archbishop, Don Juan de Aragón, their mother's brother and the grandson of His Catholic Majesty, Ferdinand of Aragón. Thus what Francis's mother had directed in her will was accomplished: "And I commend to the excellent lord archbishop of Zaragoza my sons and daughters, and I assign my lord as their tutor, earnestly entreating His Excellency to take these my children and have them trained and reared in his house and court."[4]

Zaragoza, Baza, and Tordesillas

In Zaragoza the archbishop sought someone to teach his nephew grammar, music, and the use of weapons. Francis's earliest biographers place considerable importance on an event at this time which strongly influenced his life. In 1522 the youth followed the lenten series in the church of Santa Engracia. One sermon he heard was on the Last Judgment and another on the Lord's Passion; both left a great impression on his mind. Ribadeneira goes so far as to state that after hearing these sermons Francis began to lead a mortified life and embraced a contempt for the things of this world. It is certain that he seemed inclined to lead such a life from an early age. But it would be premature to date from this particular time his plan to renounce the things of this world.

Not long after he came to Zaragoza Francis made a trip to Baza, a city in the kingdom of Granada where his paternal great-grandmother lived. Doña María de Luna, widow of Don Enrique Enríquez, had a keen desire to see her great-grandson before death took her; since the archbishop of Zaragoza did not oppose these wishes, Francis and his sister Luisa traveled to Baza. Here Francis fell gravely ill. Recovery was a long-drawn-out affair. To complicate the situation an earthquake rattled the kingdom of Granada, the greatest destruction occurring at Baza itself. This meant that for some forty days the convalescent had to be nursed in a tent set up outside the city walls.

Once Francis recovered, María de Luna decided to take a step which promised to open to him the doors to the court of Castile. With the approval of the archbishop of Zaragoza, she arranged to have him sent to Tordesillas where the deranged queen Juana ("la Loca"), Charles's mother and the eldest daughter of Ferdinand and Isabel the Catholic, lived a life of forced retirement, cared for by her daughter Catherine, who was still a young girl. Charles V desired that, as long as his young sister had to put up with this isolation, she should have the companionship of boys and girls her own age. Francis was one of the boys selected for this assignment; so he bade farewell to his own sister and went off to Tordesillas, where he remained from 1522 to 1525, the year Catherine left for Portugal to become the wife of John III.

As we shall see, thirty years later, in 1554 and 1555, while he was commissary general of the Society of Jesus in Spain, Francis returned to Tordesillas to assist and console Doña Juana during the last days of her unhappy life.

By the time he returned to Zaragoza to dedicate himself to serious, uninterrupted studies, he was already fifteen. The archbishop assigned him a tutor, Gaspar Lax, a former professor of the Montaigu College in Paris with a reputation as an outstanding philosopher. Francis studied philosophy under him for two years.

All evidence indicates that during these years at Zaragoza he underwent a very serious spiritual crisis. His age, his "ruddy complexion and amorous disposition," about which Ribadeneira speaks,[5] the very freedom he enjoyed, the bad example and advice to which he was exposed—all these put his virtue in danger. If we are to look for a time in his life during which he might have committed the sins that later aroused in him feelings of confusion and repentance, we would suspect that it was during the days he spent at Zaragoza, even more than during his time at court; for according to witnesses he led a most chaste life prior to his marriage, which took place soon after he arrived there. Still, if we are to give credence to his brother Tomás's statement, which is the basis for Vásquez's and Ribadeneira's opinion, we must conclude that Francis emerged from the Zaragoza trial unscathed. In his testimony, transcribed and given at the end of the following section, Tomás affirmed that his brother was a virgin when he married. Even though we cannot know the secrets of his heart, we can well believe that such was the case. His strength to resist the seduction of evil came from the sacraments of confession and Communion which he received with frequency and devotion.

At the court of Charles V

In 1528, when he was eighteen, Francis began serving in the court of Charles V. The duke of Gandía wrote to the emperor on February 8 of that year, saying that he was sending his firstborn, to be followed by his other sons once they reached the proper age.

> Don Franciso goes to begin to serve you, so that these sons whom the Lord has granted me to give for Your Majesty's service may start to do so. Don Francisco [Francis] is coming now, as will the others when they are of age, to where they can start learning to employ themselves with their slight strength in duties in which I would wish to be employed with all the strength in the world. For I deem this the great-

est happiness I could have on my own or their behalf.[6]

It was with affection that Charles V and Empress Isabel welcomed the newly arrived Francis at their court, and there is no doubt that from the very beginning they felt for him that warmth of friendship and trust which they so often expressed during the course of his life.

As for the young courtier, he busied himself with the services entrusted to him, all the while endeavoring to round out his academic and human education. It is said that at this time he became very fond of riding and hunting, soon gaining the reputation of a good horseman who emerged victorious in jousts and tourneys. Even though actively engaged in court festivities, however, he remained faithful to his principles. No contrary insinuation ever darkened his good reputation.

In the beatification process his brother Tomás summed up his early days in the following words:

> During all the time of his youth no one ever detected in him an inclination for games or unseemly activities, but they noticed he showed a great inclination towards matters devotional, to the extent even that they feared he would leave the world. For this reason they tried to send him to the court of Castile. There he progressed in the life of perfection. Emperor Charles V and Empress Isabel took note of this and they gave him for a wife Leonor de Castro, an illustrious woman, the first lady-in-waiting to the empress and the principal mistress of her wardrobe.
>
> His qualities and all the attentions he received not only failed to make him prideful in his own eyes; rather, humbled himself with great modesty and moderation of soul. He was loved by all. Everyone trusted his integrity, so much so that, even though the ladies were always carefully watched and despite the fact that he was young and comely, there was never a door closed to him day or night. Whenever he had to hold converse with a woman he put on a hair shirt. For this reason it is believed that he arrived a virgin at the bridal bed. No one saw aught in him but chastity. He frequented the sacraments of confession and Communion often. Often too he hunted, and during the chase he would lift up his thoughts to the Lord.[7]

Married life and children

When the duke of Gandía sent his firstborn to court in 1528, he granted him half of the barony of Llombai as well as the title baron. On July 7, 1530, Charles V elevated the barony to a marquisate; from that time until Francis inherited the title Duke of Gandía in 1543, he used the title Marquis of Llombai.

It was between these dates that the marriage took place between Francis and the Portuguese lady Leonor de Castro. Leonor, daughter of Alvaro de Castro and Isabel de Meneses, Barreto y Melo, had been one of the ladies Empress Isabel brought with her from Portugal when she came to the court of Castile to marry Charles V. The empress felt a special liking for Leonor, which prompted her to take the initiative in arranging her marriage. Her choice for the match fell on the baron of Llombai. Charles V approved, although he could see that her plan would meet with some opposition from the duke of Gandía, who probably would have preferred that his heir marry a young lady from Valencia, or at least one from the realm of Aragón. As a matter of fact, the duke did offer some hesitation to the empress's choice, but finally approved the match. Charles V showed his gratitude in a letter to the duke, in which he praised him for his desire to serve him and at the same time promised a dowry for Leonor de Castro.

> Although this [marriage of your son] is something favorable to you, your house, and your son, still I accept and very much appreciate your will and resolution [to serve me] and I hope that you realize that it was more profitable than stretching out negotiations. Therefore, considering this fact and my desire to show favor for Doña Leonor de Castro, I wish to give her a dowry of eight million *maravedís* in addition to what she already has.[8]

The emperor also promised an *encomienda* of the Order of Calatrava to another of the duke of Gandía's sons.

Francis and Leonor's wedding took place in the summer of 1529. The empress appointed Francis her master of the horse, entailing a sizable stipend, and designated the marquise first lady-in-waiting to the empress. From that date on the newlyweds enjoyed a highly privileged position at court, even though Francis was not yet twenty. According to his brother Tomás's testimony cited above, there were no doors closed to Francis. For his part, he showed himself worthy of such trust.

Although less than totally spontaneous in its inception, the wedding of Francis and Leonor de Castro was not a marriage of convenience. The marquis always loved his wife, took care of her during her illnesses, and mourned her at her death.

The correspondence between Queen Catherine of Portugal and her brother the emperor indicates that, despite the panegyrics her husband's biographers have lavished upon her, Leonor de Castro had a difficult temperament, or at least a personality that did not strike the fancy of the queen. This personality was the source of problems when Charles V wanted to appoint the marquis and marquise majordomos to María, the daughter of Catherine and John III of Portugal, at the time of her marriage to the Spanish prince, the future Philip II. We shall treat this matter later.

Meanwhile, eight children, four boys and four girls, were the fruit of this marriage between Francis and Leonor. They came into the world in various Spanish cities to which the service of the imperial court had taken their parents.

The oldest was born in Madrid in 1530 and received the name Carlos in honor of the emperor. His godparents were the empress and Prince Philip, who at the time was a child of three. After his father renounced his title, Carlos became the fifth duke of Gandía. In 1548 he married María Magdalena de Centelles y de Cardona, daughter of the count and countess of Oliva.

Born at Medina del Campo in 1532, Isabel in 1538 married Francisco Gómez de Sandoval y Rojas, marquis de Denia and count of Lerma. This alliance fulfilled Alexander VI's wish for union between the house of Gandía and that of Denia. The eldest son born from this marriage, Francisco de Sandoval-Rojas y de Borja, had the satisfaction of seeing Philip III raise the marquisate of Lerma to a dukedom. He was the duke of Lerma, the favorite of Philip III, who became so well-known in Spanish history.

The third child, Juan de Borja, later first count of Mayalde y de Ficalho, was born in 1533 at Bellpuig (Lérida) while his parents were on their way to Monzón to take part in the Cortes of the realm of Aragón. In 1522 he married Lorenza de Oñaz. She was the granddaughter of St. Ignatius's oldest brother, the lord of Loyola. Her father had no male heirs, so she succeeded him to the entitled estate of Loyola. Juan and Lorenza became the parents of Leonor de Oñaz y Loyola Borja, who succeeded her mother to the claim of the Loyola estate. When her mother Lorenza died in 1575, Juan de Borja remarried in 1576, choosing Francisca de Aragón y Barreto to became his second wife. Subsequently he became Spanish ambassador at Prague; later, when he returned to Spain, he was majordomo first to the empress María Hapsburg and afterwards to Margaret of Austria, wife of Philip III. In the world of letters he is known as the author of a book entitled *Empresas morales,* published in Prague in 1581. He died in the Escorial in 1606.

Alvaro was born in Toledo in 1534/35; Juana, in Madrid in 1535/36. The latter married the marquis of Alcañices, Don Juan Enríquez de Almansa y de Rojas. Their daughter and heiress, Elvira Enríquez de Borja, in turn married her uncle Alvaro de Borja, son of St. Francis. Therefore, for some time the marquisate of Alcañices remained associated with the Borja family, under the name Enríquez de Borja.[9]

Francis's sixth child was Fernando, born in Madrid in 1537. By order of Philip II he accompanied his father on his trip to Spain in 1571. Dorotea was Francis's seventh child. She was born at Valladolid in 1538 and later entered the convent of the Poor Clares in Gandía, thereby continuing a tradition that that convent always numbered at least one representative from the family of the dukes of Gandía. Lastly, there was Alonso, born in 1539; in Gandía he married Leonor de Noroña, widow of Don Luis de Osorio.

Life at court (1529-1539)

After his marriage the marquis of Llombai continued to perform his duties in the court and to enjoy very high esteem. He also continued to deport himself in an exemplary manner, showing himself particularly generous in providing for the poor and needy.

In the years between 1529 and 1533 Spanish domestic affairs passed through difficult times, especially because the emperor was away campaigning against the Turks and defending his own interests in Italy. In 1532, while Francis I of France was striving to dominate the Italian peninsula, Vienna nearly fell to the Turkish threat.

Charles went out to counter this onslaught; but before leaving Spain he appointed his wife regent and handed over the administration of the realm to Cardinal Juan de Tavera, who was archbishop of Toledo as well as president of the Council of State. The empress's constant preoccupation was the threat of the Berbers; in her letters to Charles there is one dominant theme—Algiers. On May 21, 1529, this position had fallen into the hands of Barbarossa, as the Europeans called Khair ed-Din, chief of the Barbary pirates (1466?-1546); so the proximity of the pirates now became a constant threat to the Spanish Mediterranean coast. Late in 1532 Barbarossa made raids on the duchy of Gandía, into areas inhabited by Moriscos. Barbarossa's power increased still more when in 1534, after being named admiral of the Turkish fleet, he seized Tunis, whose king was a vassal of Charles V. The empress, Tavera, and the Spanish people in general wanted Charles to give preference to the African question because it was of more vital concern to them than the quarrels that kept him in Italy.

The marquis of Llombai traveled about with the empress as she moved from one Castilian city to another. These frequent moves were to a great extent motivated by the royal lady's many ailments. She had spent the winter of 1529/30 in Madrid; and during one part of 1531 we see her in Ocaña and later at Avila. From December of that year until the following August, she made the castle of La Mota in Medina del Campo her residence; but the plague forced her to retreat to Segovia, where she convened the Cortes before pressing on to Madrid, wintering there until February 17, 1533. Next she left for Barcelona to await her husband's return. Charles had met with Pope Clement VII about the matter of convoking a council and then let it be known that he was returning to Spain.

Finally landing at Rosas on April 21/22 of that year, toward the end of the month he was at last able to greet his wife in Barcelona. During the latter half of the year, the Cortes of the realm of Aragón met at Monzón; and the marquis of Llombai, accompanied by his wife, attended its sessions. As we have already noted, it was while passing through Bellpuig bound for Monzón that Leonor gave birth to their third child, Juan.

During all of 1534 and the first half of 1535, Charles traveled throughout Spain, giving Francis the opportunity of dealing with him on a day-to-day basis. There is a tradition that the emperor showed a strong desire to study mathematics, history, and cosmography with his favorite. This was the procedure they followed: each morning Francis went to the emperor's cosmographer, Alonso de Santa Cruz, for an explanation of the lesson of the day; then in the afternoon he repeated what he had learned to his distinguished fellow student. Reportedly, the two of them followed this schedule for six months.

The conquest of Tunis and the Provence campaign

The most noteworthy event in imperial politics during this period was the capture of Tunis, a city of crucial importance for the defense of Sicily and Naples. It is enough to recall that in 1534 Barbarossa, the master of that African city, had landed on the coast of Italy, pushing up as far as Fondi, about halfway between Rome and Naples. On May 30, 1535, the imperial forces sailed from Barcelona bound for Sardinia. Once they arrived there they headed toward the African coast, where they disembarked on June 16. The high point of this expedition was the capture on July 14 of La Goleta, a town that commanded the whole Gulf of Tunis. After this victory, coinciding as it did with a revolt against Barbarossa by some of the townsmen inside the city walls, the capture of Tunis was an easy matter.

The marquis of Llombai did not take part in this expedition, either because he was laid low by fever or because his presence was thought more useful at court. He had left Barcelona for Madrid, where he fell ill, but on August 6 he joined in the public festivities celebrating the victory at Tunis.

What was the emperor's strategy going to be now? Continuous petitions came to him from Spain, begging that he follow up the success at Tunis by seizing Algiers, thereby striking the decisive blow against Barbarossa. But Charles V was thinking only of Francis I. He was aware that the king of France, forgetting all the agreements made at the Peace of Cambrai, also called the Paix de Dames (August 5, 1529), was plotting revenge for the defeats he had suffered at Charles's hand in 1521, 1525, and 1529. The crux of the dissension was possession of the duchy of Milan. In order to face up to Charles, Francis had made an alliance with the Turks and was doing everything possible to bring the pope over to his side. His meeting with Clement VII in 1533 resulted in the marriage between the duke of Orleans, the future Henry II, and Catherine de' Medici, a relative of Clement. Against the peaceful inclinations of the Catholic Montmorency, Francis opted for war, providing Admiral Chabot with the military strength to prepare an attack in Italy. Savoy was to be the point of encounter between the two forces. By the end of 1535 there were alarming rumors about this newest war between Spain and France.

Charles V spent September and October of that year in Sicily, then he crossed over to Naples. In early April he entered Rome in great triumph, passing through the arches of Titus and Septimius Severus. On the 8th he had an audience with the pope, to whom he proposed that the duchy of Milan be turned over to King Francis's third son, the duke of Angoulême, who should in turn marry the widowed duchess, Christine of Denmark. But Francis I spurned the plan. On Easter Monday, April 17, Charles gave his famous discourse in Spanish before the pope, in which he openly declared his plans. The next day he left Rome, having failed to get Clement to abandon his neutrality. War was imminent.

It seems that Charles had first planned to cross the Alps at Montgenèvre and attack Grenoble and Lyons. But he finally decided on a simultaneous sea and land campaign, relying for support on the fleet under the command of Andrea Doria. Doria's plans, seconded by the emperor, were to seize the port of Marseilles. If this succeeded the emperor's hold over the western Mediterranean would be uncontestable, and the conquest of Algiers, which had been left for the follow-up operation, would be greatly facilitated.

At the head of a powerful army, Charles V passed through the Col de Tenda on July 17, 1536, and on the 25th, the feast of St. James the Apostle, he entered Nice.

The marquis of Llombai, who had not been able to participate in the operation at Tunis, was present at this campaign in Provence. It is reported that the emperor, seeing him bathed in sweat and panting under his heavy armor, still more unwieldy because the bearer was so overweight, told him to take it off.

The commander of the French army was Constable Montmorency, who employed tactics that wonderfully supported his plans. He entrenched himself at Avignon and, instead of engaging in battle with the enemy, made use of the scorched-earth policy. The imperial army continued its march, occupying Antibes and Cannes. On August 2, it entered Fréjus, but the closest it ever came to its objective was Aix-en-Provence. Montmorency's tactics soon paid off for the French; as each day passed it became more difficult for the imperial army to secure provisions for men and animals from countryside and cities that had been ravaged and stripped of anything edible. Armed raids in search of food meant going into areas protected by the French, resulting in still higher casualties. Disease became rampant. Diego de Leiva, the hero of Pavia, died of exhaustion on August 15. According to reports dysentery claimed more casualties from the imperial ranks than Montmorency's weapons. So it was that, without ever fighting the real battle he had sought, the emperor was forced to admit defeat and left with no option other than to order retreat.

One of the insignificant events that took place as the army retreated was an assault on the Tower at Muy. This trivial engagement took the life of the great poet Garcilaso de la Vega, who was fighting in the ranks of the retreating army. His friend Francisco de Borja assisted him during his last moments and helped him die a Christian death.

On November 16 Charles V sailed for Spain, quartering in Barcelona from the 6th to the 31st of December.

The death of the empress Isabel

The empress Isabel died May 1, 1539, at the palace of the count of Fuensalida in Toledo. She was only thirty-six years old. The shock was overwhelming, especially for Charles, who had lost not only his life's companion but also a loyal and intelligent collaborator in the task of governing. Grief-stricken, the emperor retired to the monastery of Sisla, remaining there from May 12 to June 26.

According to her wishes Isabel was to be buried in the royal chapel at Granada, where the mortal remains of Ferdinand and Isabella lay interred. The escort chosen to accompany the empress's body to the tomb was made up of the cardinal archbishop of Burgos, Fray Juan de Toledo, who acted as president; the marquises of Villena and Llombai, and the bishops of León, Coria, and Osma. On Friday after the Ascension, May 16, the cortege entered Granada and moved in procession to the cathedral to read the nocturns from the divine office. The bier remained exposed during the whole night.

Solemn funeral ceremonies lasted nine days. On the 17th the cardinal of Burgos offered the burial Mass, but before the interment there had to be the verification of the corpse. It was at this point that the scene took place that has been described by all of Borgia's biographers, the scene that the Malagueñan painter José Moreno Carbonero depicted on his famous canvas. The empress's body was unrecognizable. She had wished not to be embalmed; furthermore, the long trip, made under deplorable conditions, could only have worsened this state of affairs. Borgia was shocked when he looked upon the disfigured face that once had been so beautiful and that six years later would be immortalized by Titian's brush. Ribadeneira goes so far as to say that Borgia could not bring himself to attest that the body he saw was once the empress. It was only when faced with the evidence that it had to be the one borne from Toledo to Granada that he was freed from doubt. God had changed his heart to the point that he uttered the expression that has become so well known: "Never more, never more will I serve a master who can die."[10] We shall have an opportunity to return to these moments and dwell upon their importance in Borgia's life.

More obsequies were performed on the several days that followed.[11] The archbishop of Granada, Gaspar de Avalos, celebrated Mass on the 18th, at which a Dominican from the convent of Santa Cruz preached. On the 19th the bishop of Osma said Mass, but we do not know who delivered the sermon. Then on successive days a number of religious orders held funeral services. It does not seem that the marquis of Llombai was present at these, because in all probability he began his return trip to Toledo on the 20th with other members of the court.

There are three points about which we cannot be absolutely certain at this significant moment in Borgia's life. The first is the influence that beholding the empress's body exerted on the direction his life was to take. The second is the role the Apostle of Granada, St. John of Avila, may have played in his conversion. And the third concerns the decisions Borgia made at that time with respect to the future.

It is certain that what he saw made a great impression on the man who for ten years had so faithfully served the empress and had enjoyed her esteem and confidence. But we must determine with precision exactly what happened. What actually moved Borgia was the fact that his sovereign had died so prematurely. In the spiritual diary he kept during the last years of his life, the anniversary he recalled was May 1, not the 16th or 17th of the month. For example, on May 1, 1564, he wrote, "Thanksgiving now for 25 years."[12] That was the number of years that had passed since the empress's death on May 1, 1539. On the same day in the year 1566, he noted: "Cons[olation] with the e[mpress], joy for what the Lord works in her and in me *through her death.*"[13] Notice the last three words that we have italicized. On May 1, 1567, he wrote: "May [15]67 and 28 [years] since the death of the empress. . . . Thanksgiving for the benefits from the same day as this in past years."[14] Seeing how death had destroyed so much power and so much beauty, the eyes of the young courtier who had watched the sheer dynamism of the empress could not but be opened to the caducity of the things of this world. What trust could he place in a life that fate could so suddenly change? Even if he did not pronounce the exact words attributed to him, we can be certain that he experienced the sentiment they express.

Ribadeneira says that the day after the burial Borgia heard a sermon preached by John of Avila and was so moved that he felt compelled to share his feelings with this preacher, who would one day be a canonized saint.[15]

The time sequence constructed on the basis of reliable documentation leads us to dismiss the hypothesis that Borgia heard John of Avila preach. According to the data we have, John preached two funeral orations for the empress, one on May 26, the other on June 6. As we have already pointed out, Borgia had probably already left Granada before these dates. But even if we do dismiss the hypothesis, we can admit that Borgia may well have taken advantage of his presence in Granada and had a conversation with a man famed for the sanctity of his life and the power of his sermons.

Did Borgia decide to cut all ties with the world shortly after the empress's death? Did he vow at that time to enter a religious order as soon as he was free of his obligations? The safest answer we must give to these questions is that this could not have been his resolution as far as the immediate future was concerned. He was married and had eight children, the eldest of whom was only nine and the youngest but a few months old. Besides these details, facts speak for themselves. A little more than a month after Borgia had returned to the court, Charles V named him lieutenant general of Catalonia. He accepted the office without reservations and gave it his total dedication for four years (1539-43). Later we see him eager to be assigned to the post of majordomo to the infanta María of Portugal, wife of Don Felipe, Charles V's son and heir to the throne. We should point out that the reasons offered for denying him this office—reasons which we will later have the opportunity to analyze—added to Borgia's disappointment at being rejected.

If he did not decide to break with the world at Granada, we can nonetheless assert with conviction that the empress's death meant the beginning of a new life for Borgia. That is, it occasioned a conversion to a holy life even in the world, characterized by a greater austerity in whatever he did, a greater practice of prayer and penance, and a more frequent use of the sacraments.

It is most unlikely that at this time he had already made a vow to leave the world and become a religious. Given his own age—he was only twenty-nine—and his wife's age, he could not have expected to escape from the responsibilities that kept him in the world. True, as soon as he was widowed in 1546, he wanted to enter the Society of Jesus. But there were other factors which led him to make this decision, and we shall have the opportunity to deal with them in chapter three.

2. Viceroy of Catalonia (1539-1543)

The appointment

On January 5, 1538, Don Fadrique de Portugal, archbishop of Zaragoza and since 1525 viceroy of Catalonia, died in Barcelona. The city aldermen that very day communicated the news of this event to Charles V. From Toledo the emperor responded, assuring them that "as soon as We are able We shall appoint a lieutenant general who will be suitable for the service of God and Ourselves and for the good of justice."[1] In a letter of March 7 he added that he was aware of the need to find a successor to Don Fadrique, and that he more than anyone else wanted to see the post filled; "but, considering the importance of the province and of this city, the delay in making this appointment means serving them better; we wish to provide for them in such a manner that God will be served and our conscience will be eased, and this shall be done very soon."[2]

Despite this promise, three months passed before the appointment was made. The choice finally fell on Francisco de Borja, marquis de Llombai, member of His Majesty's Council. The document announcing the appointment was dated Toledo, June 26, 1539.[3] Charles V conveyed the name of this choice to the members of the standing committee for watching over the government of Catalonia, known as the Generalitat; he explained the reasons that had persuaded him to appoint the marquis of Llombai to this position, listing the qualities of the elected, the love and trust he bore him, and his conviction that under the new viceroy "the country shall be well ruled and governed and that justice will be properly administered." He exhorted them to show him respect and obedience, "by which We shall be served by you."[4]

Francis Borgia at this date was twenty-nine years old. His appointment spelled the end of commissioning prelates to the viceroyalty and the beginning of selecting them from the ranks of the non-Catalan nobility.

As they informed the emperor in their letter of August 4, the Barcelona aldermen were delighted with Francis's appointment. They expected that

Francis's "prudence and knowledge" would work to the advantage of the principality, the county and the city of Barcelona, and they dispatched the sub-syndic, Juan Lunes, to Tortosa to meet him. Finally, they did not hesitate to remind him that the viceroy would be expected to repeat in the city of Barcelona the same oath he had taken when he entered the principality.[5]

Charles V's instructions to the new viceroy

According to custom Charles V gave the new viceroy detailed written instructions that bear the same date as his appointment.[6] The first recommendation was that the viceroy attend to the problem of criminal justice, of paramount importance because "the rugged mountainous terrain" made it easier for bandits and miscreants to enter the country. He listed the captains of the principal bands that were pillaging the land. Then he got down to specifics. He urged Borgia to contain the ringleaders because without their leadership the bandits would be powerless to commit crimes. He wanted to be kept informed about everything that had to do with the public order. The viceroy was to distinguish between ordinary trials and those reserved to the Crown, being mindful that the barons and churchmen as well as the laymen always tended to reduce the number of the latter. He should not absent himself from the meetings of the council or audiencia. He was reminded that, in virtue of the new law, the ordinary citizens were forbidden to bear arms. He should stop the practice of having recourse to ecclesiastical immunities; the defendants should seek an apostolic brief for each immunity.

Everything pertaining to civil law was to be dealt with according to the Constitutions of Catalonia. The viceroy was to see to it that members of the audiencia fulfill their duties without sluggishness or partiality. He was advised to preside over one of the two chambers, as his predecessor had done. If at any time he was prevented from being present at a session, he should ask for an account of the proceedings. Trial cases should be "regulated like a clock."

As we can see, the emperor focused his attention primarily on the administration of justice. He likewise made recommendations about the excise tax, the Barcelona fortification works, the road project between Urgel and Barcelona, bread making, street cleaning, the vice of gambling, and so forth.

As had been done for his predecessors, "a base salary of two thousand ducats and two thousand for financial help" was allotted to the viceroy. Borgia will later say that his pay consisted of "five thousand ducats as salary"; he realized that, given the many expenses of his post, he was not well remunerated, but he cared more for the king's purse than for his own.[7]

Oath-taking at Tortosa and Barcelona

The new viceroy made his entrance into Tortosa on August 14, 1539. Before the main altar of the cathedral he took an oath that he would observe and see to it that others observed all of Barcelona's *usatges* (customs), the constitutions, liberties, and privileges of Catalonia. Immediately afterwards he ordered the reading of two documents, the first by Juan Lunes, sub-syndic of Barcelona, and the second by Pablo Renard, notary and syndic of the Generalitat, the autonomous government of Catalonia. Both "protested" that the new viceroy should respect the Constitutions of Catalonia and that he refrain from making use of his power to convene the Cortes and to refer to the king's tribunal cases that should be handled locally. The power to make such decisions was crucial and should be employed by the sovereign alone. It was under these conditions that the emissaries would receive the viceroy's oath of office. In response the viceroy agreed to accept the "protestation" if and to the extent that it did not countervail the faculties and powers granted him by his appointment.[8]

The formalities were over, but Borgia did not wait until he arrived in Barcelona before implementing his commission. On the following day, August 15, he took action against "some very ugly occurrences that had transpired in the city of Tortosa" and ordered the guilty imprisoned. Instead of being the place of shelter and defense for the king's vassals, the castle had become a den of thieves. He cleared it out and deposed the castellan, who was one of the first to be imprisoned.

The new viceroy made his formal entrance into Barcelona on August 23. The aldermen, mounted on horses and accompanied by the city magistrates and by many knights, townsmen, and merchants, paraded from the Plaza de San Jaime through the streets of the Call, the Hospital, and the Puerta de San Antonio to the Cruz Cubierta. Here they awaited the viceroy. Once he arrived the retinue marshaled itself, the chief alderman or *conseller en cap* taking his place on the viceroy's left. Now the assembled dignitaries set out, crossing the Puerta de San Antonio and proceeding through the streets of El Carmen and of La Puertaferrissa. From here they went by way of the Plaza Nueva and the Puerta de Nuestra Señora to the episcopal palace. They marched into the cathedral, where the viceroy renewed his oath of office in accordance with the city's privileges.[9] Two days later the aldermen and other leading citizens presented themselves to the viceroy at the episcopal palace, where he had taken up his lodging.

This last detail from the *Dietari del antich Consell barceloní* requires some modification.[10] Francis did not live in the episcopal palace, but rather in the

archdeacon's house next door to it, which today houses the Instituto Municipal de Historia of the city of Barcelona. Charles V himself had asked the
bishop to rent this building as the viceregal residence.

The viceroyalty

The letters of Charles V and the Consejo de Aragón to Francisco de
Borja were usually addressed in the following manner: "To the illustrious
marquis de Llombai, our cousin and our lieutenant general in the principality of Catalonia and in the counties of Roussillon and Cerdaña." Although
we use the term viceroy, which became common after the time of Charles V,
the title lieutenant expresses exactly the nature of Borgia's office. As the
name implies, he was the monarch's representative, his *alter Nos*, the one
needed to take his place during his prolonged absences from the principality.
As Charles wrote to Borgia on October 24, 1539, the viceroy governed with
delegated jurisdiction, "with the customary authority which you have from
Us to rule and govern the said provinces."[11] Borgia's residence was not the
royal palace, lacking as it did the necessary facilities, but rather a house of
the duke of Cardona on the Calle Ancha. But, as we have already explained,
he resided in fact at the archdeacon's house. In the presence of the viceroy
nobody, not even the duke of Cardona, the sole grandee of Spain living in
the principality, was permitted to sit on a dais or in a curule chair.

Fernando II of Catalonia and Aragón, better known as Ferdinand the
Catholic of Spain, created the lieutenancy as a permanent office. Its primary
function was to exercise judicial authority; in the administration of justice it
was assisted by a council or audiencia, established in 1492 and made up of
eight doctors of the law, whose number was increased to twelve in 1521. The
council's first concern was maintaining law and order. That same year, 1492,
the king also created the position of governor general of the principality. His
job was to visit the cities and borderlands of the principality and to be
always at the service of the viceroy. The county of Roussillon had its own
captain general; during Borgia's viceroyalty this post was filled first by
Francés de Beaumont and then by Juan de Acuña.[12]

As the Crown's representative in the political structure of the principality, the viceroy was the highest magistrate, a fact which easily put him on a
collision course with opposing forces, in particular, with the Cortes, the
General Deputation, also known as the Generalitat, and with the Consell de
Cent, Barcelona's municipal government. As time went by, long after
Borgia's tenure of office, the viceroy gradually became a mere territorial
functionary, an intermediary between the king and his council and between
local Catalan officeholders. He had some influence with regard to the

appointment of *vegueres*, who were similar to magistrates, bailiffs, and castellans. That is, he would propose to the king the name or names of those he considered qualified for the office.[13]

Borgia addressed his reports either to Charles V himself or to the emperor's secretary and right arm, Francisco de los Cobos. At times he would also write to Cardinal Juan de Tavera, archbishop of Toledo and president of the royal council. Answers to his letters came from the same officials to whom they had been addressed or from the Consejo de Aragón. Letters from the Consejo were sent in the name of the king and were always signed either by the vice-chancellor, Miguel Mai, a native of Barcelona, or by the secretary, Juan Comalonga, who was from Perpignan.

As we have already seen, the viceroy had to take an oath to respect the Constitutions and privileges of Catalonia. A prerequisite for holding office, this oath was taken either in Tortosa, Lérida, or Perpignan, depending upon where the viceroy entered the principality. Moreover, no matter where he first took the oath, he always had to repeat it in Barcelona. Finally, since the viceroy's jurisdiction was suspended each time the king came into the principality, he had to repeat the oath after the king's departure. Retaking the oath was done often during the tenure of Borgia's predecessor, Fadrique de Portugal, and we shall see that Borgia had to repeat his oath after the Cortes of Monzón in 1542. On that occasion Charles V was present in Barcelona while his son, Prince Philip, heir to the crown, swore to respect Catalonia's Constitutions and privileges.

The historical background

To appreciate what Borgia had to deal with during his viceroyalty, we should keep in mind what was taking place in Spain in general and in Catalonia in particular between 1539 and 1543.

Still reeling from the blow dealt him by his wife Isabel's death, Charles V on May 1, 1539, had to face the Ghent rebellion against the administration of his sister, Mary of Burgundy, in the Low Countries. Once again he was forced to leave Spain. But this time he could not rely on the remarkable skill of the empress, who had acted as regent when he had found himself in similar predicaments on three other occasions between 1529 and 1533, 1535 and 1536, and finally in 1538. This time he called on Prince Philip, a boy of twelve, assisted by Cardinal Tavera, to fulfill the regent's role. In a letter of October 24, 1539, Charles communicated to Borgia the news of his latest journey to Flanders, adding that his gentleman of the bedchamber, Luis de Zúñiga, would apprise him of the reasons for his going. We know that, besides punishing the Ghent rebels, his motives were to confer with his brother Ferdinand and his sister Mary about whether or not the Low Countries should be governed by their own princes. According to the sentence handed down on April 29, 1540, Ghent was duly punished by being deprived of goods and defenses and stripped of her liberties, and even of her coat of arms.

The rivalry between Spain and France—the everlasting cause of distur-bance during the whole of Charles's reign—was at this date enjoying a period of relative calm, after the ten-year truce agreed upon at Nice. This peace had come about as a result of the mediation of Pope Paul III during May and June 1538 and the successful meeting of Charles V with Francis I at Aigues-Mortes on June 14, 1538.

At the beginning of 1540 hopes for a lasting peace were a reality. Both Constable Montmorency of France and Granvelle, Charles's secretary and counselor, were inclined to be optimistic regarding such a prospect. The emperor's visitation to Flanders and journey through France, where he was warmly received, were highly encouraging. He wrote to Borgia on February 14, 1540, "We received excellent treatment in France from the king, our brother."[14] So there was hope for true peace and lasting progress throughout Christendom. But in fact the balance between the two powers was unstable. People lived in a perpetual state of war during which respites of peace merely served to give opposing sides time to catch their breath in order to resume hostilities. The duchy of Milan was the key to the problem because the hegemony of Europe depended on who occupied Milan.

Faced with recurrent outbreaks of hostilities, the sovereigns had to fortify their frontiers. One of these was in Roussillon.

During the period that concerns us there were no military engagements properly so-called until the summer of 1542, apart from a few skirmishes which are not worthy of notice.

Unquestionably, one reason why concord between Christian princes was so desirable was that it permitted each one to consolidate his energies for the struggle against the Turks. This particular goal and the pacification of religious factions in Germany were Charles's two greatest ambitions; howev-er, Francis's alliance with the Turks, the common enemy of Christendom, was one of the reasons why the emperor's objective could not be achieved. Charles's dream was to launch an offensive at the very heart of the domain of Suleiman I ("the Magnificent"), that is, directly against Constantinople. Borgia alluded to this objective in a letter to Francisco de los Cobos on August 12, 1540, when he wrote, "May it please God that what has been started may be realized so that His Majesty, through his customary victories, may fix his imperial standards in the East just as they are in the West."[15] For the time being, however, this undertaking was not considered feasible, because ever since the naval battle at Preveza on September 25, 1538, the victorious Turks were assured domination of the eastern Mediterranean, a situation that obtained until the middle of the century.

The victors were allied with the Barbary pirates captained by Barbarossa. In 1534 he was named admiral general of the Turkish fleet, and from this date on the Barbary corsairs became a formidable power, making the Mediterranean coast vulnerable to their own and the Turks' striking power. Maintaining constant vigilance and securing all positions considered unshielded against the enemy's attack were matters of high priority.

After the capture of Tunis in 1535, the principal strongholds dotting the Barbary coast from Oran to Tripoli were under the control of the emperor, the one exception being Barbarossa's lair, Algiers. According to the policies of Ferdinand and Isabella and of Charles's wife, the empress Isabel, an attack on Algiers should have been the logical follow-up to the victorious campaign launched at Tunis. But, as we have seen, ever since Francis I had invaded the duchy of Savoy, occupying Turin and other important Piedmontese cities, Charles preferred to focus attention on his contest with the king of France. Such was the background to Charles's invasion of Provence in the summer of 1536, which saw his army halted before Constable Montmorency's defenses in the Rhone Valley. Charles had hoped that this southern drive would be supported by a second invasion from Flanders and by a third across the Catalan frontier, but the setback he suffered in Provence canceled out this joint action.

After his defeat in this punitive action against France and after learning of the disappointing results that came from the meeting with the Protestants at the Diet of Regensburg in 1541, Charles decided the moment had arrived for undertaking the long-desired assault against Algiers. He threw himself into this project, disregarding the advice of Prince Andrea Doria and of the marquis del Vasto, commander of the troops in Milan, and of Pope Paul III. Doria and del Vasto argued that 1541's fall weather did not favor such an enterprise. As everyone knows, the battle was a disaster for the emperor; the winds and the waves conspired against him. A good part of the fleet was destroyed, making it impossible to supply food and munitions to the troops that had already disembarked. Algiers proved itself invincible and Charles did not try to attack it again.

After the Algiers debacle Charles returned to Spain, landing at Cartagena on December 1, 1541. On the 14th of the same month he summoned the Cortes of Castile, which convened at Valladolid in 1542. At this meeting the unanimous desire of the representatives and the express will of the towns and cities were clearly stated: the king should establish his residence in Spain, leaving matters of war to his military officers. After this Cortes was adjourned, that of the realm of Aragón was convened that same year. We shall have the opportunity to discuss what took place at this Cortes later in this book.

Depicted thus in broadest strokes are the principal events of Spanish history at the time when Borgia was summoned to fill the office of viceroy of Catalonia. Now let us take a look at the particular state of affairs in the principality.

Conditions in Catalonia

As far as territorial boundaries were concerned, the counties of Roussillon and Cerdaña were always united to the principality of Catalonia, creating a total area of 13,740 square miles. According to the *fogatge* or census of 1553, the inhabitants totaled 363,765, giving the principality a population that did not quite reach 28.6 inhabitants per square mile. This census, which was the one closest to the date of Borgia's appointment, shows that Barcelona counted 32,160 inhabitants, followed by Perpignan with 8,775. According to the dates Father Pedro Gil gives us, it was in 1600 that the principality was divided into fifteen *veguerías* or magistracies, to which we must add the three from the counties of Roussillon and Cerdaña. In Catalonia at the time Borgia undertook his duties, there were eight bishoprics, including that of Elna in Roussillon but excluding Solsona, which was not set up until 1593.

As far as demography and economics are concerned, we should keep in mind that the depression which began in the fourteenth and fifteenth centuries perdured, except that now, even though the population of Catalonia tended to increase, the economy remained static. This phenomenon was one of the reasons why poverty held the country in its grasp: the food supplies simply did not keep pace with the increase of population. Aggravating the problem were the persistent droughts; indeed, as we shall see, one of the greatest challenges the new viceroy had to face was obtaining sufficient grain supplies.

Most of the land was in the hands of the barons and lords, among whom antagonisms flared up easily. Hoodlums put themselves at the service of this noble or that one, thereby perpetuating a kind of banditry among the noble classes. This, along with a brigandage drawing its membership from the common people, encouraged the presence of highwaymen, thieves, and assassins, and constituted one of Francis Borgia's greatest concerns. Then there was the isolation of the local nobility from the rest of the peninsula; linked with the chronic economic crisis of the members of this class, this isolation seems to have been the chief cause for the constant state of agitation so endemic to this part of Spain. The lords and gentlemen had few possibilities of acquiring positions in the government and their outlets for trade were limited; so they lived in a state of continuous frustration that gave rise to feuds and factional disputes.

Catalonia's geographic position tended to make it a "march." It was an enclave, shut off in the northeastern tip of the country with two frontiers difficult to protect—its seashore exposed to raids from the Turks and corsairs and its land border contiguous to France. Borgia synthesized the condition of Catalonia in a few words when he remarked that it was a "land that needed help both because of its bandits and because of its borders and shores."

In his handling of domestic affairs, the viceroy had to proceed tactfully to avoid offending the local authorities, the deputies of the Generalitat and Barcelona's *consellers*, jealous as they were of their privileges and liberties. As we have already seen, they would not even recognize the viceroy until he took an oath to respect these privileges and liberties. Writing to Charles V on August 27, 1539, Borgia asked that his letter not be shown to the members of the Consejo de Aragón, much less to its secretary, Comalonga, "because he is from Perpignan and some of the others are Catalans, and this land is so full of codes of etiquette and precedence that it could be that matters dealing with the service of Your Majesty would not get done as they should. Even in these few days I have been here I have had trouble in this business with some of the people about me."[16] We can say in general, however, that relations between the viceroy and the local authorities were good. On November 8, 1539, Charles wrote to the *consellers*, advising them that the viceroy was "very pleased with you."[17] On May 8th of the following year, he asked them not to act without previous consultation with the viceroy.

But Borgia's main problem in dealing with the Catalan authorities and the local clergy had its origin in an area other than local privileges. To implement what the Cortes had legislated in regard both to the affairs of the Crown and the fortification of the cities, Borgia had to rely on available funds. The dire economic condition of the country, however, made for opposition and foot-dragging on the part of the authorities.

Approximately nine percent of the principality's inhabitants were concentrated in Barcelona, which the Venetian ambassador, Andrea Navagero, described after his visit there in 1525 as "bellissima città e in bellissimo sito."[18] He was struck by the city's many beautiful gardens, its churches and convents, and its houses constructed of stone, unlike the adobe houses in the rest of Catalonia. He did not fail to admire its shipyard, Las Atarazanas, where so many galleys had been built, even though in that year, 1525, none were under construction.

As we learn from contemporary maps, a wall extended around the whole city, leaving only its seashore unprotected. This exposed shoreline was one of the areas the emperor ordered the viceroy to remedy.

When Borgia arrived in Barcelona, the city could finally boast of a university, founded in 1533. In 1536 actual construction was begun on the building situated at the extreme end of the Ramblas, near the Puerta de Canaletas.

The bishop of Barcelona at that time was Juan de Cardona, about whom we shall have occasion to speak.

During his administration Borgia followed the norms the emperor had given him. Accordingly, he centered his activities in three areas: the suppression of unruly gangs and brigands, the defense of the land and sea frontiers, and preparations for a possible war with France.

Gangs and brigandage

Rivalries among the gentry and ordinary brigandage were two distinct phenomena, but they were related one to another and they contributed in wreaking considerable havoc upon the inhabitants of Catalonia. We already touched on the causes for this when we presented the conditions in Catalonia during the era under discussion. Of course, brigandage was not a plague peculiar to Catalonia alone; rather, it was widespread throughout the Mediterranean countries. At the time when Borgia assumed his office, it had already reached alarming proportions; but thanks no doubt to the viceroy's firmness, it can be said that, if it was not totally eradicated, at least it was certainly curbed. In his letters to Charles V and to Cobos, the viceroy reported with satisfaction that the land was pacified. He also frequently repeated that, if it were not for a few of the ringleaders—a Cadell, a Roca, a Pujades, or a Sentmenat—the people would live in peace. But he had no illusions; he knew that, if he suppressed one of the centers of criminal activity, another would pop up in a different part of the country. Obviously, Borgia did not stop brigandage; in fact, this evil assumed an even more dreadful form in later years.

He was able to rely on an efficient legal instrument when he acted with firmness, namely, the sanctions against brigandage decreed by Charles V on March 7, 1539, five months before Borgia assumed the duties of the viceroy.[19] The harsh tone of this document, written in Catalan, is in itself a testimony to how serious an evil brigandage represented throughout Catalonia.

Let us now look at a few specific areas. The so-called "affair of the vice-county of Castellbó" was one of the most vexing problems the viceroy had to face. Nestled in the Alto Urgel, this vice-county embraced within its confines such towns as Castellbó proper, Castellciutat, Organyá, Rialb, and Tirvia. In 1512, after Castile annexed Navarre, Ferdinand II confiscated Castellbó from its proprietor, the count of Foix, and in the following year he granted it to the count's wife, Germaine de Foix. She in turn gave it to Luis Oliver de Boteller, castellan of Peñíscola. At Germaine's death in 1538, the Cortes of Monzón decreed that the vice-county should revert to the Catalan-Aragonese crown. Borgia was in charge of settling the case, which had become all the more urgent because in the interim Castellbó had become a sanctuary for hoodlums. But despite all his efforts, Borgia was not able to achieve his objective, and the vice-county did not return to the Crown until 1548.

Among all the highwaymen that ravished the countryside and the cities of Catalonia, those who gave Borgia the most trouble were Juan Cadell, Gaspar de Lordat, Antonio Roca, and Moreu Cisteller. Cadell, the lord of Arséguel in the *veguería* of Puigcerdá, belonged to a family of bandits who passed on their deadly skills from father to son. At one time Borgia referred to him as "the greatest scoundrel in the land." Charles V added that "he kept the whole of Cerdaña without either freedom or justice." It was urgent, therefore, to apprehend him and to confiscate his castle of Arséguel. Realizing that he was being hunted down, the brigand fled to France, leaving a certain Fusteret as the chief of his gang. Borgia succeeded in apprehending him. In a letter of June 28, 1540, Borgia communicated to Cobos that "I have sent him to be quartered because the evils this man has done are infinite in number."[20]

Gaspar de Lordat and Antonio Roca created trouble for the viceroy because they were "crowned ones," that is, tonsured clerics. The bishop of Barcelona acknowledged Lordat as a member of the clerical state and consequently protected him. This fact made it all the more urgent for the viceroy to obtain a pontifical brief granting civil authorities the right to pursue and punish trouble-making clerics.

Antonio Roca was one of the most notorious Catalan criminals during the first half of the sixteenth century, perpetrating his misdeeds in the region around Vic. Borgia pursued him relentlessly and in March 1542 he personally left Barcelona to hunt him down. Even though partially successful in his endeavors, he was never able to capture this desperado. More successful was the marquis de Aguilar, Borgia's successor, who had him put to death in Barcelona in 1546. Lope de Vega wrote one of his dramas about him, *Antonio*

Roca; or, The Most Fortunate Death, in which the criminal was represented as a Robin Hood-like desperado, the essence of civility, who had become a bandit because of a matter of honor.

Borgia was not successful in tracking down Moreu Cisteller either. He was one of the most fearsome bandits, a native of Prat de Llobregat; however, no sooner had the viceroy been relieved of his office in April 1543 when Cisteller, along with a thief named Biscaio, his second-in-command, and sixteen of his men, was captured at Vilafranca del Penedés and put to death at Barcelona on June 18 of that same year.

The feuds between members of the landed gentry were just as much a problem for the viceroy as the bandits were. References to gangs captained by Pujades and Sentmanat come up constantly in Borgia's correspondence. To put an end to their feuding, he suggested that the emperor have both chiefs, or at least one of them, leave the principality. Charles agreed, ordering Pujades to take part in the Algiers expedition of 1541. But Pujades did not accept the order. Borgia then succeeded in making a temporary truce between the two rival factions. In many cases this seemed to him the most viable solution. He said that setting up truces like this allowed matters to move along more smoothly than they did when many men were killed. Unfortunately in this case, however, success was short-lived, for the two gangs clashed once again.

Another difficult matter for him was the duke of Cardona's lawsuit against his brothers. Borgia did all he could, relying on the help of the duke's confessor and friend, Bernardo Margarit, prior of the Carthusian monastery of Montalegre, "who is the one who can bring him to reason when he becomes too excited, and also he is my friend." The audiencia passed sentence on the duke, forcing him to pay 77,000 *libras.* He died in 1543, a year after the sentence was handed down.

Defending the frontiers

Against the Turks and pirates – In presenting the European panorama during Borgia's tenure as viceroy in Catalonia, we stressed the urgent need of defending the sea and land frontiers against the Turks and pirates, and of preparing for an ever-possible break with France. A good measure of Borgia's efforts were focused on these objectives.

The most immediate danger lay in the frequent raids of Barbary corsairs, who on a number of occasions attempted landings. On October 27, 1539, Borgia sent news that some five or six lateen-rigged barges loaded with Moors had reached the coast. In February 1540 they seized several Spanish vessels not far from Ibiza. In August of that same year corsair ships were sighted off the coast of Garraf. Borgia prepared to go out and fight them if necessary. At this same time a lone ship from Algiers had arrived at Blanes. Another, ladened with wheat, had been captured near Tarragona. In August 1540 Borgia wrote that Prince Andrea Doria would be most welcome in Catalonia, since his intention was to clear the coast of pirates. More serious, and beyond the Catalan borders, was the assault and sack of Gibraltar that took place in September of that year. The viceroy believed he had to be alert in responding to preparations then being made in Algiers. The Spanish ambassador in Rome, the marquis de Aguilar, had informed him about these preparations, although Borgia did not think the Turks would attempt a serious raid during the course of 1540.

Coastal fortifications of Barcelona — On October 3, 1539, Charles V wrote to Barcelona's *consellers*, urging them to try to work in cooperation with the viceroy on "the works that remain to be done at the coast so that they will continue according to plans, for it is not right that so necessary and so important a matter as this should remain at a standstill." He ordered them to give themselves completely to this project "without withdrawing their hands from it."[21] In his instructions to Borgia he insisted on the same thing.[22] He urged him to show the same enthusiasm for this project as his predecessor, Don Fadrique de Portugal, who had begun the bulwark on the south side of the shore near the Torre Nueva.

Borgia in turn recognized the need "for forging ahead with this project, for being walled is as important for the city as is the bread people eat."[23] He set to work with such vigor that on May 10 he could write that he did not busy himself with anything other than the works. He went personally to inspect them and almost never left the house to go anywhere else. On March 16, 1541, he wrote that he was speeding up the project and that every day he sent prisoners condemned to the galleys to work on the fortifications. The stretch around the shipyard of Las Atarazanas was the part that lagged behind schedule. Charles V, who was informed regularly about everything, congratulated the viceroy on the progress he was making with the works.

As a matter of fact, however, the project proceeded at an exceedingly slow pace, primarily because of the difficulty in finding the necessary moneys to fund it. The city had to finance its own fortifications and therein lay the problem. In his correspondence with Charles V and with the emperor's secretary, Cobos, Borgia went into minute detail about his negotiations with both the *consellers* and the canons and clergy, who were also expected to contribute to the defraying of expenses. In both groups Borgia found little desire to cooperate. Charles V encouraged his viceroy, warning him that if he was not persistent the *consellers* would always postpone the works and would raise obstacles to its completion. Here we have a clear picture of the tight economic bind in which the city found itself.

The shore wall was not completed during Borgia's administration, but some of the witnesses at his beatification process in 1611 mentioned the project in their deposition. One of these, Miguel Querol, a pharmacist, said that the marquis of Llombai negotiated with the *consellers* and with the Consell of Barcelona over the wall's completion, adding that during Borgia's tenure of office a considerable part of it was constructed. On one occasion, when the viceroy went to inspect the wall, he came upon some workmen who were idle. He asked them what they were doing standing around stargazing and preventing other workmen from doing their jobs; then he told them that if they did not want to work, he would have them taken off the job.[24] Another witness, Pedro Ausiàs March, said that he remembered very well when there had not been any wall on the entire section of the southern part of the shoreline, and that he also recollected clearly that it was during the marquis de Llombai's viceroyalty in the principality of Catalonia that they had begun to build and construct this section of the wall.[25]

Barcelona and its fortifications were not the only project that occupied Borgia; he also took care of different coast towns such as Mataró, Tarragona, Tortosa, and others. "I am struggling to fortify them," he wrote. On Las Alfaques he undertook the construction of a tower which he considered "very necessary." He also tried to have defense works put up along the shores of the Ter River for the protection of Gerona.

The construction of galleys

Charles V had manifested to the viceroy his wish that new galleys be built at Barcelona; already on October 27, 1539, Borgia wrote back to the emperor, detailing the steps that he had taken in response to his orders. The main problem was the high price the shipbuilders had demanded, specifically Berenguer D'Oms and Enrique Centelles. The former reported that he was ready to construct six galleys, while the latter promised he would have four completed by April 10, 1540. Miguel Fiveller agreed to build at least one, maybe more. On February 2, 1540, the viceroy wrote an instruction in which he declared, "All possible vessels and ferryboats will have to be maintained, without expense to the royal court."[26] Caravels had to weigh from seventy to eighty tons; in no case could they go beyond one hundred.

Specifically, Charles V entrusted the viceroy with the preparation of three galleys, and work on this project began in earnest by the beginning of 1540. On March 6 Borgia personally paid a visit to Las Atrazanas dockyards.

The three galleys were launched during Easter week the same year in the presence of Bernardino de Mendoza, commandant of the Spanish fleet. Mendoza sailed with these "very well appointed" ships for Mallorca on June 5. Borgia had another one, a "bastard galley," built, and he made frequent references to her construction in his letters, going so far as to say that she would be "the most graceful galley ever on the sea." Mendoza went to see her and found her just right, as Borgia informed the emperor on February 26, 1541.[27] On July 5 he added that three days later she would be in the water.

In none of these letters is there any mention of the purpose for which these warships were being prepared. Everything was done in secret. But there is no doubt that they were designed to serve in the contest against the Turks, more precisely, in the Algiers campaign which the emperor was then planning.

The Algiers expedition

The word *jornada* (expedition) is used repeatedly in Borgia's correspondence to designate the ill-fated campaign launched in the fall of 1541 to capture the key Mediterranean city of Algiers.

The news about the emperor's plan to make a direct attack on this stronghold did not begin to circulate until mid-1541. But Borgia had received no official dispatch either from the emperor in Germany or from Cobos at the court. He regretted that the imperial plan — "if it is going to take place" — had become divulged, "because it will be used to warn the enemy to be better prepared." He suggested starting a rumor contrary to the one in circulation because, "in this country people quickly start talking and quickly fall silent."[28] But the events did not allow for subterfuge. In August the viceroy knew that Charles had in mind leaving Germany to join his troops in Spain.

The viceroy was responsible for providing the emperor with tents, a project that demanded his attention during the whole of that summer. The tents were taken from Tortosa to Cartegena, then on to Mallorca, where the fleet had its rendezvous. He also had to get stores for the army; but, though successful in procuring a great quantity of wine and other provisions, he had difficulty finding wheat, always a scarce commodity in Catalonia. Finally he was able to scrounge up about four thousand bushels.

On October 15 Charles V wrote to Borgia from Mallorca. He informed him that he had found the fleets of Genoa, Naples, and Sicily gathered there, adding, however, that the Spanish fleets, which according to a letter from the duke of Alba should have been in Mallorca at the end of the previous month, still had not arrived. Because his intention was to set sail from that port on the 17th, he would not wait for them. The Spanish vessels would now head directly for Algiers. Charles ended this letter with expressions of confidence in God, "for the cause is His and is of great profit for Christendom."[29]

Borgia was pleased to learn that his father, the duke of Gandía, would be taking part in the expedition with two vessels and some other lateen-rigged barges, carrying many Valencian gentlemen. Francis wrote, "God knows the envy I have because I am not able to do the same." In a letter to the marquise of Llombai, Charles V wrote that "the marquis would achieve with the same will [what your father-in-law has done] if the post he had did not prevent it."[30]

The failure of the expedition is well-known. On October 23 the troops began to disembark on the Algerian coast, near the capital city of Algiers. But during the night of the 24th/25th a tremendous storm blew up. One after another the ships carrying munitions and provisions, indispensable stores for the soldiers stranded on the land, were destroyed until their number reached almost one hundred and fifty. Still, the winds and waves continued to rage; under such circumstances catastrophe was inevitable.

The news of the failure reached Borgia after the usual delay. In a letter of November 22, he demonstrated his chagrin to the emperor for "the fate that befell Your Majesty's fleet near Algiers and how the lack of provisions has caused the suspension of the undertaking until the spring." We see here that Borgia considered the incident to be a suspension of the assault, which could be repeated at a more favorable time of the year. His admiration went out to his sovereign, who had determined to conduct the enterprise in person and allowed nothing to prevent "Your Majesty from placing your imperial person in this holy expedition, inasmuch as all that could humanly be done was put into execution." His reaction to the debacle was a resolution to serve his emperor with more will than ever before. As a good Christian he took recourse in spiritual causes for the defeat:

> Furthermore, I believe our Lord was merciful to us because He showed us that only our sins prevented the realization of Your Majesty's holy intention. And it could be that He permitted this so that from it could result an amendment of our lives such that we will be worthy of being heard when in the future we pray for Your Majesty's victories.[31]

In Barcelona there was a procession organized to thank God for preserving the emperor from harm.

Visitation to Perpignan

One of the orders Charles V had given Borgia in his first instruction was to make a visitation personally to the county of Roussillon. The immediate reason for this was to correct a very difficult state of affairs that had developed in Perpignan. Borgia wrote that it was "a business that was of great importance and which requires diligence in rectifying the problem."[32] What was it all about? Some very serious failings in discipline had taken place at Perpignan against Francés de Beaumont, the city's captain general. The first step taken was to dispatch Juan Vaquer and a president of the Court of Justice, Arnaldo de Gort, to conduct a trial there. Borgia had examined the case, but he had to acquaint himself personally and on the spot about all its details.

However, he decided not to undertake this trip immediately. He believed Barcelona should be the place from which he governed "because I am at midpoint along the coast and can go anywhere I may be needed, all the more so because the greatest danger is within nine leagues from Barcelona, including Mataró and other weak places."[33] What would happen if he was in Perpignan and the pirates landed to raid Tortosa, for example? Moreover, he was afraid that his presence in Roussillon might be read in France as a gesture of distrust. Finally, the Barcelona authorities tried to dissuade him from leaving the city.

But the order from the emperor, seconded by the Consejo de Aragón, remained in effect and he had to comply with it. So, judging the mood of Catalonia to be peaceful, he made the journey, leaving Barcelona on October 20, 1540, even though his wife has just undergone a most difficult childbirth, and he had just then received the news of the death of his brother Cardinal Enrique de Borja at Viterbo on September 16. Believing that a change of air would be beneficial for his wife, he brought her along, but subsequent events would prove that this journey was deleterious to the lady's health.

Prior to Borgia's arrival twenty-eight people "and most notably the consuls" had been taken into custody; soon six more were arrested. Their trial was a difficult one because of the silence on the part of the townspeople.

> The whole group is so determined to die rather than to tell the truth about what happened that I myself would not have believed it had I not witnessed it; because all are unanimous in believing that to act against the loyalty of their town is an important point of honor, as if it were a matter of life for

each one individually.

The fear of justice had caused many to leave the city, so that there were more houses there that were bolted up than occupied; but this situation did not prevent justice from following its course. After some of the accused confessed, others could be arrested, and thus "I hanged one of the principal scoundrels of this revolt because he was more or less the leader of those who killed the soldier Hontiveros, and the day the sentence was carried out, according to what some have told me, the women wept and the men cursed Don Francés."[34]

The court ordered the city to pay a fine of 6,200 *libras*, an amount which was to be used to reinforce its bulwarks, although Borgia was afraid that this money could not be collected in its entirety.

Once these measures were taken, Borgia's policy was to grant an amnesty to all "with the exception of some persons who were most guilty." And so the matter was settled. The emperor's pardon arrived December 15, 1540. Borgia was able to conclude that this business "has given me more grief than if it were the most important in all Catalonia."[35]

Even though he had written on November 25, 1540, that the border with France was quiet and that a Catalan coming from Marseilles had reported that he had heard nothing about the war, it was natural that Borgia should want to inspect the fortifications, as Cardinal Tavera had recommended. Consequently, he inspected the castles of Perpignan and Salses; before departing he left a very detailed set of instructions with Juan Muñoz de Salazar, "inspector of the Perpignan frontier," pointing out in minute detail what had to be done to secure the frontier zone.[36]

Borgia left Perpignan on December 17, 1540, and on the 23rd was back in Barcelona. On the eve of his departure he had written Charles V informing him about everything that he had done in Roussillon.[37] The emperor answered through his Consejo, praising him for "the skill with which you acted in everything and the good advice you left at the works and in all places where it was most fitting."[38]

Conditions that awaited him on his return to Barcelona convinced him that he had had good grounds to fear being absent from the principality's capital. He lamented that what he had achieved in a year had been lost in two months, so that he had to begin anew.

Borgia and the Barcelona church

Juan Cardona was the bishop of Barcelona during Borgia's viceroyalty, the third and last member of this illustrious family to occupy that see. The viceroy, so upright in his own life-style, could not look with approval on the indiscretions of this prelate, who had been raised to the bishopric in 1531 but by 1539 had still not been ordained bishop. The pastoral care of the diocese was delegated to titular bishops. Borgia wanted Cardona "to be consecrated and the time he spent in gambling be employed in his office. . . . This is how I wish to pay the rent for his houses: by seeing to it that God dwells in his house."[39] We have already noted that the viceroy lived in the residence that belonged to the archdeacon. Charles V shared Borgia's concern and urged that the bishop "by all means be consecrated and do what he should for the service of God, and Ours, and for himself personally."[40] But Cardona did not receive episcopal ordination until 1545, five months before his death on February 1, 1546.

The chief problem Borgia had with the ecclesiastical authorities was with the "crowned ones," or those who had received the tonsure and later taken refuge under the Church's privilege to escape civil justice. Borgia reported that clerical immunities were so widespread in Catalonia that the ordinary judges could hardly administer justice at all. He insisted with the emperor and with the Roman ambassador that he had to have a pontifical brief limiting the cases of clerical immunity. This brief arrived but was of little use because, as the viceroy wrote on May 5, 1540, "it comes with some clauses very detrimental to the administration of justice."[41] So he had to obtain another one, which, in fact, arrived in Barcelona that same year. "The brief dealing with the 'crowned ones' has arrived here tonight. May God grant that it be better than the last one."[42]

But the bandits, with the approval of the clergy, employed yet another stratagem, namely, abusing the custom of sanctuary. Because there was a plethora of churches and hermitages scattered throughout the country, some of them abandoned, it was not difficult for the bandits to escape justice. The Roman ambassador petitioned the pope to impose limits on this ecclesiastical privilege or at least to restrict it to churches and chapels still actually used for religious worship.[43]

In his instruction of 1539 Charles V had made reference to the delicate matter of reform of the monasteries, especially those of nuns:

> The dissipation, the bad habits, and excessive freedom which exist in some monasteries of monks and nuns in Barcelona and in Catalonia cause disservice to God and dishonor and disrepute to the same city and to the country, as well as ignominy to religion; and it is a burden to one's conscience to allow it to continue thus without a remedy.[44]

On December 9 of the same year Borgia could write to Cobos that the fruits of his intervention were beginning to be seen.

> The [monasteries] that are under the supervision of the bishop of Barcelona were enclosed in such a way that neither the nuns go out nor men go in; but [the condition of the monasteries] still should be better than it is. And in other monasteries which are under different prelates the nuns were simply warned and asked to attend carefully to the matter of their going out of the monastery and having others come in, because it seems injurious to God and to society.[45]

As we can see, what primarily needed reform was the observance of cloister. Borgia added that it was necessary to act tactfully, because reform was a problem that had been entrusted to the cardinals of Toledo and Seville and to the bishop of Tortosa. He proposed that in the case of Catalonia these prelates should delegate their mandate to the bishop of Gerona and to the inquisitor Fernando de Loaces.

Even after he had given up his office of viceroy, Borgia continued to take an interest in the reform of Barcelona's monasteries and convents; but by then it was in response to the suggestions of St. Ignatius, who always showed a great interest in this sensitive issue. Borgia was able to write to Ignatius from Gandía on June 7, 1546, about the diplomatic way of procedures they had agreed upon in these matters.[46]

Conflicts

Unquestionably, the Barcelona establishment cordially received the newly appointed viceroy, Francisco de Borja. An indication of this fact were the words addressed to him by the *consellers* of Barcelona in a letter of August 4, 1539: "We have felt, and we still do feel, a special pleasure . . . because Your Excellency . . . is endowed with so much prudence and knowledge" that they could hope his administration would redound in "praise of God, service of His Imperial Majesty, in beneficence, concord, joy, and consolation for all the towns of this principality and these counties."[47] A chance phrase of Borgia's in a letter of 1541 enables us to deduce that this cordiality was not merely a first impression: "although they [the *consellers*] show goodwill toward me." In turn, Charles V told the *consellers* in a letter addressed to them on November 8, 1539, that his viceroy proved "to be very happy with you, something which has given Us great pleasure."[48] If there were problems these existed to a large measure because the viceroy had to collect the city's payment for the upkeep of its own fortifications.

As to dealings with the Generalitat, we read in Borgia's correspondence this noteworthy phrase: "seeming to me that the concerns of the Generalitat should be favored." Here too, however, the main problems had an economic origin. Borgia had to get the *diputats* to pay the *residuo*, a tax imposed on the Generalitat by the Cortes of Monzón. In a letter of June 18, 1540, to Cobos Borgia said that he had

> extracted one thousand ducats from them, but I still have reason to complain about them [the *diputats*] and I will see if I can get more. I assure Your Excellency that, considering the effort it takes to get money from them, even if God gave me authorization for it it would take the rest of my life to get a penny out of them; for coin, even belonging to His Majesty, is so hard to extract from them that I almost have to use hooks to do it.[49]

Borgia showed courage in confronting the nobles and gentlemen when he considered that justice demanded it. He remained firm in implementing the prohibition against exporting horses from Catalonia, even at the cost of

> having many complain against me and even losing some friends, among whom is the viceroy of Sardinia [Antonio de Cardona] to whom, however he and his brother [Pedro], the governor, importuned me, I refused permission to embark a horse. I disregarded their insults, for I was doing my duty.[50]

On May 3, 1564, Borgia noted in his spiritual diary, "I give thanks to God for the crosses of this day so many years ago."[51] There is no doubt that he was alluding to the events that took place twenty-three years previously, on May 3, 1541. This was the day, consecrated to the Exaltation of the Holy Cross, that the people of Barcelona celebrated the dedication of their cathedral. To be sure, it was a great festive day and a joust was organized at which the viceroy was asked to act as referee. Before the tournament began Borgia noticed that a dais had been erected in the plaza for the duke of Cardona and his wife. This was a violation of the explicit regulations mentioned earlier in this book, prohibiting the use of curule chairs and daises in the presence of the viceroy. Borgia canceled the joust. The duke was terribly incensed; but even worse, the action occasioned the clash between the viceroy and Luis Enríquez de Girón, the count of Módica. While the tournament did not take place on that day, the viceroy allowed it to go ahead on the following day, when his attendance at a meeting of the audiencia prevented him from being present at it.

But it was at the gala dinner given during this fiesta time that the count of Módica became even more enraged. The viceroy took his stance at the door of the dining room where he prevented any gentleman from entering until all the invited ladies had been seated. The count drew his dagger in a threatening manner and down in the streets his retainers caused disturbances. The upshot was that the count had to face court charges and was put under house arrest.

In his letters informing the emperor and the secretary, Cobos, about these events, Borgia insisted that he never once acted from feelings of passion, but only to defend what he had judged to be "royal preeminence."

The Consejo de Aragón must have thought that the viceroy acted with little diplomacy by punishing a man of the count of Módica's rank. Not only was he the count of Módica, he was also duke of Medina de Rioseco, the sixth admiral of Castile, and count of Melgar. Without repudiating the viceroy's actions, the Consejo made this recommendation to him: "We ask and advise you to avoid such matters in every way that you can." In the future he was to abide by the judgment of the Consejo. There was no doubt that Borgia was ready to obey whatever he was ordered. When he was informed that Charles V had pardoned the count, his reaction was shown in these sentences in his letter to the emperor, March 14, 1542:

> Here I have learned how Your Majesty was pleased to pardon the count of Módica, which was a great favor to the marquise and to me. And this you can believe: that if there were anything that could increase the desire we have of serving Your Majesty it would be this. Because [the pardon] was for us one of the greatest favors which we could have received from Your Majesty.[52]

The wheat problem

The dearth of wheat was the object of constant preoccupation for the viceroy. Its cause was "the sterility of the land," about which he was always lamenting, aggravated by a persistent drought. On August 22, 1539, he wrote to Charles, "At any time you came to Catalonia you must have seen the want of grain, like wheat, barley, and oats, that the whole province suffers and how in most places there was no harvest this year."[53] This was a scarcity that was experienced to some degree in every region of Spain, so much so that, when grain was taken out of one place, the natives would suffer want. This is what happened in Roussillon when it exported grain to Barcelona in 1541. One particularly fertile region was the plain of Urgel.

Sometimes the wheat scarcity became acute and grain had to be brought in from outside the principality. In 1540 three thousand *fanegas* were imported from La Mancha. Wheat was also imported from France. The viceroy was ready to permit iron to be exported to France in hopes of persuading the French to lift their embargo on wheat. The wheat scarcity also affected prices considerably, making them skyrocket; over a number of years it had a catastrophic effect upon the weak Catalan economy. During our period wheat was becoming more and more expensive, supposing that it could be found at all.

On the other hand, conditions were favorable for wine and other agricultural products.

The French attack at Perpignan

During the early years of Borgia's viceroyalty, the Roussillon border was relatively quiet, although peace between France and Spain was always precarious. In June 1541 an incident occurred which jeopardized relations between these two powers: some imperial soldiers were accused of having killed Antonio Rincón, a Spaniard, and Cesar Fregoso, an Italian, both emissaries of the French king in his dealings with Suleiman the Magnificent. In retaliation French authorities arrested and held in custody George of Austria as he was traveling through France. Bastard son of Maximilian I, Charles V's grandfather, the prisoner was also archbishop of Valencia. Meanwhile, Juan de Acuña, captain general of Roussillon, reported that France was making preparations for war; and on August 30, 1541, Borgia relayed this news to the secretary, Cobos, asking him to send troops, particularly cavalrymen, into Roussillon. Then he awaited instructions. Borgia feared that the French, seeing the emperor preparing a great fleet, would think that he was going to launch an attack on Marseilles or some other city along the coast. Thus, as a countermeasure, they might invade Roussillon, "seeing themselves powerful and us without resources."[54] On September 18, he reported that "this business keeps getting bigger. I mean in preparations and in the number of soldiers."[55] He believed that between Narbonne and Aigues-Mortes there were twenty thousand troops and three thousand others between Narbonne and Leucate.

Charles V in turn wrote to the viceroy on September 19, telling him that he wanted to keep the truce with France; but, given the fact that France was rattling the sword before Perpignan and Fuenterrabia, one had to keep on the alert. He urged Francis to order Captain General Juan de Acuña "to have good spies in France to know what was being done."[56]

Periods of calm followed these moments of alarm. "The French business seems to be settling down, because the border activity is not what it used to be," Borgia observed. At any rate, he was ready to send a good number of men from Ampurdán to Perpignan if there was any danger. On October 5 he wrote that "the border situation . . . is quieter and there is less bustling of armed men; . . . at any event, we are taking every precaution."[57] On the 12th of the same month, he showed that he did not put too much faith in the lull because "Your Excellency [Cobos] knows the way of the French, and the king has come to Lyons. I would not want them to start something."[58] On December 19 he wrote, "I am informed that everything is peaceful as far as France is concerned."[59]

In this uncertain atmosphere the Cortes of Monzón was convened in June of 1542. During its sessions the principality offered the emperor, in addition to the customary services and general levies, the sum of 250,000 *libras* to support his war effort, and Barcelona gave him twelve large bronze cannons to be used at Perpignan.

Faced with an attack on this border, Charles V named the duke of Alba captain general of the army. He also offered to send, as the historian Felíu put it, foreigners—Germans, that is—to Perpignan. But Catalonia refused them, saying that the Catalan militia would be sufficient. Rogation prayers were offered in Barcelona and a procession was organized.

On August 31 the war began. Henry, the dauphin, invaded Roussillon at Leucate, bringing with him a great number of men and cannons. After meeting some resistance, he pushed on to Perpignan, where he set up a siege that lasted nine weeks. But the resistance offered by the Catalan defenders finally forced him to retreat, and the news that the siege had been broken was published in Barcelona on October 4. The preparations undertaken at Perpignan were successful; its fortification works held.

Despite everything, the danger was not forgotten. In Barcelona they continued to dig moats and to build ramparts, putting great efforts into these projects during the early months of 1543 under the constant supervision of the viceroy, who urged authorities to allocate sufficient men and money.

On February 24, 1543, Charles V informed the viceroy that, according to Juan de Acuña, the French had made new plans to invade Catalonia, this time through Conflent, in an endeavor to attack Puigcerdá.[60] Francis received orders that all places, but especially Puigcerdá, were to be well supplied with defenses "in accord with the confidence we have in you." It was essential to supply Puigcerdá with provisions that would enable it to hold on for six months, supported by one thousand infantrymen stationed before the city, with an additional thousand backing them up at Elna, and four hundred more at Cotlliure. Moreover, the three companies of Germans that were stationed at Puigcerdá were to be moved up as close as possible to Perpignan. The troops at Ampurdán were also to be reassembled. Finally, the artillery was to be under the command of Captain García Carreño. But this invasion attempt as well proved unsuccessful.

The Cortes of Monzón in 1542

There had been talk about calling together the Catalan-Aragonese Cortes at Monzón ever since the beginning of 1542. One of Charles V's reasons for doing so was to present his eldest son, Prince Philip, and have him take the oath to protect regional privileges and be recognized in turn as heir apparent to the throne. According to Borgia, some of the experts were of the opinion that the oath need not be taken in the Cortes, where there might be difficulties. In any event, according to the Catalan privilege, the prince had to renew his oath in Barcelona, whether he had taken it in the Cortes or not. Charles V insisted that the ceremony take place during the Cortes, and so it was done. But later the consensus was that the prince should renew his oath in each of the capitals of the confederation, Zaragoza, Barcelona, and Valencia. By March, plans for summoning the Cortes were agreed upon, and so the viceroy postponed some of his business affairs in deference to it. In April he said that he was doing nothing else but preparing for the meeting. He asked that the Franciscan convent be reserved for his lodgings. Because his predecessor, Don Fadrique de Portugal, had stayed there during the last convocation, he was under the impression that this convent was reserved for the viceroy of Catalonia. But when he was informed that Don Fadrique had lived there in his capacity as archbishop of Zaragoza and that the convent was already reserved for the archbishop, he asked that another place be found for him and for his father, the duke of Gandía.

The convocation was set for May 15, but there was a postponement and Borgia did not leave Barcelona until June 12. The Cortes was in session until September 25; during that time Prince Philip did take his oath and the representatives approved a more than usually generous subsidy (*servicio*) to the king. We have already pointed out that the emperor received 250,000 *libras* for his war effort. Governmental affairs were discussed during the sessions, and the administration of the viceroy did not escape criticism. One particular problem that was treated, of course, was that of brigandage; and on October 5 a law was passed against bandits, thieves, and other malefactors.[61] By a special order of the emperor, the viceroy and other authorities of the principality were ordered to be particularly on the lookout for malefactors and bandits coming into the valley of Aran and vigilantly to ensure the security of the people living there.

During the long sessions at Monzón, Charles V and his representatives in Catalonia had the opportunity to deal with the affairs of the principality. Did they discuss the matter of relieving Borgia of his job as viceroy so that he could be appointed first majordomo to Princess María of Portugal, whose wedding with Prince Philip was imminent? They could have, but the sources do not say. The fact is that once the sessions were adjourned Borgia returned to Barcelona, where he carried out the duties of his office with the same vigor that he had always demonstrated.

On October 16, Charles V also left for Barcelona. Here Prince Philip joined him on November 8, after taking his oath at Zaragoza and promising to protect Aragonese privileges. After he had repeated this same oath in Barcelona before the Catalan authorities, he left for Valencia, where on the 21st of that same month he took a third oath in the presence of his father.

On December 2, Borgia had to repeat the oath he had taken when he first became viceroy, not in order to prolong his term of office, but simply because his jurisdiction had been suspended during the emperor's presence in Barcelona. The *consellers* did not come to pay their visit to him until ten days after Charles had quit the principality.

Borgia's private life

There is a contrast between the picture of Borgia that we get from archive documents and the portrait left us by his first biographers, Dionisio Vázquez and those of a similar approach, Ribadeneira and Nieremberg. The documents show us an administrator preoccupied with grain supplies, meting out justice, maintaining public order, defending cities, and making preparations for war. Without neglecting all these aspects of his life, the biographers focus their attention on the saint, who accepted the position of viceroy purely in compliance with the will of Charles V and who devoted himself primarily to prayer and pious practices. A compromise between these two extremes is detected in the testimony of the fourteen witnesses participating in Borgia's beatification process held in Barcelona in 1611.[62] During these proceedings they responded to questions posed by Father Pedro Gil, the procurator of Borgia's cause; and, even though they had not lived with Borgia in Barcelona and at times based their depositions on what they had read in the biographies of the authors we cited above, they were nevertheless close enough to the facts and therefore capable of testifying to the mood, tendencies, and inclinations prevailing in the city with regard to Borgia. Two of their number, Gabriel Olsina and Miguel Juan Amat, were city archivists and could have consulted the very same documents that are at our disposal today.

In capsule form, what do the biographies say? They tell us that Francis frequented the sacraments, going to confession and Communion once a week; that he dedicated five or six hours a day to prayer, getting up at two or three in the morning to do this; that he recited daily the six canonical hours or said the corresponding Our Fathers and Hail Marys that were his obligation as a knight of the military Order of Santiago; that while he recited this vocal prayer he meditated on the mysteries of Christ's life, just as he did when he said the rosary; that he fasted on many days, and that one year he observed two lents, the first from November 4 to Christmas, and the other in preparation for Easter; that during this period he would take nothing more than a bowl of herbs, a slice of bread and a glass of water; that from this time on he gave up eating supper altogether; that, as a consequence of these prolonged fasts, he who had once been enormously fat became so thin that he could fold his skin over on himself and that a jacket which had fitted him perfectly before he had begun these fasts became more than sixteen inches too large at the waist; that he examined his conscience twice a day, in addition to making a brief reflection each time the clock struck; that he performed harsh penances which included hairshirts and disciplines. All in all, as Ribadeneira observed, "his life was more that of a very penitent religious than that of a lord and governor who was young, married, and reared in luxury and opulence."[63]

Although we do not take all these assertions literally, we cannot help but see a semblance of truth in them. One thing is certain: ever after his Barcelona days Borgia lived a life of prayer and penance, noteworthy for the exercise of virtues.

Speaking of his fasts, Vázquez tells us that Francis had three reasons for performing them: (1) to do penance for the excesses formerly indulged in, (2) to save time so that he could dedicate it to prayer, and (3) "to enable his body to lose weight, for it was too fat."[64] As far as this last consideration is concerned, we know that he was overweight because Borgia himself tells us so. We should recall that he himself remembered the effort it required, thanks to his "pottle belly," for him to go down roads and up mountains in hot pursuit of hoodlums. Moreover, it is certain that, even though he lost weight because of these excesses, he did not do so without serious harm to his health. Vázquez says that "his stomach was damaged . . . and developed violent indigestion, building up such excessive gas that to expel it he had to spend two hours daily exploding it through his mouth."[65] This malady remained with him throughout his life.

As far as Borgia's spirituality during this period is concerned, suffice it to say that some hints of the behavior his biographers describe can already be seen outlined in the *Six Very Devout Treatises* which he published in 1548 but which beyond doubt was the fruit of his experiences long before this date.[66] Also, his *Mirror of a Christian's Works* shows us how he sanctified each of his actions, while what he wrote in his *Method for Reciting the Holy Rosary* harmonizes with what Vázquez, Ribadeneira, and Nieremberg told us about the devotions he practiced in Barcelona.

For matters of conscience, Borgia had recourse to two Dominicans, Father Juan Micó, his confessor, and the provincial, Father Tomás de Guzmán. He also shared an intimacy with the Franciscans from the Jesús Convent, where St. Salvador de Horta lived, as did Fray Juan de Tejeda, a somewhat enigmatic lay brother. Indeed, Francis had such affection for Fray Juan that he persuaded his superiors to send him to Gandía. He also knew the future St. Peter of Alcántara at this same convent. In 1541 Peter was on his way to take part in the Franciscan general chapter at Mantua when he fell ill and had to stop over in Barcelona. It was during that same chapter that the new general, Giovanni Maltei de Calvi, issued a document dated June 1, 1541, admitting Francis, his wife, and his children into the brotherhood of the order ("in nostrae fraternitatis consortium").[67]

But those who exercised the greatest influence on his future were the early Jesuits sent to Barcelona. The first of these was Father Antonio de Araoz, who spent a few days in the ducal city in 1539, and then returned for several months in 1542, devoting himself with considerable success to the priestly ministry. He had dealings with the marquise of Llombai, who introduced him to her husband. They conversed with one another, quite naturally, about the Society and its founder. Borgia was so delighted with what the young Jesuit was doing in Barcelona that while attending the Cortes at Monzón he wrote to Ignatius on July 18, 1542, asking him to keep Araoz there so that he could continue his apostolate in that city.[68]

In February and March of that year Peter Faber and his two companions stopped in Barcelona on their way to Germany. Borgia treated them with signs of singular affection, as Faber informed Ignatius on March 1. "We arrived here in Barcelona last Saturday evening [February 26] and were put up by the viceroy, the marquis of Llombai, who is very fond of us, as is his wife the marquise; and for this reason you should keep Their Excellencies very close in your remembrances."[69]

We have few facts about the intimacy of Borgia's family life. His many occupations and preoccupations certainly could not have left him much time to enjoy the peace of the archdeacon's house, which he called his home, sharing it with his wife Leonor and their eight children, the youngest of whom was Alonso, born in 1539, the same year his father was appointed viceroy. When we consider that the oldest was born in 1530, we see that all of the children were at this time very young, needing the care of both mother and father. Also part of the viceroy's household was Borgia's sister-in-law, Juana de Meneses, whom he always mentioned in his greetings to the secretary, Cobos, and his wife, María de Mendoza.

To support such a large family, Borgia relied on the resources he listed in a letter of August 26, 1549, to the secretary Juan Vázquez de Molina.

> After I was married, having made the expedition to France with His Majesty [1536], he granted a life pension of 400,000 *maravedís*, which I have; and when our lady the empress, who is in heaven, died, His Majesty bestowed on me the post in Catalonia, with 5,000 ducats as a salary. And when I arrived in Barcelona, he granted me the Huélamo *encomienda*, which afterwards His Majesty ordered improved by [granting me] the *encomienda* of Reina, which I now have. . . . And what was done for the duchess [Leonor] was that our lady the empress upon her death bequeathed her a life pension of 250,000 *maravedís* which, with the other pension of 500,000 given her when she married, was forfeited at her death.[70]

His income did not always arrive in Barcelona on time, and Borgia was forced to write more than once to Cobos, humbly asking that he remember what was due him and his wife, clearly explaining, however, that "we have nothing else with which to serve His Majesty, and we do not want it except for his service." Occasionally he asked for a pension for one of his children. In 1541, he learned of the death of Bernardo Rovira, abbot of Santa María del Estany, a royal-patronage monastery, and he also heard that the diocese of Córdoba had remained vacant; so he ventured to ask that the rents from those two church properties be granted to one of his children as a pension. From all this we gather that Borgia not only lived uncomfortably but also put up with an austere life-style, always enduring it courageously and always bearing in mind the incentive for his actions, the service of the emperor.

3. Duke of Gandía (1543-1550)

Succession to the duchy

Francis's father, Juan de Borja y Enríquez, the third duke, died in Gandía on January 8, 1543. He was only forty-nine years old. The city *jurados* communicated the news to Francis in a letter written on the day of his demise. After expressing their condolences on his loss, they asked him for instructions about "the order that we must have in the government and management of the said town."

In his answer on January 15 the then viceroy of Catalonia notified them that "the affairs of this post and the business His Majesty has entrusted to me, and those which arise because of the war, are of such importance that in no way would I dare leave here without His Majesty's permission."[1] In the meantime, he delegated the widow, Duchess Doña Francisca de Castro-Pinós, to care for all that had to be done in Gandía.

Francis considered that his first duty was to inform the emperor of his father's death. In his letter he expressed the "need to inspect the house so as to put some things in order."[2] So it was not a question of submitting his resignation as viceroy, but simply of requesting leave to make a tour about his lands to inspect the condition of his estate. In a letter from Madrid on January 22, Charles V extended his condolences.[3] His grief for his father's loss would be mitigated by the joy of his being next in line to succeed him. The emperor trusted that Francis would continue serving him with the same fidelity he had manifested up to the present time. As far as the trip to Gandía was concerned, the emperor ordered him to put this off until his own arrival in Barcelona, where he was thinking of spending the whole month of March. As a matter of fact, the situation at the time was tense. Charles V wrote the viceroy of Catalonia a second letter the same day, ordering him to have the borders well prepared against a possible French attack.

In the midst of mourning his father's death, Francis must have experienced great consolation from a letter of condolence sent by Paul III. The pope expressed sympathy for the loss of Don Juan, whom he loved because he was the grandson of Alexander VI, "from whom our exalted position has its origin," and because of the virtues of the deceased. He exhorted Francis to conduct himself as befitting such a father.[4] Borgia answered the pope on April 21, telling him that he would like to be able personally to show his appreciation by kissing his foot, but that the service of the emperor prevented him from doing so. However, whatever the circumstances, "I consider myself to be as much a creation of Your Holiness as of the duke my father."[5] We shall have the opportunity to see other examples of deference shown Borgia by Paul III, as well as of the esteem that the pope entertained for him.

Majordomo to Princess Maria?

As eldest son of the deceased duke, Francis became the fourth duke of Gandía, the title he henceforth used whenever he signed his name. But there remained an uncertainty: Would he continue serving as viceroy of Catalonia or would he leave this office to devote himself to the governance of Gandía? Charles V had plans that offered a third option, plans he must have communicated to Francis when he came to Barcelona on April 11. These included naming Francis chief majordomo to the infanta María Manuela, daughter of the Portuguese monarchs and fiancée to Prince Don Felipe of Spain. This position would entail the same duties that the count of Miranda had exercised for the deceased empress Isabel. Francis's wife would be the mistress of Princess María's wardrobe. On April 22, 1543, the imperial secretary, Francisco de los Cobos, sent Francis the credentials of his nomination.[6]

On April 18 of that year, Francis had left Barcelona for Gandía, and the marquis of Aguilar, Juan Fernández de Manrique, was named his successor. Though he felt a sense of relief on leaving the viceroyalty of Catalonia, he must have experienced sadness in quitting Barcelona. On January 20, 1543, he had written Cobos, "Barcelona needs no other proof of her worth than the pain men feel when leaving her."[7] But there was no doubt that for him the departure was a blessing that he could still remember in 1564, because on April 18 of that year he wrote in his spiritual diary, "Thanksgiving for leaving Catalonia, which took place twenty-one years ago this day."[8]

He should not have had to remain in Gandía any longer than it took for him to tidy up a few family affairs and to attend to some administrative business. After that he was supposed to have gone to the court. Philip II signed the marriage contract with Princess María at Lisbon on December 1, 1542, and on the following November 13 the royal couple were married in Salamanca. As it turned out, however, Francis stayed on in Gandía for seven years, until 1550. What had happened? Princess María's parents opposed

Charles's plan; or, more exactly, her mother was against it and would not give her consent to it. A number of reasons have been put forward to explain this stubborn resistance. For example, that Francis's appointment had been made without consulting the bride's parents, or that the Portuguese monarchs thought it would be preferable to give a Portuguese the position that had been offered to the duke of Gandía. As a matter of fact, they did select the Portuguese Alejo de Meneses and his wife, Margarita de Mendoza, to be María's majordomo and mistress of the bedchamber. But judging from the correspondence between Queen Catherine and her brother, Emperor Charles V, we gather that Francis's wife, Leonor de Castro, was a persona non grata with the Portuguese queen. It is difficult to see if this dislike resulted from Leonor's domineering and difficult disposition or from a personality clash between the two women; but the fact is that Catherine made her misgivings known to the interested parties through King John III's brother, the infante Don Luis.[9]

The situation being what it was, there was no alternative but to wait and see how things would turn out, and this is what Borgia recommended that Charles do. Besides, it would be awkward going to Portugal without the approval of that country's king and queen. But the emperor was determined and carried on as if his decision was a fait accompli. Besides other pieces of evidence, this curious incident offers proof of Charles's attitude. In the instruction the emperor left his son in 1543, he recommended that after their marriage Philip and his wife be moderate in their sex life; and he advised the prince's majordomo, Don Juan de Zúñiga, to make sure Philip heeded this counsel, adding, "I have also ordered your wife's dignitaries, the duke and duchess of Gandía, to be faithfully vigilant" in carrying out these instructions.[10] If Charles had remained in Spain, perhaps matters might have taken a different turn; but after spending the whole of April between Molíns de Rey and Barcelona, he sailed for Italy on May 1 and did not return to Spain until 1556, after he had abdicated.

These months must have been filled with anxieties for Borgia because of the uncertainty of his immediate future, more than because of any ambition to fill a position that would open doors for him to a most attractive future at court. In the fall of 1544 he still believed that he would be going to court, all the more so because the prince wanted him at his side. His wife's poor health was one more factor added to his list of uncertainties, but we can be sure that during these months his desire was more to serve the emperor than to realize his own personal advancement.[11] At any event, all this bewilderment can only have contributed to detaching him more from the things of this world.

Events that followed put to rest all his doubts. On July 8, 1545, Princess María gave birth to Prince Don Carlos, destined to be all too well known in history; then four days later she was taken away by a premature death. So it was that the problem of choosing a majordomo was solved; but, as we shall have the opportunity to see, the matter came up again at a later date.

In 1543, Charles exchanged the *encomienda* of Reina (Badajoz) for that of the Order of Santiago's *encomienda* of Huélamo (Cuenca), which he had given to Borgia. Francis thanked him for this in a letter of June 10, 1543.[12]

The task of governing

The new duke of Gandía committed himself to administering his vast holdings. The properties that Francis had inherited at the time of his father's death were those named in his father's last will and testament, drawn up at Gandía on February 28, 1538:

> We, Don Juan de Borja, Duke of Gandía, lord of the castle of Bairent; of the castle and barony of Corbera and other small towns there, such as the town of Albalat on the banks of the Júcar; of the barony of Castelló de Rugat, and of the town of Pobla and of other hamlets in the same barony; of the castle, barony, and estate of Rois; of the castle and the village of Chella; of the castle and the valleys of Gallinera and Ebo, and of the villages located in them, and of the towns of Real and Las Almoines, Bellreguart, Miramar, Jeresa and Alcodar, and other villages of the same region; of the barony, the estate, and the castle of Navarrés . . .[13]

Besides the town of Llombai, those of Catadau and Alfarb were part of the marquisate of Llombai.

Gandía stood out among the other towns because of its importance and because of the number of its inhabitants. The saintly duke continued to fortify this walled city against possible raids by Moors and corsairs. In 1543 he wrote to Prince Philip, "I hope, trusting in God, to defend Gandía with the fortifications I am putting up in it."[14] He also contemplated constructing defenses for Valencia and even for the island of Ibiza, which he considered the port of entry to the old kingdom of Valencia. He believed that he had to take steps to prevent the kingdom's Moriscos from escaping in ships that the Moors and Turks might land on the Valencian coast.

We should not forget that a large part of the population of the duchy was made up of Moriscos, the Moors who had remained in Spain after the reconquest and received baptism. The Moriscos predominated in one quarter of the city of Gandía and constituted the sole inhabitants of some of the neighboring villages.[15] It was an acnowledged fact that these New Christians were an industrious people; when they were expelled, the economy of the country suffered greatly. Nevertheless, they created many problems because they did not prove to be culturally assimilable and their religious conversion was merely a pro forma rite. This Morisco problem was one of the most difficult Borgia had to face. He was both a political figure and a Christian, so his ardent desire was that the Moriscos live in peace as good Christians. In 1545 the viceroy of Valencia acknowledged that this was precisely what Borgia was trying to achieve. Rather than attempting to coerce these people, he tried to win them over by teaching them and catechizing them. Finally, the college of Gandía, which we discuss later, and the monastery of Llombai, which the duke would entrust to the Dominicans, implemented Borgia's earliest plans to provide a Christian education for the Moriscos.

The most prominent building in Gandía was the principal church, dedicated to the Blessed Virgin Mary, which Alexander VI in 1499 raised to the rank of collegiate church. Constructed in the second half of the four-teenth century, it is a Gothic edifice with only one nave and two side chapels. Unfortunately, a great part was destroyed by fire in August 1936. Among other priceless artifacts that perished was the precious reredos of the main altar, a work by the Lombard Pablo de San Leocadio. Fourteen canons and thirty-seven benefice-holders constituted the clergy of this collegiate church. During Francis's time the dean of the chapter was Francisco Roca, to whom he entrusted on more than one occasion the management of his affairs in Rome. It goes without saying that during his viceroyalty, Borgia endeavored to promote the splendor of divine worship.

The ducal palace of Gandía, which the Borgias had chosen for their residence, had belonged to the kings of Aragón. In 1890 the Society of Jesus purchased it for a novitiate and residence. Today one can still visit this palace and admire its wide portal, surmounted by an escutcheon bearing the Borja and Oms coats of arms. An outside staircase leading from the main patio opens upon the spacious Hall of the Crowns; from here a visitor can go into what was the saint's office, now converted into a chapel. Next door was the "holy chapel," to which Francis would retire for prayer and pen-ance. This chapel was constructed in the shape of a coffin; its walls were covered with paintings depicting the mysteries of the rosary.

The monastery of the Poor Clares

In the city of Gandía there was a monastery of Poor Clares which enjoyed a role of singular importance in the history of the reform of Franciscan nuns. In the second stage of this history, that is, from the first part of 1457 on, the monastery housed French nuns from the monastery of Lézignan, located in the diocese of Narbonne. These women subscribed to the reform of St. Colette of Corbie (d. 1447), who had adopted the primitive rule of St. Clare. From this date on the Gandía monastery diffused authentic Franciscan spirit into various cities of Spain. The Borgia dukes were benefactors of this monastery; but after María Enríquez de Luna, widow of the second duke of Gandía, became a nun there in 1511, taking the name María Gabriela, the connection between the monastery and the ducal family became very close. From this date until at least the time of the tenth duke, Pascual de Borja y Ponce de León, at least one daughter from the ducal family lived within its monastic cloister.[16] Limiting ourselves to close relatives of our saint, the Poor Clares in his family, besides his grandmother, María Enríquez, were his aunt (Sister Francisca); his sisters María (María de la Cruz), Ana (Juana Evangelista), Isabel (Juana Bautista); and his half sisters, María (María Gabriela), Ana (Juana de la Cruz), and Magdalena (María Magdalena de Jesús).

In 1533, St. Francis Xavier's oldest sister, Magdalena, died in this monastery. Already a nun before he was born, at her death she was the abbess of Gandía.[17] The Apostle of the Indies never had the opportunity to meet this sister of his.

For the good of his subjects

Borgia loved his subjects and, motivated by sentiments of social justice, was concerned for their welfare. Extrapolating from testimonies offered at his canonization process, we have abundant evidence that he was particularly generous toward the poor and needy.

He fostered two industries which depended on the crops most widely cultivated at that time, sugar and silk. These constituted the source of prosperity for the region. Planted in the vast fields, sugar cane ensured a source of wealth for the country, because from November to January the duke's sugar-refining mills provided work for more than five hundred hands. After the Moriscos were expelled in 1609 and American sugar came to be imported, this industry died out; but the silk industry remained active, and mulberry trees, food for the silk worm, continued to thrive in Gandía's irrigated plains. Sugar and silk had made the duke of Gandía one of the richest men in the land, and they also provided bread and work for many of his subjects.

He restored the hospital of San Marcos with the view to improving the health of the citizens.

Composer and ascetical writer

From his ancestors Borgia had inherited a penchant for his favorite sports, hunting and horseback riding. But perhaps his greatest love, one that he shared with Charles V, was for music. Not only did he take pleasure in singing and in playing musical instruments, but he also composed a number of secular and religious pieces. There is one nonreligious cantata attributed to him, and he was certainly the composer of a mass for four voices as well as of several motets that still survive. The mass is better known for the vividness of its expression than for the artistry of its composition. The motets were composed to accompany the representation of Christ's passion and resurrection performed on Good Friday in the Poor Clares' monastery, as the Blessed Sacrament was carried from the altar of repose, and on Easter Sunday, during the procession which made its way to the collegiate church and back again to the monastery. On August 4, 1550, before leaving for Rome, Francis presided over the meeting of the collegiate chapter at which the nuns set down directions for staging this ceremony and specified the wages due to each of the participants.

Borgia's great love of music is reflected in his spiritual writings, where frequently he made use of musical images; for example, contrasting the docility of organ pipes toward the player at the console with man's rebellion against the action of God, or the harmony flowing from well-tuned instruments with the disorder that is wrought by sin. We cite here an example taken from his treatise *Pattern of the Soul of Christ*:

> Grieve for your blindness; behold the horrible dissonance; let human ears be stopped as you consider that, when the fingers touch the keys of a wooden or a tin pipe and when the bellows have been inflated, the notes are immediately produced. Though the Lord's fingers touch the heart of man in diverse ways, and though he is an instrument finer than wood, of greater quality than tin, and though the Holy Spirit sends his breath in varied ways, man alone fails to respond to the artist who created him.[18]

His efforts as an ascetical writer began during his Gandían period. In addition to a method for saying the rosary, which reflects the practices of his Barcelona days, and a sermon on humility, which dates from 1546, during this period Borgia wrote six brief treatises in which the main themes were self-knowledge and confusion over man's lack of response in the face of God's kindness. He apparently alludes to these writings in a letter to Peter Faber on September 15, 1545, in which he reports giving thanks to God for permitting him "to finish these little works which I have begun."[19] Father Oviedo informed St. Ignatius in a letter of January 26, 1547, that "the booklet which His Excellency wrote has already been printed and it is very useful because it deals with humility and self-depreciation which His Excellency has practiced and in which he is proficient."[20] He was probably alluding to the treatise entitled *Spiritual Eye Salve*. This treatise, and perhaps other treatises as well, was published in a separate edition about which we know nothing. In 1548, the printer Juan de Mey published all of them together at Valencia under the title *Seys tratados muy deuotos y vtiles para qualquier fiel Christiano, compuestos por el illustriss. S. don Francisco de Borja Duque de Gandia y Marques de Lombay, etc..*[21]

Meanwhile, as he continued studying theology according to the method of St. Thomas Aquinas, he got the idea of converting the matter of his lessons into prayer. So he composed some Latin litanies asking the Lord for graces corresponding to the various dogmas of the Christian faith.[22]

Family problems

One of Borgia's major preoccupations was the education of his many children. As he wrote to Francisco de los Cobos, January 20, 1543: "With this [the death of his father] eight more children, not counting those I already had, were born to me. God will provide for all."[23] He did not include in this number the children of his father's second marriage who had either already died or had embraced the ecclesiastical or religious states. But his principal problem concerned his stepmother's demands about her dowry and, above all, about the payment of the debts the third duke of Gandía had left behind. It was not possible to reach an agreement over these matters, so they both had to go to court. Francis had no problem about giving his stepmother back her whole dowry and all her personal belongings, but the parties reached an impasse regarding a debt of 24,000 ducats. Borgia believed he and his stepmother should assume equal responsibility for settling it. If he were to pay the whole amount, it would mean that either he would have to draw money from the entailed estate (*mayorazgo*), a procedure that would be illegal, or else he would have to pass on the debt to the Borgia children. "The sorrowful widow of Gandía," as Francisca de Castro-Pinós referred to herself, appealed to Philip II in a letter of October 15, 1546, asking him to intervene so that the Real Consejo would not judge against her.[24] Actually, the first sentence handed down was in her favor; but Borgia, advised by experts, believed he should appeal what he considered an unjust decision. In an undated letter he informed Ignatius about it. What he asked was that

> Her Ladyship be kind enough to pay the remainder of the debts of the duke, My Lord, as was just, and that I would be satisfied and would not ask for anything more; only that the debts be finally paid, which come to twelve or fourteen thousand ducats, in addition to the same amount which I have already paid. Her Ladyship did not want to accept this, much to the astonishment of many.[25]

The appellate sentence was likewise against Francis, but his reaction was what would be expected from a man already totally detached from the things of the world. If we are to believe Father Vázquez, he went to the convent of the Poor Clares and told them what had happened, as if it were good news. The important thing was to look ahead.

Vocation to the Society of Jesus

When St. Ignatius admitted Francis Borgia into the Society of Jesus, he told him that his decision should remain secret "because the world does not have ears to hear such an explosion."[26] Ignatius knew very well what it meant for a man who enjoyed the confidence of Charles V, occupied a privileged status in the court, and was a duke and grandee of Spain to enter a new and scarcely known religious order like the Society. St. Ignatius's request was respected, but the extraordinary fact is that Borgia entered the Society. What were the steps, then, that led to this decision?

Ultimately, everything begins with Empress Isabel's premature death and her burial at Granada. As we have already seen, the empress's death was a terrible shock for him, irrespective of whether he made the decision then to enter the religious life as soon as he was free from his commitments or whether he did not formulate these intentions with any precision. From that time on, he saw the world through different eyes.

His failure to be named chief majordomo to Princess María Manuela, Philip II's first wife, gave rise to his second disenchantment with the world.

The third blow came with the death of his wife, Leonor de Castro, on March 27, 1546. Leonor's health had always been delicate, at least since her Barcelona days. She was gravely ill in Gandía during the course of 1544; as soon as she was able to leave the house, she and her husband went to the nearby monastery of San Jerónimo de Cotalba to pass the winter there. By mid-1545 her health seemed to have improved, but in reality, after a series of ups and downs, she was rapidly approaching the end of her days. On March 20 she wrote her last will and one week later she surrendered her soul to its Creator. Writing to Araoz, Borgia said that "in her sickness she was wonderfully mortified and in her passing away she was wonderfully blessed."[27]

As we have already said, Francis sincerely loved his wife, and he was affected by the thought of her approaching death. According to his own report, while fervently praying before a crucifix that she be spared, the figure on the cross answered him that whatever he wished would be done; it cautioned, however, that it would not be to his advantage if his wife should be cured. Francis resigned himself to the will of God, so clearly manifested.

His granddaughter, Sister Francisca de Jesús, a Poor Clare from the Descalzas Reales convent in Madrid, testified in the beatification process that the figure on the cross spoke to Borgia. "It was a well-known fact that a crucified corpus spoke to the said servant of God and that this witness saw the crucifix because Señor Don Juan de Borja had it brought to this house so that they could see it."[28] Francis gave the crucifix to his sister-in-law, Juana de Meneses, and she in turn gave it as a gift to Juan de Borja, the saint's son and the witness's father.

Borgia's feelings after his wife's death were expressed in the letters he wrote to Paul III and to St. Ignatius with the news of this event. He told Ignatius that with her death "my love for her has been doubled because she is more loved by the Creator."[29] He addressed a letter dated June 11 to Paul III, confident that the pope shared in his sorrow over his wife's death "because we are all of us the creatures of Your Holiness." Begging his blessing for the deceased, he requested that he "make her a participant in the sacrifices of the universal Church."[30]

After this, one event followed on the heels of another in rapid succession.[31] In May of that year, 1546, Borgia made the Spiritual Exercises under the direction of Father Andrés de Oviedo, rector of the college of Gandía. At the climax of the Election he made his decision, and on June 2 he made a vow to enter the Society. The text of the formula has been preserved for us:

> In the name of our Lord Jesus Christ, I, Francisco de Borja, duke of Gandía, have made the vow of chastity and obedience to the superior of the Society of Jesus, seeking to be received for any office, porter, or cook, etc., once I have settled the business to which I am in conscience bound to attend. This vow to belong to the Society if they accept me I have made on July 2, vigil of the Ascension.
>
> The Duke of Gandía.[32]

(The reader will note that he got the date wrong: the vigil of the Ascension cannot fall in July. He meant June.)

This vow is comparable to the one which those intending to enter the Society would make once they had finished their probation and before they began their studies. For Borgia there was no mention of poverty, since he still had to hold on to the ownership of his properties, as well as the use and administration of them, for as long as he was bound by his office. But it seems that Francis considered the day he took this vow as the beginning of his religious life, for in the entry for May 29, 1565, he wrote, "Ite[m], I began the twentieth year in the Society, and instead of joy, sorrow and tears for the passion of Christ."

There is no extant letter from Borgia asking St. Ignatius to admit him into the Society. Perhaps it was lost, or perhaps his request was transmitted verbally to the general of the Society by Peter Faber, who conversed with Borgia when he passed through Gandía on his way to Rome during the month of May of that year, 1546. Faber arrived in Rome on July 17, a few days before his death on August 1. But we do have a long and beautiful undated letter in which Ignatius informed the duke that he has been accepted into the order. "And thus, in the name of the Lord, from this moment on, I accept and receive Your Lordship as our brother, and as such my soul will have for you that love which is due to one who, with so much generosity, gives himself to the Church in order to serve the Lord more perfectly in it." He added the following guidelines covering what he should do in the meantime: arrange for the marriages of those daughters who were old enough to marry and entrust his other sons and daughters to the care of their oldest brother. The duke should leave the works he began in Gandía in good order; moreover, since he already had a good foundation in learning, he should begin to study theology and, if possible, take a doctorate from the university of Gandía.[33]

Why did he choose the Society?

The dealings Borgia had had in Barcelona with Fathers Faber and Araoz, the first Jesuits in Spain, greatly influenced his vocation. He established an intimate relationship with Araoz, as the correspondence they kept up attests. More intimate, although of a shorter duration, were his links with Faber. When the gentle Savoyard came to Gandía in early May of 1546 to participate in ceremonies for laying the cornerstone of the Society's college there, he spent almost one whole day conversing with Borgia. On this occasion Borgia could have given shape to the decision he formalized during the Exercises he began later that same month.

It was through these two Jesuits that Borgia came to know St. Ignatius, with whom he very quickly began a familiar exchange of letters. Borgia laid open to him his questions concerning the spiritual life and Ignatius sent back his answers. This student/teacher relationship, which Borgia maintained with such great humility throughout his life, was established at this time between these two souls, so different in character but united in a common desire for sanctity.[34] Ignatius, in turn, was aware of the virtue and qualities of his correspondent.

The Exercises, made according to the Ignatian method, put Borgia to the decisive test. We have already seen that it was at the time of the Election, the high point of the Exercises, that he decided to enter the Society. So it can be said that the Spiritual Exercises brought him to the Society, as they had brought so many others.

A contributing motive was the fact that the Society was a new order, little known and still criticized by some. If he wanted to lead a hidden life in the eyes of men, it is clear that he could achieve it more easily in the Society than in one of the larger orders, especially because the Society did not permit its members to accept prelacies. Therefore, it would be more difficult for someone to force a miter or a cardinal's hat upon him if he was a member of the Society. Fernando Solier attested to this in Borgia's beatification process. When Borgia went to visit Charles V at Yuste, he said, the emperor asked him why he had not entered an older, established order. Borgia answered that he became a Jesuit because in another order he would have been given signs of esteem and consideration for having left the world, whereas in the Society all were equal.[35]

Solemn profession

He made his solemn profession binding himself definitively to the Society on February 1, 1548. How do we explain that he made such a vow as this, granted to so few, considering that he had been admitted to the order little over a year earlier? Something must have moved Ignatius, even prescinding from Borgia's exceptional qualities and his extraordinary vocation.

The documents are not very helpful on this point, most certainly because everything was done with the greatest discretion. The one who treats the subject in greatest detail is Polanco in his *Chronicle* of the Society, written long after these events took place and at a time when one could express himself with greater freedom.[36] This first historian of the Society takes as his point of departure the Argonese Cortes convoked at Monzón in 1547. Philip II wanted the duke of Gandía in attendance and would accept no excuses for his absence. Also present was Father Antonio de Araoz, who, accustomed to following the court, was now in Monzón looking for ways to reform convents of women religious in Catalonia. According to Polanco, Araoz discovered that Philip II was thinking of naming Francis Borgia his major-domo. Araoz quickly communicated to Ignatius what plans were afoot. To save Borgia's vocation, he recommended that the duke make his solemn profession, but continue to manage his duchy and administer his family affairs for as long a time as necessary. The plan seemed good to Ignatius, who obtained permission from Pope Paul III for Borgia to make his solemn profession, with a proviso that for three years he could continue to look after the business that kept him in Gandía.

Without denying the basic premise contained in Polanco's account, some points need qualification. Even if we grant the supposition that admission to the profession did not originate with Borgia, the fact is that he accepted it voluntarily and enthusiastically. Andrés de Oviedo wrote from Rome May 31, 1547: "About Señor R[afael, the code name for Borgia] I wrote a note to Your Paternity concerning Your Paternity's reply to the licentiate Araoz about the possibility of getting permission from the pope. He [Borgia] feels great consolation over this and wishes to have it if it is agreeable with Your Paternity."[37]

According to Oviedo's letter, negotiations for the pope's dispensation took place before July 5, the date the Cortes at Monzón was called to order. It is very possible that during the sessions of the Cortes Araoz realized that there were plans to give Borgia a position at court. Philip II must have entertained such thoughts ever since the death of his first wife, María Manuela, in 1545, because shortly after she died the principal officials Charles had appointed before he left Spain to serve his son followed her to the grave: Cardinal Tavera in 1545, shortly after the princess; Juan de Zúñiga, Philip's tutor and majordomo, in 1546; and the secretary, Francisco de los Cobos, on May 10, 1547. So it would not be at all surprising that Philip II considered giving the duke of Gandía a post vacated by one of these individuals, perhaps the position which Juan de Zúñiga had once occupied.

Moreover, we should keep in mind that, after the death of Princess María Manuela, there was still a possibility of Philip's being united to the Portuguese royal family through a marriage with another of his cousins, María, daughter of Manuel I ("the Fortunate") and his third wife, Leonor, the eldest sister of Charles V. But this marriage with María ("the Aban-doned," so-called because she never wed) did not materialize. If it had, Francis might well have filled the post to which he had been appointed for

Philip's first wife.

The reason for granting Borgia the solemn profession was not so much to secure his vocation as to block the court's designs that might thwart that vocation. Clearly it would have been difficult for Philip to succeed in attracting to his service a man bound by solemn vows taken after a papal dispensation for their immediate effectuation.

The permission Ignatius received from Paul III, as a matter of fact, was for an unspecified person to make his profession in secret and then, for three years beginning from May 1548, to continue managing the affairs which tied him to the world. In a letter to Ignatius on December 27, 1547, Borgia spoke of a "business" which could not have been anything other than his profession. After "our Lord was pleased to take me out of the Babylon of Monzón," he added, "I did not want to cease giving thanks to the Lord for his favors and for the manner he gives them: Blessed be his holy name. It is impossible for me to express my sentiments about this, at any rate in a letter." He was awaiting Araoz' arrival. Upon his coming, "we will write to you about what I have not included, giving an account of the business as Your Paternity has requested."[38] So, the "business" he referred to is in all probability his profession. Because he had fallen ill in Barcelona, Araoz was not able to be present at the ceremony; but without waiting any longer Borgia made his profession in the presence of three Jesuit priests from the College of Gandía and the Franciscan Juan de Tejeda. The formula he used is as follows:

> Jhs. I, Don Francisco de Borja, R. [duke] of Gandía, an abominable sinner and unworthy of the call of the Lord and of this profession, trusting only in the goodness of the Lord, which I now hope to receive, do solemnly vow poverty, obedience, and chastity according to the statutes of the Society, using the permission and dispensation sent me by Father Ignatius, superior general. For this I beseech the angels and saints in heaven to be my advocates and witnesses. And I ask the same of Father Master Andrés, Father Master Francisco Onfroy, Father Master Saboya, and Father Fray Juan Texeda, here present. At Gandía, St. Ignatius's day, first of February 1548.[39]

Note, in this formula, the absence of the fourth vow of special obedience to the Roman pontiff when sent by the pope to the infidels or to the faithful. Even though we are on safe ground when we surmise that this vow was implicitly included in the words "according to the statutes of the Society," still it is more probable that Borgia pronounced this vow explicitly, in the words of the formula as we know it, either on that same day or on some later occasion. The important thing is that he made reference to this fourth vow and felt bound by it in a quite difficult situation that we will have occasion to discuss later. In 1561, when the pope ordered him to quit Portugal and come to Rome, he left in writing that he did so at a sacrifice "in consideration of the vow I had taken at the time of my profession to the sovereign pontiff in obedience to go wherever His Holiness would order me to go."[40]

In chapter five, we shall deal with fact that it was not until August 22, 1554, that Borgia pronounced the simple vow of the professed about not accepting ecclesiastical dignities; at that time we will also explore the reasons for this omission.

On the day of his profession, Borgia expressed his feelings in a long prayer that Vásquez inserts into Ribadeneira's *Life*, first published in 1592. It begins with these exclamations: "My Lord and my sole refuge, what did you discover in me to take notice of me? What did you see in me to want me in this Company of your companions?" Francis continues pondering with great affection his unworthiness for the grace received, thanking the Lord for his vocation to and profession in the Society.[41]

It was from this moment on that Francis became definitively incorporated into the Society. Only the repeated attempts to make him cardinal could threaten to separate him from the Society. In chapter five we shall discuss these attempts. Meanwhile, he continued living his ordinary life of prayer and study. But between 1547 and 1549 some noteworthy events took place, among which were the elevation of the college of Gandía to university status, the decision handed down in the suit with his stepmother, and the spiritual crisis of Fathers Oviedo and Onfroy.

"My college and university of Gandía"

This is the way Borgia referred to one of the projects he so doggedly undertook for the good of Gandía. The first college of the Society in Spain was at Valencia, planned and founded by the Valencian Jesuit, Juan Jerónimo Domènech. In 1544 another Valencian, Diego Miró, from Ruzafa, and three companions came to the city and opened up the college for Jesuit students. Favorably impressed by this enterprise, the duke of Gandía got the idea of raising funds from the duchy to set up a similar college. As early as November 1544 he had discussed the project with Antonio Araoz, at first regarding it as a college for the duchy's numerous Moriscos. Later on he broadened this concept to include lay students from every social stratum.

Gandía was the first college of the Society where Jesuits conducted classes for students who were not members of the order. As we shall see, in 1547 the college acquired university rank, and as such was the world's first Jesuit university.

On March 14, 1545, Ignatius wrote Borgia, giving his approval to the project. On May 28, Borgia thanked the general for this good news and declared that he was now ready to put up the college building and to provide the necessary income to support the professors and students. He asked Ignatius to send a master of arts and several students. Ignatius complied by assigning Andrés de Oviedo to the college. This father arrived from Rome on November 16 that same year, 1545, accompanied by five young Jesuit students.

Borgia had chosen a block contiguous to the church of St. Sebastian as the site for the new college building; because of this the college took the name of this holy martyr. Construction was begun in 1546, and the ceremony for laying the cornerstone took place on May 4. One of the participants present was Peter Faber, who had accepted Borgia's warm invitation to attend. At the time Faber was making his way toward Rome and then on to Trent, where he had been called to take part in the Council. He arrived in Gandía on May 2, the Sunday after Easter, and he spent one of his two days there conversing almost uninterruptedly with the duke, who certainly apprised him of his own personal intentions. They would never see one another again, because Faber, shortly after arriving in Rome that same year, died a saintly death. He had written to Araoz describing the dedication ceremony: "The morning I left Gandía, very happy and having left all very happy, I first said Mass in St. Sebastian's, which is where the college is being built, and after Mass, at which the duke and his children assisted, we went to lay the first stone of the college with special blessings which I solemnized with seven psalms."[42] Peter Faber laid the first stone, the duke the second, Andrés de Oviedo the third; then the duke's children each added a stone.

While the building of the college progressed, Borgia was entertaining the idea of converting it into a genuine university. This was one project, among several others, which shows how close were Borgia's connections with both Pope Paul III and Charles V. The pope gave him what he had requested when he issued the bull of foundation for the university on November 4, 1547, granting to this new center the same privileges enjoyed by the universities of Valencia, Salamanca, and Alcalá. The emperor likewise gave his approbation to the new institution, and St. Ignatius declared in a decree dated March 20, 1548, that the Society accepted and assumed responsibility for operating the college and university.[43] At the same time, Ignatius determined the number of chairs to be filled. There would be eight: three of grammar and humanities, three of arts or philosophy, and two of theology. He authorized the duke-founder to reduce this number if he thought it advisable. As a matter of fact, on November 16, 1549, the number of chairs was reduced to five: two of grammar and Latin, two of logic and natural philosophy, and one of scholastic theology.

The construction of the new college-university was finished in 1548, and on May 9 the Jesuits moved into the new building. On the following day, the feast of the Ascension, Mass was offered for the founder and the Blessed Sacrament was enthroned in the new church. In the evening, Father Diego Miró, who had come down from Valencia, presided over an academic exercise in which Francisco Onfroy defended a thesis in theology and Master Pedro Canal one in philosophy. The Jesuits installed in the new residence numbered thirteen; ten Moriscos lodged in separate quarters.

The duke managed to raise funds needed for the maintenance of professors and students. At first operating costs came to some five hundred ducats; but the following year they had gone up to eight hundred and the projection was that in a short time they would increase to a thousand. Within the limits imposed by this budget, he hoped to support some twenty-five students, in addition to the neophytes.

In this year of 1548 classes were off to a good start in all the disciplines. On February 4, 1549, Oviedo wrote that "theology classes have begun and there are many students and good exercises; the brethren are making progress, and the lord duke is one of the students; and after he has heard the lessons His Lordship and I repeat them."[44]

The first rector of the college and university was Father Andrés de Oviedo, a native of Illescas in the diocese of Toledo. In a letter of July 29, 1547, Ignatius directed the Gandía Jesuits to elect a superior from one of their number. Oviedo, who at that time was thirty years old, was their unanimous choice.

After this first election a second was made by Ignatius in the form of a letter dated January 12, 1549, and addressed to the same Oviedo.

The official act in which the new rector was installed took place March 1, 1549, with Araoz, the provincial of Spain, presiding. This date was considered the official beginning of the university, although, as we have seen, classes had already begun. The new rector installed the professors in their chairs. Father Jerónimo Pérez was called from Valencia to fill the chair of theology, a subject which he had been teaching for twenty years; but unfortunately he died shortly after undertaking his new assignment and was succeeded by Father Bautista de Barma. The Portuguese Manuel de Sá and the Frenchman Jean de la Goutte taught philosophy. Francisco Saboya and Juan Ferri taught Latin and rhetoric.

Ignatius sent instructions to Father Oviedo to draft statutes for the new university in the same way that Father Jerome Nadal had done for the university of Messina. After Oviedo's draft was eventually sent to Rome and revised, the first statutes of the university of Gandía were promulgated between 1549 and 1550.[45]

Unpretentious as it was, this tiny university had its days of evident splendor. The *Libro primero de la Universidad de Gandía* preserved in the Municipal Archives at Valencia lists the names of those who graduated between 1549 and 1645, including that of Francisco de Borja, who received a doctorate in theology on August 20, 1550. The university continued to function even after Charles III expelled the Society in 1767. In 1867 Gandía's municipal government invited the Piarist Fathers to take charge of the college, which continued to be dedicated to St. Sebastian.

The Gandía affair

This is the name given to an episode of distorted spirituality that took place in Gandía between 1547 and 1549. It was an anomaly that seriously plagued St. Ignatius and required that in order to resolve it he apply the strong arm that he reserved only for gravest occasions. The episode seems to have clarified the position of the Society and its founder regarding matters of such great importance as the relationship between the interior spiritual life and apostolic zeal, between contemplation and action; it also indicated the attitude one must have when faced with such preternatural phenomena as visions and prophecies. Francis had an important role in settling the crisis and was the instrument Ignatius finally used to resolve it.[46]

The chief protagonists were Fathers Andrés de Oviedo and Francisco Onfroy. Becoming withdrawn and preoccupied with his own spiritual progress, Oviedo shut himself up in the hermitage of Santa Ana on the outskirts of Gandía. Consoled by this experience, he and Onfroy addressed a letter to Ignatius dated February 8, 1548, in which they requested permission to retire to a wilderness for seven years to give themselves completely to prayer, because it seemed to them that the hours they devoted to prayer in the college were too few.[47] In his answer on March 27, Ignatius prudently prepared the ground for a negative response, declaring that "it was a serious matter and a dangerous precedent for the manner of proceeding in the Society."[48] The phrase "manner of proceeding in the Society" (*modo de proceder de la Compañía*) recurs frequently in Ignatius's writings and shows his strong determination that no one in the Society should deviate from the basic path of its Institute. The provincial Araoz was told in a letter that "our Father was very far from agreeing to such a thing, rather he thinks it quite repugnant to our Institute and our manner of proceeding."[49] Full powers were given to the provincial, including powers to dismiss from the Society those who refused to obey.

As the history of the Church has shown, movements such as this recur from time to time. This one in Gandía was related to the Franciscan reform movement that began in the fifteenth century and grew to a degree of intensity during the first half of the sixteenth century. In Gandía there was a marked Franciscan influence, first of all because of the books which were probably accessible to those who lived at the college, especially those of Herp and of Bernabé de Palma; second, because of the relationship the Jesuits had with the Franciscan lay brother Juan de Tejeda, a native of Extremadura, the center of the Franciscan reform movement in Spain; and last, because of the Poor Clares, who, as we have seen, had transplanted the severe, reformist spirituality of St. Colette to the Gandía convent. The penchant for retreating to hermitages clearly had a Franciscan stamp about it.

Fray Juan de Tejeda was in Gandía, taking theology courses to prepare himself for the priesthood. The Jesuits from Rome already knew this friar because he had been in Rome trying to get permission to be ordained a priest. Although they recognized in him a devout and pious man, they could not have been much impressed by the way he went about laying plans for his priestly ordination while sidestepping his immediate superiors. The fact is that they saw him as the one chiefly responsible for what was happening in Gandía. "Here it is thought that the one who has rendered them so contemplative, etc., is Fray Juan de Tejeda; our Father Ignatius is not happy about his converse with the members of the college, and much less with his living there with them."[50]

Even though this strife was confined to the college of Gandía—with some repercussions at the college in Valencia—Ignatius regarded it as serious. But the storm blew itself out in a short time, thanks to the firmness of the general and to the docility of those involved. Oviedo had always submitted his projects to the decision of obedience.

Appreciating what part Borgia played in all this conflict is our concern here. Despite his love for prayer and penance, he did not let himself get involved in what took place. We are unable to find any complaint from Ignatius about Borgia's conduct. But more importantly, by giving him instructions and by keeping him informed about what he had sent to Araoz, the general relied on him in solving the problem. As far as Tejeda was concerned, Borgia wrote to the general on May 4, 1548, indicating that, even before they had received the order prohibiting the friar from living in a house of the Society, they had made a decision along these same lines.[51] In a letter of March 29, 1548, Ignatius sent Borgia guidelines on how to deal with Fathers Oviedo and Onfroy.[52] One solution would be to disperse some of those involved in the affair among different cities. Another would be to forbid them to talk among themselves about anything other than their studies and to prohibit them from having any dealings with the students. Ignatius sent Borgia two blank pages with his signature attached, authorizing him to use these as he saw fit. As the years went on, Borgia would continue to develop the discretion and tact that he had demonstrated in this Gandía case. Meanwhile, those involved in the affair submitted; and he noted that the devil had lost more than he gained. "Therefore we get the merit of the desert and the sacrifice of obedience."[53] Little by little, the waters returned to their channel. Father Oviedo preached every morning to the people, and then after the noon meal he taught them catechism, much to their spiritual profit. He also devoted himself to hearing confessions. Onfroy continued teaching philosophy, while at the same time studying theology.

No sooner had this predilection for the wilderness been arrested when another fancy no less dangerous arose. It was the credulous belief in visions and prophecies. Here too, the person chiefly responsible seems to have been Tejeda. He went so far as to say that Borgia would be the "angelic pope" destined to reform the Church.[54]

After calling a meeting of experts to Rome on July 9, 1549, St. Ignatius sent an instruction on visions and revelations to Gandía.[55] This instruction is a model of its kind. In its pages Ignatius applies the rules for spiritual discernment to judging prophecy and other such manifestations. Before believing in the truth of a prophecy one must examine it thoroughly to see whether it accords with Catholic doctrine and serves for spiritual edification. Until this fact is established one should suspend judgment. Should we find anything contrary to right reason or to good doctrine in the prophecies, we should reject them. This was the category in which Onfroy's prophecies belonged.

Ignatius sent Araoz a copy of this instruction, and another to Borgia, along with a letter in his own hand, containing some sobering thoughts. The general believed "strongly and without any possibility of doubt [that the prophets] were off the path, deceived, and incited by the father of lies." He charged Borgia to "watch and take necessary steps, not tolerating these matters that can cause so much scandal and do so much damage in so many places, but turning everything to the service of His Divine Majesty and seeing that [the prophets] be healed in every way for God's greater service, praise and glory, world without end."[56]

Oviedo was removed from his office as superior and Father Saboya was appointed on a temporary basis. The litigation with his mother-in-law took Borgia away from Gandía for some time; and when he returned he was able to inform Ignatius on October 17, 1549, that "I have employed the best means I could to the end which Your Paternity ordered, and the problem is all but completely resolved, and very soon, I hope, it will be completely resolved."[57] He gave him still more encouraging news on November 30, informing him that "with what Your Paternity wrote me I made use of Your Paternity's authority, and 'in thy name (after our Lord) I have changed men.' He is now quite consoled and an excellent student." He was referring to Oviedo. He went on to urge Ignatius to write him, "consoling him and rejoicing about what I tell you here because, after all, he is a true son of the Society, although because of this naiveté he wishes to be 'like some lonely bird on a roof.'"[58] Ignatius did not have to apply drastic measures, and following Borgia's advice he wrote Oviedo a letter. Later Borgia told him, "Your Paternity's letter has given him a new lease on life, so much so that he keeps kissing Your Paternity's name and signature where it is found in the documents or writs, and now he talks another line. Blessed be God for everything."[59] A little later Oviedo was named rector of the college at Naples; and in 1553 he was appointed auxiliary bishop to the patriarch of Ethiopia, Father João Nunes Barreto. At Nunes Barreto's death, which took place in Goa without his ever having set foot on Ethiopian soil, Oviedo succeeded him in this assignment. Even though he was able to enter the Ethiopian kingdom, he was not able to accomplish his mission and was forced to live in extreme solitude and poverty until death took him in 1577.

Onfroy was not in Gandía when all this was taking place, and he probably never knew about St. Ignatius's instruction on visions and prophecies. Suffering from advanced tuberculosis during the winter of 1549, he was moved to Valencia, where he died in June 1550.

One month later Fray Juan de Tejeda left Gandía, never to return. Borgia had asked him that in his travels through Castile he apprise the duke's relatives of his intention of going to Rome to gain the concession of a plenary indulgence during the Holy Year. He asked him to deliver this same message to his sister Luisa, the countess of Ribagorza, who lived in Pedrola, most assuredly notifying her of his intention to declare openly his entrance into the Society. But Tejeda was not able to fulfill this commission because he suffered a stroke while he was in Valladolid on the feast of the Transfiguration; two days later he died.

Approbation and publication of the book of the Exercises

Both because of what he had heard from a number of sources and because of his own experiences, Borgia knew that great fruit was to be obtained from the Spiritual Exercises. But he was aware that there were not wanting those who criticized this method of spiritual renewal as novel and suspicious.[60] To counter past opposition and to stave off new attacks, Borgia resolved to take advantage of his influence with Pope Paul III. On January 2, 1547, he got the pope to grant *vivae vocis oraculo* a plenary indulgence to anyone who showed sorrow for his sins and confessed them to a priest of the Society.[61] Although, as he wrote to Ignatius, the pope did not expressly mention the Exercises "as was requested, it seems to me His Holiness has granted us something more than we asked for."[62] Paul III probably omitted the name "Exercises" because he did not wish to irritate those who held them in low esteem, but Borgia was not satisfied. He sent Canon Diego Sánchez to Rome, requesting the pope to have the book of the Spiritual Exercises examined by the master of the sacred apostolic palace. Then he requested that the pope approve it if the examiner found nothing objectionable in it and, using his apostolic authority, grant indulgences to whoever made the Exercises.

Paul III submitted both the Latin translation by Father André des Freux, called the *Vulgate,* and the Latin *versio prima* of the *Spiritual Exercises* to the verdict of the Dominican cardinal Juan Alvarez de Toledo and the master of the sacred palace, Egidio Foscarari. Not only did they fail to find anything objectionable in the book, but they judged that the Exercises were of great value to souls. The pope's vicar in Rome, Filippo Archinto, gave the *imprimatur.*[63]

After this favorable report, the pope issued the brief *Pastoralis Officii Cura* on July 31, 1584, approving the book of the Exercises.[64] As Nadal would note at a much later date, it was a great and rare privilege in the Church for a Pope to approve a book in so solemn a fashion.[65] Not satisfied with having obtained the papal approbation, Borgia now promoted the printing of the *Spiritual Exercises* and offered to defray the expense. The first edition of five hundred copies was printed at Rome in 1548. The cost of twenty-two ducats was paid by Borgia.

4. First Trip to Rome (1550-1551)

Motives for the journey

The pope proclaimed a plenary indulgence for those who would come to Rome for the Holy Year of 1550. This presented Borgia with a good opportunity and an excellent pretext to leave Gandía without divulging his real motives for going to Rome. It would obviously be easier for him to make his public entrance into the Society away his homeland. But he had other motives for undertaking the trip. St. Ignatius had manifested his intention of calling together during this Holy Year all the first Fathers and professed of the Society who were able to come to Rome. Borgia was one of these. Ignatius wanted to present for their consideration the text of the Constitutions of the Society, and for reasons of health he was also going to submit his resignation as general at this meeting. His intention was kept secret until the occasion presented itself, but it was one more reason for Borgia's going to Rome. We should mention here that Ignatius did tender his resignation in an autograph document signed on January 30, 1551,[1] but the congregation did not accept it.

Among the major determinants for Borgia's undertaking this trip was his desire to know the Society's founder personally and to place himself for some time under his direction. Needless to say, Ignatius approved of this objective.

By March 1549 it had become clear that the duke of Gandía could be freed from his obligations within a year. Some questions remained which consultation by mail over a period of several months attempted to resolve. The first problem had to do with timing. Should the duke make the voyage in March 1550 or after the summer? Ignatius recommended that he not arrive in Rome until October because travel in mid-summer would prove very injurious to his health. Other questions were: (1) Should the duke give up all his income before he left Gandía or retain some of it to contribute to the cost of building the new church planned in Rome and of establishing the college the Society wanted to found there? Subsequent history has shown us the second alternative was the one for which they opted. (2) Should Borgia be ordained a priest or not? A document from Rome was obtained under date of January 9, 1550, authorizing any bishop to ordain him and declaring him free from any censure he might have incurred.[2] As we shall see, he was not ordained in Gandía but in Guipúzcoa in 1551. (3) Should he receive a doctorate from one of the faculties before his departure? We have already seen that he was granted the doctorate in theology on August 20, 1550, eight days before his departure for Rome. (4) Should he travel as a Jesuit and be received as a guest in the houses of the Society? Actually, he traveled incognito, although many people he met on his way must have realized that there was something unusual about this pilgrim.

His last official act in Gandía was the drawing up of his will. He did this closeted in the room reserved for him in the college, and on August 26, 1550, he signed it before the notary Onofre Pérez de Culla. Two days later he attached two more codicils.[3]

The three years the pope had given Borgia for keeping his religious profession secret would expire in May 1551; but he left Gandía on August 30, 1550,[4] eight months prior to the deadline. Visibly reflected on his countenance was the joy he felt at the step he was about to take. The three other professed who were in Spain at that time, Fathers Araoz, Miró, and Oviedo, made the trip with him, along with other Jesuits and several persons in the duke's entourage, bringing the total number to between twenty-five and thirty persons. They made the journey overland and on horseback, taking almost two months to do so.

He was not given any particular instructions about the itinerary; but Ignatius had a letter sent to him to the effect that, if he passed through Parma, he should find out whether Madama Margaret of Austria was there. She was Charles V's daughter and "very devoted to the Society." And in Bologna he might meet the city's pontifical vice-delegate, Gerolamo Sauli, who was also Genoa's archbishop. The two of them could talk about the Society's college in that Mediterranean city. In Florence he could visit Duke Cosimo and his wife, Duchess Eleanor of Toledo.

On October 10 Borgia wrote a letter to Ignatius from Bologna telling him that he was doing all that Ignatius had requested him to do.[5] In Parma "I kissed Madama's hands and she gave me much news about Your Paternity, and I was very pleased to see what a true and devout daughter to Your Paternity she is." On the 11th he wrote: "I leave for Ferrara and there I shall learn about the affairs of the college, according to Your Paternity's orders, and in three or four days I shall return here and we will deal with the vice-delegate [Gerolamo Sauli] about the Genoa business. After that I shall go on to Florence." Although Borgia did not mention it in his letters, we know the duke and duchess of Ferrara received their cousin cordially. We should note that Ercole II d'Este was the son of Lucrezia Borgia, sister of Juan de Borja, Francis's grandfather and second duke of Gandía. But what Francis was interested in was not the hospitality of the court but rather the affairs of the college in the city of the Estes. The same can be said of his journey through Florence. Here he spoke with the duke and duchess about setting up a college of the Society either in the duchy's capital or in Pisa.

Just as the nobility of the various cities through which Borgia passed had received him with honor, so did the Roman nobility when he arrived there on October 23. Although it is not known how they found out when he would make his entrance into the city, many cardinals were on hand to greet him. The Spanish ambassador, Diego Hurtado de Mendoza, came out to receive him. The cardinal of Burgos, Francisco de Mendoza, was among those who invited him to remain as a guest in his house, and Pope Julius III himself offered him lodgings in the Vatican. But Borgia wanted no other dwelling than the humble Jesuit house of Santa Maria della Strada. Part of the house was reserved for him and his entourage. It was next to the church and separated by a patio from the living quarters of the Fathers. In this same patio or "little garden" Ignatius began in 1553 to dictate his autobiographical memoirs to Father Luis Gonçalves da Câmara. Thanks to Father Gonçalves da Câmara we know that that "house or dwelling" continued to be called "the duke's."

Three months in Rome

The sources tell us nothing about it, but we can imagine the emotion the two saints, Ignatius and Francis Borgia, must have felt when they embraced for the first time. During the three months that followed they must have conversed frequently, if not on a daily basis. Close contact enabled Ignatius to come to know this man who had renounced such a privileged position in the world to enter the Society. Assuredly he instructed him about everything concerning the Institute of the Society and about the Constitutions upon which he had been working without respite. Borgia must have admired more than ever the great qualities and virtues he saw in the general of the Society. For him these three months were a veritable novitiate.

Besides his conversations with St. Ignatius, during these three months Borgia was involved in fulfilling the conditions required to gain the jubilee indulgences, as well as visiting or receiving visits from cardinals and other personages. He had an audience with Pope Julius III, who renewed his invitation for him to take up lodgings in the Vatican, but Francis continued to live happily in the humble house of the Society. There he gave everyone examples of his virtue, appearing once, for example, in the Fathers' refectory and waiting on table.

Rome's church and college

Among his other interests two principal projects engaged his attention, the construction of a new church for the Society and the funding of the Roman College, which was about to go into operation.

The old church of Santa Maria della Strada was too small to accommodate the many faithful who came to hear the Fathers preach or who wanted to make their confessions to them, so it was agreed that a new church should be built. Besides the financial hurdle, there were bureaucratic problems that had to be surmounted. The municipal authorities would not give permission to construct a new church in the same neighborhood. However, very likely owing to the influence Borgia exerted even before his arrival in Rome, permission finally came on October 1, 1550, to construct a church according to the plans of the Florentine Nanni de Baccio Bigio. During Borgia's stay in Rome, sometime toward the end of 1550 or the beginning of 1551, Ignacio de Villalobos, bishop of Squillace, laid the cornerstone in the presence of Borgia and Ignatius. But additional stones were slow to follow. This was the first inauguration of what was to become the church of the Gesù. Two more such ceremonies would take place after other benefactors and other architects had been found.

The Roman College was one of Ignatius's most brilliant creations. It was a center not only where young Jesuits received an effective cultural formation, but also where a large number of lay students would be educated in the learned professions and in good moral and religious principles. This college would serve as the model for others of the Society, in the same way that the church of the Gesù would in time become the prototype of churches the Society would erect in Europe and overseas.

Even before leaving Gandía, Francis sent a financial contribution which marked the beginning of this enterprise. In his second codicil of August 28, he provided that fourteen thousand ducats should be sent "to the college for students of the Society of Jesus that I plan to be built and constructed soon in Rome."[6] In a written memorandum to Ignatius on the eve of his departure from Rome, he specified a number of donations and pledges he had collected "so that the holy undertakings of the church and college may get started." He left 3,200 gold escudos in ready money, to which another 1,500 were added the following April. His son and heir, Don Carlos, would make an annual contribution of 500 escudos as long as he lived; his second son, Juan, would pledge 500 escudos annually for six years. Other contributions were to be collected from the emperor, the bishop of Squillace, from Tommaso del Giglio, and from Cardinals Ippolito d'Este, Francisco de Mendoza, and Durante de' Duranti. Borgia would have liked to leave the management of this fund with Ignatius, but when the latter refused Borgia appointed Luis de Mendoza as his executor.[7]

On February 22, 1551, eighteen days after Borgia left Rome, a "free school of grammar, humanities, and Christian doctrine" opened up on the Via d'Aracoeli, at the foot of the Capitol. In fact, however, only classes in Latin and Greek were offered, but in the beginning of 1553 courses in philosophy and theology were added. For this reason, 1553 is rightly considered the year when what was to become the Gregorian University came into being. Ignatius created the college; but, from the monetary point of view, its founder was Francis Borgia. He renounced the title of "Founder" because titles of honor did not interest him. These events were just the beginning. Borgia, however, did not cease to be interested in the Roman College during the course of his life. We will have an opportunity to see this in chapter six.

Because his sojourn in Rome was drawing to a close, Borgia now did what he considered was his duty: he advised Charles V of his intention concerning the future, and "as your vassal and your servant and as *comendador* of the Order of Santiago,"[8] he asked for the emperor's permission to enter the Society. This letter, dated January 15, 1551, was dispatched to Augsburg, where the emperor was at the time. Enclosed in the letter was a memorandum in which Borgia outlined his wishes on some concrete points.

In his response of March 10 Charles wrote, "I understand your determination to enter the Society of Jesus and the reasons that have moved you to do so."[9] He thanked him for having apprised him of his resolve, "and as far as putting it into execution, there is nothing more to answer except to tell you that you may do so, however and whenever seems best to you." As for the contents of the memorandum, Charles promised to take them under advisement. Specifically, he allowed him to continue to receive for a period of five years the 400,000 *maravedís'* pension that Borgia had been awarded for life. It seems that the saint turned over this pension to the Roman College. Borgia did not let his advantage pass without asking the emperor to favor the Society. Charles V assured him that he should "have confidence that because this is both something that is pleasing to our Lord and will show consideration to you, I shall do so gladly."[10] The concrete details would be discussed by the Consejo del Reino.

Borgia likewise communicated his intentions to Prince Philip in a letter of January 17. We know this because of Philip's answer, also from Augsburg, on February 21. He thanked Borgia for "the information you so kindly gave us about everything," and he was delighted about his plans "because I hope in our Lord that it will be for his greater service and for the peace of your soul."[11]

5. Apostle to the Basque Country (1551-1552)

Francis found his three months' stay in Rome long enough for him to finish all the projects that had brought him there. And now where should he go? Most certainly he discussed the matter with St. Ignatius. They decided on the Basque country; more particularly, on the province of Guipúzcoa. Inclined to hide from people's eyes, Borgia thought he could do this better in the Basque mountains than in any other place. According to Nadal, he contemplated making a pilgrimage to Jerusalem, but Ignatius had dissuaded him from doing so.

Polanco tells us in his *Chronicle* that Borgia began getting everything together for his return to Spain in January 1551, but that Ignatius held him back until the first part of February.[1] Still, we are left with several unanswered questions. Why did he not wait for Charles V's answer to his request to renounce his estates? Why did he not publicly declare in Rome that he had entered the Society? Why was he not ordained a priest there? Why did he set out on a journey in the dead of winter? The sources answer only the last question for us. Borgia left Rome when he learned that the pope wanted to make him a cardinal. We shall return to this subject; for the time being, suffice it to say that he began his return trip on February 4, 1551, at night to avoid being noticed.

Ignatius counseled Borgia before the latter left Rome, but he did so with the tact and deference he always used when dealing with Francis, leaving him complete freedom of movement. Borgia remained exempt from the jurisdiction of Araoz, the provincial of Spain, and depended exclusively on the general. In a memo dated January 2, 1552, we see this indicated. "To Don Francisco. One [exemption] from Father [Ignatius], that he may go wherever he judges right in the Lord."[2] Later, in a letter of August 12, 1553, this exemption was stated explicitly for him:

> The second [thing] is that, although Your Reverence may, for
> your own satisfaction, consult with Father Doctor Araoz

concerning your movements and other matters you consider appropriate, you are not obliged to do so, nor are you obliged to follow his advice; and this was the intention our Father Ignatius had in mind when he exempted Your Reverence from obedience to all provincials or any other person in the Society except the general: you should follow your devotion and spirit because he [Ignatius] hoped that God our Lord will guide Your Reverence's affairs so that your own person, without other instruments, will serve him.[3]

It goes without saying that Borgia used this freedom with great discretion. He was predisposed to obey Ignatius, not only in cases where the general gave express orders, but even at the merest sign of his will. There were no clashes with Araoz, but sometimes Borgia found himself confronted with the dilemma of deciding between what he understood was Ignatius's mind and the provincial's judgment. We shall have the opportunity of seeing that as time went on this tension increased.

From Rome to Oñate

The retinue that accompanied Borgia was made up of some thirty persons, among them almost all the Jesuits who had made the trip to Rome except Oviedo, who stayed on in Italy to become rector of the college at Naples. On the other hand, Miguel Ochoa, first rector of the incipient college of Oñate, remained in Borgia's company.

As we said above, they left Rome on February 4, 1551. In his spiritual diary Borgia recorded this anniversary in 1564. "On this [day], the thirteenth anniversary of my departure from Rome to Spain, etc. Day of consolation."[4]

On April 4, they arrived in Azpeitia. Here in St. Ignatius's native town Borgia did not neglect paying a visit to the house of Loyola, where he met Juana de Recalde and her two daughters, Lorenza and Magdalena. Juana de Recalde was the widow of Ignatius's nephew, Beltrán de Oñaz. We do not know the precise moment when Lorenza, at that time mistress of Loyola, became acquainted with Francis's second son, Juan, who accompanied his father on this journey. But the fact is that the next year, August 7, 1552, Juan and Lorenza signed their marriage contract, thus joining together the Borgia and Loyola families. We do know that Ignatius did not want to get involved in this wedding, nor did he take an active part in showing favor to any of the suitors who were asking for the hand of the mistress of Loyola. We also know that Juan de Borja's marriage did not please Ignatius, because when this young man was in Rome he had given indications of having a vocation to the Society. Although Francis did not attend the marriage ceremony, which was celebrated by Araoz, he took advantage of the first opportunity that presented itself to go to Loyola to bless the newlyweds.[5]

The provincial Araoz determined where Borgia and his entourage were to set up their permanent residence. "After having gone for more than fifteen days around the countryside of Oñate, as well as that of Vergara, inspecting the lay of the land, [he] resolved . . . that the place for our settling down should be the hermitage called the Magdalena," as Borgia wrote to Ignatius on April 23.[6] This place was selected because the Society was going to open a college in Oñate. In no time a little house was built alongside the hermitage, and it was here that on September 8 Borgia, Miguel Ochoa, and eight other Jesuits settled in. On the 14th the relics which had been brought from Rome were carried in procession to the hermitage.

Life in a hermitage, isolated from the populated center of Oñate, offered Borgia the opportunity to spend long hours in prayer and penance, at least at the beginning of his stay. A little later, he began to receive a number of requests from various quarters that he take up his favored ministry, preaching. For this reason and because the Jesuits had formed a small community there, as we have already seen, it would be wrong to suppose that Borgia led a solitary life at Magdalena. The hermitage had become his winter headquarters, from which he sallied forth on apostolic campaigns. He devoted to prayer and to the composition of spiritual tracts the time that remained free from the apostolate. Some of his surviving writings date from this period; one of these is a tract on the way a lord should govern his estates.[7] During one of his excursions in 1553, Borgia met the constable of Castile, Pedro Fernández de Velasco, who asked him for this tract; but because it was not yet finished, Francis could not give it to him.[8]

Very soon Borgia's reputation spread far and wide. Here was a man renowned for his noble birth and influence at court who had renounced honors and privileges to become a religious. Requests for him came from all over; everywhere he went he was accorded the same signs of friendship and admiration. Bishops, nobles, and civil authorities received him warmly and the people flocked to his sermons.

On April 6, 1551, he was in Vergara, where he paid a visit to the house of Ozaeta. The lord of Ozaeta was Juan López Gallaiztegui, son of St. Ignatius's sister Magdalena and hence his nephew. Vergara competed with Oñate for the privilege of extending hospitality to the illustrious guest. Borgia visited the town several times, and it was here that he preached sermons that were attended by great crowds of the faithful.

In May he received Charles V's consent to his petition to renounce his estates.[9] Now that he had the emperor's permission, there were no further obstacles to making this renunciation, as he was so eager to do. Accordingly, before the notary Pedro López de Lazarraga and several witnesses, he put his signature to the formal document on May 11.

His ordination to the priesthood and first Mass

Holy orders followed. The bishop of Calahorra, Juan Bernal Díaz de Luco, was busy with the affairs of the Council of Trent; so, taking advantage of the permission he had that allowed him to choose any bishop to ordain him, Borgia prevailed upon the acting bishop of the diocese, Juan Gaona. He shaved off his beard and put on the Jesuit cassock, and then during the ember days after Pentecost he was ordained. On Wednesday, May 20, 1551, he received minor orders; on the 21st and 22nd, the subdiaconate and diaconate; and on Saturday the 23rd, the priesthood. On Trinity Sunday, May 24, "His Lordship [Borgia] was at the sermon [of Father Araoz] and that was the first [day] that he went out as one of Ours, robed and shod as one of the Society." So wrote Manuel de Sá to St. Ignatius on May 28.[10]

He wanted to celebrate his first Mass on the feast of Corpus Christi, which that year fell on May 28; but St. Ignatius asked him to postpone this public and solemn function until a special indulgence could be obtained for all those assisting at the Mass.[11] On May 29 Bishop Gaona consecrated the altar at the hermitage. On June 29, feast of St. Peter the Apostle, Francis preached a sermon in the parish church of Vergara, whose patron saint was Peter; on this occasion people flocked to the church from miles away. Toward the end of July St. Ignatius's letter arrived at Oñate, informing Borgia that the Holy See had granted the requested indulgence for all who assisted at his first Mass.

Before this public Mass Francis wanted to offer a private Mass on August 1, 1551. He chose to say it in the oratory chapel at the house of Loyola. The chasuble his sister Luisa, the countess of Ribagorza, made with her own hands for this occasion is preserved to this day beside the altar in the oratory.

Borgia celebrated his first public Mass in Vergara on Sunday, November 15, before more than ten thousand of the faithful. Since it would have been impossible to fit such a crowd into the parish church, the decision was made to stage the event in the open air, in front of the hermitage of Santa Ana de Rotalde. It is said that more than 1,200 people received Communion at the Mass.[12]

A case can be made that this was the first important apostolic ministry that Borgia performed in Guipúzcoa. Others followed. He preached in Oñate on the first Sunday of Advent, November 29; on the second Sunday in Mondragón; on the feast of the Immaculate Conception in Segura; on the third Sunday in Vergara; the fourth again in Oñate; and during Christmas vespers in Vergara.

The town of Vergara was not satisfied merely to hear Borgia's sermons; the people put pressure on the Society to open a college there. They pledged that they would donate a house and provide it with the needed income. Borgia was favorable to the enterprise and supported it in a letter to Araoz on December 4, 1551.[13] Two days later, the city's council, tribunal, board of governors, gentlemen, and hidalgos addressed a letter to the general formulating their desires.[14] They chose Ignatius's nephew, Beltrán López de Gallaiztegui, lord of Ozaeta, to be their advocate; on that very day he wrote to his uncle supporting their project.[15] But their hopes were not to be realized at this time, for Vergara had to wait until 1593 to have its college of the Society.

One of the cities beyond the Guipúzcoan borders that showed an especially great desire to see and hear Borgia was Pamplona. To facilitate his coming, Bernadino de Cárdenas, viceroy of Navarre and duke of Maqueda, sent Borgia an invitation, offering to meet him at the kingdom's frontier; but Borgia, who shied away from pomp and circumstance, appeared in Pamplona without any advance notice. In the cathedral of that city he preached a number of times to large congregations.

We now come to the year 1552. On January 7 we see Borgia in Azcoitia. From there he moved on to Loyola, "where we found very good and recollected ladies who desired the arrival of the Fathers in such a way that we could not put them off," as Borgia's companion, Father Miguel Ochoa, wrote to Ignatius from Loyola. The ladies in question were Juana de Recalde, the widow of Ignatius's nephew Ignacio Beltrán, and her two daughters, Lorenza and Magdalena. He also saw Martin García, Ignatius's other nephew, "who was always sick," and Isabel de Araoz, the Spanish provincial's sister, a nun in the convent of the *beatas* of Concepción. He did not accept hospitality in the house of Loyola but rather in the Azpeitian hospital of the Magdalena, where Ignatius had lodged in 1535. Ochoa continued his letter, saying that Borgia "wanted to eat at the same little table where Your Paternity ate and to sleep in the same room where you slept." He then adds a curious detail: "We also discovered the pony Your Paternity left this house sixteen years ago; it is now quite fat and sleek and serves the house very well to this day. It enjoys great privileges in Azpeitia: even though it goes into the grain fields they tolerate it."[16] Evidently he was referring to the "little horse" which, as St. Ignatius tells us in his autobiography, his friends bought for him in Paris so that he could travel to Azpeitia.[17] When Borgia begged for alms in the streets of Azpeitia, he and his companions gathered so much that they could not carry it all by themselves and had to be helped by the neighbors.

He also visited Bilbao in February of 1552, after stopping to preach at Vitoria on Septuagesima Sunday, the 14th of that month. While in the Vizcayan capital he followed his custom and lodged in the hospital of the poor. The people in Bilbao offered him a permanent residence for the Society, placing at his disposal either the church of St. John or that of our Lady of Begoña. Between Quinquagesima Sunday, February 28, and the first Sunday of Lent, he preached four sermons in Vergara.

A visit to Portugal

In February 1552 St. Ignatius entrusted Borgia with a sensitive mission that took him to Portugal. In the Society's Portuguese province a difficult situation had arisen, which led to Father Simão Rodrigues's removal on December 27, 1551, from his post as provincial. It seems that the reason for sending Borgia, who knew Portuguese affairs so well and who had such excellent connections with the people at the court, was to calm the situation. Obedient to the orders he had received, he set off from Oñate on March 19, 1552, accompanied by two priests, Bartolomé Bustamante and Pedro Domé-nech.

Two events deserving comment took place on this journey. At Casa de la Reina, a village in La Rioja, the duchess of Frías wanted to discuss with him the possibility of bringing Poor Clare nuns from Gandía to found a convent. The idea for this venture came from Francis's aunt, Sister Francisca de Jesús, who wanted to move on to a more distant place because she felt "surrounded by her own blood inside and out" of the convent at Gandía,[18] where she had one cousin and six nieces. She considered that Casa de la Reina, which was under the protection of the duchess of Frías, who was also the wife of the constable of Castile, would be ideal for her purposes. This noble lady was willing to spend between ten and twelve thousand ducats on the project, but Borgia talked her into limiting herself to some two thousand ducats. Already in September 1549, using Ignatius as the go-between, he had negotiated for permission from Rome to allow the move. Rome, however, rejected this request.

Borgia continued his journey through Leiva and Belorado to Burgos, where, even though his plans had not included a halt, he stopped over for two or three days. On Passion Sunday, April 3, he was in Valladolid, where he met his son-in-law, the count of Lerma; together they journeyed on to

Tordesillas. On April 10, Palm Sunday, while they were in Toro, Princess Juana, the daughter of Charles V and fiancée of the heir to the Portuguese crown, summoned him. During the course of Holy Week the princess made "a short form of the Exercises," as Bustamante wrote to Rome.[19] There were indeed "light" exercises as described by Ignatius in the eighteenth annotation of his book, so-called because they did not last a month or aim at complete results, but they were practiced with intensity. Borgia conversed with his directee for two hours in both morning and afternoon. It was during this time that he began to exercise that influence over Princess Juana which was to continue; we shall deal more extensively with this in chapter six. One practical fruit of these exercises was that the princess gave up playing cards, which she used to enjoy greatly; she also gave up reading "profane books." The cards she destroyed and the books she handed over to Father Francis.

On April 16, Holy Saturday, he set out toward Salamanca, where he remained until the 23rd. There he learned his trip to Portugal was not necessary, "being advised that the business he was going to treat had been settled well and as Your Paternity [Ignatius] desired, and thus I concluded that there was nothing else to be done about it." He returned to Oñate, where he spent the remainder of 1552.

It was a pity that Borgia's trip to Portugal had been thwarted at a moment so crucial for the Portuguese province of the Society. Had he been on hand, perhaps a solution would have been found to the crisis that resulted from the removal of Father Simão Rodrigues from the province he had founded. Showing himself to be very much up to date on the Portuguese question, Borgia wrote a carefully nuanced letter to Ignatius on September 19, 1552.[20] In a veiled way he registered his disagreement with the transfer of Rodrigues to become provincial of the province of Aragón. "If Your Paternity was advised and informed, I doubt that he would have taken" that measure. But since the decision could not be rescinded, he recommended some solutions to the general which guaranteed that Rodrigues's departure from Portugal could be dispatched without his losing face.

The journey earlier cut short was undertaken the following year. Father Gonçalves da Câmara sent Borgia an urgent invitation in the name of King John III to come to Portugal "because of the need His Highness had to communicate both his own affairs and those of the Society,"[21] as Father Bustamante explained to Ignatius in a letter of September 20, 1553, in which he related in detail all the stages of the journey.

Borgia made his definitive departure from Oñate on Holy Saturday, April 1, 1553, and traveled to Calahorra where the local bishop, Juan Bernal Díaz de Luco, wanted to establish a house of the Society. Arriving at Burgos, he learned of the arrival in Spain of Jerome Nadal, who on April 10 had been appointed commissary general for Spain and Portugal. Among other things, the commissary general was responsible for making the Constitutions known in Spain and Portugal. Borgia set out for Medina del Campo to meet him, but by the time he got there Nadal had already left for Portugal. In Medina Francis laid the first stone of the Society's college. From here he went on to Salamanca, arriving on August 4 and remaining there for twelve days. At Salamanca he preached two sermons, one at the monastery of the nuns of St. Ursula on the feast of the Transfiguration, and the other on St. Lawrence's feast in the chapel of the Jesuit residence before a group of laymen, among whom were distinguished professors from the university. On August 16 he departed for Coimbra, stopping off for a short while at Ciudad Rodrigo, where the diocesan bishop, Pedro Ponce de León, came to pay him a visit. From August 23 to 28 he was in Coimbra, to the great consolation and edification of Jesuits and lay people there. On the 27th he preached before a huge congregation, among whom were the distinguished Doctor Martín Azpilcueta and other professors from the university of Coimbra.

He arrived in Lisbon on August 31, where he was received with great warmth.[22] It can be said without exaggeration that the court turned itself upside down in welcoming him. Borgia always had very close ties with Portugal. His wife had been Portuguese; Portuguese also was the empress Isabel whom he had served so faithfully. When he entered the room where the king and queen awaited him, they arose and took a few steps forward to greet him. The king doffed his hat; Borgia in turn fell on his knees. At the end of the audience the king and queen accompanied him to visit Princess Doña Juana and the infantas María and Isabel. On the following day the infante Don Luis, the king's brother, the apostolic nuncio, the archbishop, the duke of Aveiro, and other personages came to the Jesuit residence to visit him. The king and queen treated him with great affection. They were aware of his illness, so they put their own chief physician at his disposition; and each day they sent him specially prepared food. Bustamante goes so far as to say that they "treated him as if he were their own son."[23]

His conversations with Philip II's sister, Princess Juana, merit a certain highlighting. Juana, who was married to John Manuel, the heir to the Portuguese crown, had been unsuccessful in fitting into the Portuguese court. In the year following these events, in 1554, that is, she was to become a widow at the age of nineteen, and shortly after her husband's death she would give birth to the hapless Prince Sebastian. We have already seen that, ever since she made the Exercises under Borgia's direction at Toro, she had led an intensely spiritual life. At that time, we recall, Borgia had deprived her of her favorite distractions, card playing and reading secular literature. Once back in the court she went one step further; she substituted for her former games others of a spiritual nature. It consisted in gathering forty-eight cards, twenty-four bearing the names of different virtues and the other twenty-four marked with the names of vices. The cards representing the virtues contained appropriate verses as well as a "confusion" for failure to practice these virtues. For example, on the card "Love your neighbor" was written

> Love and esteem in this world
> the lowly and rejected,
> for they are loved by God.
> *(Confusion)*
> I opened my door to the darling rich,
> and shut it on the poor and dejected.

On the card assigned to the vice "backbiting" was written:

> The tongue kills more than the knife.

Hands of seven cards were dealt. Whoever ended up with the greatest number of vice cards lost and had to perform some mortification. Whoever picked up a virtue card confessed confusion for not having practiced that particular virtue. An innocent game, but it gave the princess and her ladies real enjoyment. The princess confessed that "she had never seen anything more pleasant in her life."[24]

Borgia's first visit to Portugal was not merely a succession of honors and courtesies; it also resulted in great benefits for the Society. Commissary General Nadal's work was expedited by the prestige enjoyed by this humble religious. Referring to Borgia, he acknowledged this work.

> This Father's goodness, humility and edification and his effectiveness in all spiritual matters is a blessing. Blessed be God. The only way I can express how much he has assisted me is to say that everything the Lord has done here he did while he [Borgia] was here; and before he came and after he went, too, because of the great veneration Their Majesties have for him.[25]

On October 5, Father Francis set out from Lisbon in the direction of Evora. He received the same reception at the College of the Holy Spirit that he had received in Coimbra and in Lisbon, and the cardinal infante of

Portugal was awaiting his arrival there. On the 10th he left Portugal and was in Córdoba on the 18th. The college in this Andalusian city had a special meaning for him because it owed its existence to the generosity of the dean of the cathedral, Don Juan de Córdoba. St. John of Avila was also connected with this college because, once he saw it being built, he said he could now sing his Nunc Dimittis. On November 25, 1553, the Jesuits moved into the building and during the following month began holding classes. Borgia wanted to become one of the masters of grammar and catechism there, and he was not easily persuaded that this was not his apostolate. On March 15, 1554, Nadal wrote about him to Ignatius:

> As I have advised Your Paternity, Father Francis gathered much fruit in Portugal and through him Jesus Christ helped us in our endeavors there in a special way. Besides this he is doing very well. The Lord is with him in his goodness, simplicity, probity, and prayer, and in his edification and effectiveness toward all. Apart from this, while he appeared withdrawn and retiring in Oñate, he is now fervent, diligent, effective, and determined to help with all his might and means the Society's progress.[26]

Up to that time, Ignatius had left it to Borgia's judgment and discretion how he was to be guided, without ever imposing any specific rules. But this freedom was not going to last long. Soon Ignatius imposed upon him the office of commissary general for Spain and Portugal. We shall deal with this matter in chapter six.

Borgia the preacher

The entire period spent in Guipúzcoa calls our attention to Borgia as a preacher, a function in which he distinguished himself all his life. A lengthy series of his sermons is still preserved; beginning with the one he preached at Gandía in 1546 and ending with the one he gave in 1571 in the cathedral at Valencia at the insistence of the patriarch, John de Ribera. The *Short Treatise on How to Preach the Holy Gospel*,[27] which undoubtedly reflects his own style of preaching, shows his great esteem for the ministry of the word.

The subject matter of his sermons was simple, not at all recherché: the Creed, the Commandments, the Gospels and the liturgy of the day. He elucidated all his sermons by a plethora of Scriptural citations that show us how seriously he took his studies in Gandía and also reveal something about his subsequent readings of the sacred text.

It was the unction of words pronounced by a man who put into practice what he urged upon others that most enraptured his hearers. Another great preacher, Father Francisco Estrada, wrote to St. Ignatius from Burgos on May 1, 1553, saying that Borgia "preaches with great ease and without much effort, and in one sermon he moves more people than famous preachers do in many sermons because the people admire the sight of a duke who is a poor man and a preacher, and in him and through him they glorify God and confound themselves."[28]

In addition to his sermons, preached in widely different circumstances, he gave the Spiritual Exercises to a number of people. Some of his exercitants decided to enter the Society. In particular, Nadal cites Bartolomé de Bustamante, a famous architect and erstwhile secretary to Cardinal Juan Tavera; also Antonio de Córdoba, the son of the marquise de Priego and countess of Feria, who at that time was the rector of the university of Salamanca and had been proposed for a cardinal's hat. Two disciples of St. John of Avila were also admitted to the Society after making the Exercises under Borgia in 1552. These were Diego Guzmán, the brother of the count of Bailén, and Doctor Gaspar Loarte, a professor of theology at Baeza. It is well-known that John of Avila wanted to direct his former disciples toward the Society. As far as the number of vocations is concerned, Polanco says that, if all who had asked had been were admitted, many more new colleges could have been filled.[29]

Danger of the cardinalate

It was considered ominous that on three separate occasions Borgia had been proposed for the cardinal's hat. Ecclesiastical dignities are not allowed in the Society, and all the professed make a vow not to accept them unless the pope expressly commands under sin that they do so. Ignatius always vigorously defended this special mark of the Society: it nipped in the bud ambitions for prelacies and guaranteed that the order would not lose its best men.

Particularly when one keeps in mind that two of Borgia's brothers, both of whom died prematurely, were named cardinals by Paul III, it is easy to appreciate that this possibility was an ever-present danger. Had the pontificate of the Farnese pope lasted longer, it would have been very difficult for Father Francis to escape from such an eventuality. Even if Julius III was not compelled by his own inclinations to enroll Borgia in the College of Cardinals, he was inclined to carry out the wishes of the emperor and the king of the Romans.

The first rumor that plans were afoot to make Borgia a cardinal spread through Rome at the beginning of 1551, during his first visit there. We mentioned that he left the Eternal City on February 4 of that year, and we explained the long trip he took to Spain during the dead of winter as the result of his determination to avoid this threatening danger.

On March 30, 1552, Charles instructed his ambassador in Rome, Diego Hurtado de Mendoza, to propose to the pope the names of four churchmen as candidates for the cardinalate. The first name was that of Father Francis Borgia. Julius III reacted favorably to this recommendation and instructed his nuncio in Spain, Giovanni Poggio, to communicate the news to Borgia, who in those days was at Casa de la Reina. The nuncio summoned him to Santo Domingo de la Calzada and notified him of the pope's offer.

From a letter to Borgia on June 5, 1552,[30] we know St. Ignatius's reaction when he learned of the plans of emperor and Pope. This letter is an example of the spiritual discernment the saint used in solving a difficult case. At first, he had "this conviction or spirit to oppose [these plans] as much as he could"; but he did not see God's will clearly. In order to discover this will he ordered all the priests in the house to offer Mass on three consecutive days for this intention; he ordered the nonpriests as well to pray that "in everything he be shown the way to the greater divine glory." During these three days he reflected on the subject for several hours, his feelings fluctuating back and forth. Sometimes he did not see clearly why he should oppose the nomination. "How do I know what God our Lord wants to do?" At other times "these apprehensions were removed." On the third day "I found in myself, during my customary prayer and ever since then, with a decision reached that was so complete, and with a determination so peaceful, and with such astonishing freedom" that it seemed to him that he would be doing something displeasing to God did he not oppose Borgia's cardinalate. However, he did not wish to impose his decision on Borgia. He simply asked him to tell the pope what seemed to him best, "leaving the whole matter to God our Lord, so that in all our affairs His most holy will be accomplished." This indeed is a letter that has the typically Ignatian stamp upon it.

Five days earlier, on June 1, the secretary of the Society, Father Polanco, had written Borgia another letter.[31] It presents us with some very interesting facts. At the time Polanco wrote, Ignatius had already made up his mind to oppose the nomination with more vigor—according to Polanco—than he had employed when Father Claude Jay was being considered for the bishopric of Trieste.[32]

According to Polanco the intention of the emperor and of his brother, Ferdinand I, king of the Romans, was known through Ferdinand's ambassador in Rome, Diego Laso de la Vega; and it was confirmed by Cardinals Mendoza, de la Cueva, and Maffei. According to Maffei the idea seemed very good because "he wanted the Society to be the seminary for bishops and cardinals."[33] Polanco added that what Ignatius did was immediately to ask for an audience with the pope. In this audience he explained the reasons why the Society rejected ecclesiastical honors. "The pope showed himself to be most understanding of what was being proposed to him," expressing the opinion that Francis's state of life was better than that of a cardinal and asserting that "he would never send him the cardinal's hat" against his will. The pope went so far as to say that he felt a kind of envy for the Fathers because they did not have the responsibility of governing the Church.

Not satisfied with this assurance, Ignatius also visited a number of cardinals, as he did at other crucial times. Although most of them wanted to see Borgia in the College of Cardinals, many conceded that this was not a good thing. Accordingly, Polanco concluded, "the business can be considered a thing of the past; Rome has had enough of it." Finally, he remarked that Borgia was ready to go "with his head bared to the sun and rain rather than accepting a cardinal's hat to shelter him."

But what was the attitude of Borgia, the principal party in all this? We have no direct knowledge of what took place in his soul because he did not speak or write about it. We have to rely on the correspondence of others, especially that of Araoz to Ignatius. Do these letters reflect the sentiments of Borgia impartially, or were they influenced by the judgments of those who wrote them? Araoz wrote twice to Ignatius, once on September 3 and again on November 22, 1552. Using roundabout phrases in the first letter and more explicit ones in the second, Araoz gives the impression that Borgia thought he should accept the cardinalate. "I have already written to Your Paternity in other letters how R[afael] resolved to accept the favors that Antonio Rión gives because he feels interiorly that he should."[34] Antonio Rión was a lay brother in Rome who gave public reprehensions (*capelos*—literally, "hats") to members of the community who had committed faults.

How much truth is there in this? Possibly human weakness may have led him to yield in a matter of such significance for his vocation. But knowing him and knowing what his attitude was at the time, such a hypothesis has to be discarded. How could he have aspired to a cardinal's hat after having renounced so privileged a position in the world and lived in an atmosphere of such intense spiritual activity, characterized by sentiments of profound humility and contempt for earthly glories? What may well have occurred was that he too was assailed by the doubts St. Ignatius experienced: Was it really the pope's desire that he should accept what had been proposed to him if he could not avoid it?

His biographers, including Ribadeneira,[35] say that, faced with the proposal that had been made to him, he was very much grieved and asked the pope not to make him accept it. The fact is that at this time the storm had died out; a contributing factor was that Julius III, while making the offer, never imposed it.

In 1554, after about two years had gone by, the same scenario repeated itself. This time it seems that the initiative came from Prince Philip. Actually, the same rumors that had circulated in 1552 made their rounds again, namely, that Borgia was inclined to accept the dignity if it should be offered to him. Fathers Polanco and Nadal manifested their concern over with this state of affairs, the first in a letter to Father Nadal on May 15, 1554;[36] the second, in another letter to Borgia himself, dated June 17.[37]

In this whole affair one detail should not be overlooked. Borgia, who had made his solemn profession on February 1, 1548, had not as yet pronounced the simple vows that go along with this profession. One of these is the vow that binds a Jesuit not to accept prelacies except under obedience to the one who has authority to oblige him to do so, namely, the pope. Borgia did take these simple vows on August 22, 1554,[38] and sent the autograph formula to Ignatius in a letter dated September 17. In his response of November 23 Ignatius wrote that, together with his letter of September 17, "we received the vow formula which by oversight had not been sent earlier. I trust that in the divine goodness it was a sacrifice pleasing to God."[39] Borgia had delayed taking these simple vows because the Constitutions of the Society, which prescribe the vows, had not yet been published. Even granting that he may have vacillated, the fact that Borgia pronounced these vows is an evident proof that by this time he had decided not to accept the cardinal's hat unless the pope forced him to do so. And we have already seen that the pope did not force him. The danger had passed and Borgia found himself at peace. Ribadeneira recounted that, once when Francis was talking with his confessor, Father Gaspar Hernández, "he told him that for many years he had petitioned our Lord from the bottom of his heart to please take him from this life rather than allow such a thing to take place." Father Hernández himself recounted this to Ribadeneira.

Ribadeneira also reported that, while Borgia was still in Rome, both Pius IV and Pius V tried to make him a cardinal, but that these plans also came to naught.[40] As a matter of fact, there was talk about it in 1566, when Borgia was already general of the Society. In a letter of June 26, 1566, the secretary Polanco informed Father Diego Carillo of the general's reaction to this proposal.

We were rather amused at how certain some people seem to

be about our Father's getting the red hat. Although there was some talk about it here, the said Father gave such a look to those who mentioned the subject that I doubt that anyone brought it up a second time. At the moment there is no mention of it at all and no reason to fear it, for honors of this sort are not usually forced on a person who not only does not want them but bluntly declares that such a prospect is more displeasing to him than an order to take away his life.[41]

6. Commissary General in Spain and Portugal (1554-1559)

Appointment, prerogatives, and exercise of the office

On January 7, 1554, St. Ignatius wrote to Jerome Nadal, commissary general for the Society in Spain and Portugal, informing him that Spain, since 1547 a single province, was to be divided into three new provinces, Aragón, Castile, and Andalucía; no changes were to be made for the province of Portugal, however. In this letter he mapped out the boundaries for each province and named those who would govern them. Francisco Estrada was to be provincial of Aragón; Antonio de Araoz, up until now provincial for all of Spain, was to be provincial of Castile; and Miguel de Torres provincial of Andalucía. Diego Miró would continue at his post as provincial of Portugal; and Francis Borgia, the newly appointed commissary general, would have ultimate authority over the whole of Spain and Portugal.[1]

In April of this year Nadal called the three provincials and the new commissary general to Medina and entrusted them with their new offices. Father Francis was to be "over them all."[2] Borgia "accepted the position; however he asked me that he not be given the care of souls along with his charge, and he also requested not to be called 'commissary general'—all of which seemed to me should be granted him in the Lord."[3] Despite this concession, we note that in fact he was given the title "commissary general," although ordinarily he was simply called "Father Francis."

Even though his nomination was communicated to him officially during the month of April 1554, as we have seen, it appears that Borgia had already known about it since March. In fact, from March on his life took on a new direction, as we see from what Nadal wrote to Ignatius on the 15th of the month:

> Besides this [Father Francis] is doing very well. The Lord is with him in his goodness, simplicity, probity, and prayer, and in his edification and effectiveness toward all. Apart

from this, while he appeared withdrawn and retiring at Oñate, he is now fervent, diligent, effective, and determined to help with all his might and means the Society's progress, concerning which he has many ideas. . . . He would like, however, to have a hermitage or house where he could retreat, some place central enough to enable him to be of service to a large geographical area. The plan was to set up [this hermitage] near Plasencia, an advantageous site for the whole of Castile, Andalucía, and Portugal.[4]

The reference to these provinces indicates that Francis considered them under his jurisdiction. By May 14 of that year Nadal concluded his impressions of the new commissary general in his letter to Ignatius:

Father Francis is in good spirits in the office that he has and he has great hope for growth. He dedicates himself to administration, to the Constitutions, and the rest, which is what we wanted. I certainly marvel and rejoice seeing him in such good spirits. He is very much in need of support, however, because of his poor health and practice of retirement. It is a blessing from God that he is so enthusiastic about founding colleges and in attracting candidates. He is held in high esteem everywhere and much fruit is derived from his example.[5]

At the time of his appointment, the authority of the commissary general was imprecisely defined. This was a touchy matter, with all the potential of creating tensions between the commissary general and the provincials. In fact, tensions did break out, at least in the case of Araoz, who felt himself somewhat hamstrung in carrying out his office, particularly in his most important duty of visiting the houses in his province. Besides this problem, another arose because the general had never given Borgia a written appointment. Such an official document may not have been of capital importance when it came to dealing with Jesuits, but it was indispensable "in official functions, such as accepting houses or colleges, etc., because people ask us for one, and the lawyers put no importance in whatever instruction Father Nadal left behind."[6] Because of this predicament, St. Ignatius sent Borgia letters patent on November 13, 1555, formalizing his commission. In this document Ignatius stated the need to have someone in Spain and Portugal with the authority of the general of the Society; for this reason he appointed Father Francis to fill the office of commissary general.[7] Thus it was that

Borgia became a kind of lieutenant for the general, just as he had been in earlier years lieutenant for Charles V in the principality of Catalonia.

Besides the territories mentioned in the document, the commissary general's jurisdiction extended to those lands overseas that had been placed under the sovereignty of Spain and Portugal. His commission was explicitly defined in letters patent drawn up on April 16, 1556, and sent to Borgia on the 21st.[8] After St. Ignatius's death in 1556, Borgia petitioned his successor, Father Diego Laínez, for "a commissioning document such as the one our Father of happy memory sent me, because it may come in handy in situations that are apt to occur."[9]

In a letter of June 1559, Borgia informed Laínez how he thought he should exercise his office. His intention was to leave the provincials the powers they were guaranteed by the Constitutions of the Society, but he would reserve the following to himself:

1) Authority to decide on those matters the provincials did not resolve or in those cases where an appeal was made over the decision of the provincials.

2) Authority to make a concrete decision when the provincial was far off and when delaying the answer was deemed unsuitable.

3) Authority to admit candidates to the Society after previous notification to the particular provincial. The rationale here was that it could sometimes happen that a particular candidate would be of no use to a particular provincial, whereas he could be well employed in another province.

4) Authority to determine the disposal of the worldly goods of those making their renunciation. Here the argument was that the person who is in charge of all could better attend to the common good.

5) Authority to establish new houses or colleges and to transfer those already established.

Borgia communicated this plan to the provincials. Their primary duty was to visit the houses and colleges to provide for the needs of each; the commissary general proposed that the provincials frequently communicate with him by letter in order to assure unity of purpose. Health permitting, he too would visit the houses at various times.[10]

Before he left, Nadal entrusted Borgia with an instruction in which he strongly recommended that the newly named commissary general exhort all to be faithful in all things to obedience and to the manner of proceeding in the Society, in conformity with the Constitutions and their declarations, and the rules.

Travels from 1554 to 1559

The commissary general did not have a fixed residence. We see him moving from one place to another as circumstances dictated; for the most part these circumstances involved founding new colleges. In 1557 he wrote, "I go about like a gypsy from college to college."[11] Although his tenure of office extended beyond 1559, we shall limit ourselves here to listing his activities between 1554 and 1559, that is, until his dispute with the Inquisition forced him to move to Portugal, when he all but totally ceased to exercise his authority. We shall deal with this matter in chapter eight.

In 1554 we find him in Medina del Campo, Tordesillas, Simancas, Avila, and Plasencia. At the beginning of 1555 he was in Andalucía, where he visited Seville, Montilla, and Córdoba. He then returned to Plasencia, from where he was summoned to Tordesillas to assist Queen Juana "la Loca" in her last hours; next he directed his steps toward Valladolid, Simancas, Sigüenza, and Alcalá. He divided 1556 between Plasencia, Escalona, Simancas, Valladolid, Alcalá, returning at last to Plasencia. In 1557 he visited Alcalá, Madrid, Avila, Simancas, Valladolid, Jarandilla, Lisbon, and Plasencia. At the beginning of 1558 we find him at Valladolid, where his accustomed stopovers at the court became more and more prolonged; yet even during this year he continued to visit such cities as Medina del Campo, Toro, and Alcalá. And so we reach the waning days of 1559.

It was only natural that a contemplative like Borgia would feel from time to time the urge to retire to a place apart. The bishop of Plasencia offered him a house or hermitage which, by coincidence, bore the same name as the hermitage at Oñate, La Magdalena. It was located at Jarnadilla, a stone's throw from Yuste, the place Charles V was thinking about choosing for his own retreat. The archbishop of Toledo, Cardinal Siliceo, urged Francis to accept La Magdalena, if for no other reason than that it would make a convenient place from which to visit the emperor.[12] St. Ignatius, always so compliant when dealing with Borgia, gave him permission to withdraw to an isolated place far from the hustle and bustle so that he could find consolation and renew his strength; the idea of accepting La Magdalena seemed good to Nadal too. He added, however, that "the name 'hermitage' should not be given to it, but rather some other appellation such as 'house' or the like, according to the established practices of the Constitutions."[13]

Writing to Peter of Alcántara in 1557, Borgia confessed that he would consider it a paradise on earth to have available a retreat like El Pedroso, the house where the saintly Franciscan had withdrawn to live a hidden life.[14]

But pressures of business rendered this dream impossible. Ignatius consoled him, saying: "We were pleased by the fact that the desire for the

hermitage has resolved itself into the exercise of charity toward the neighbor. May it please Him to impart the fruit and even the very savor of the
hermitage to Your Reverence in the midst of outward activities."[15] In these
words we see the epitome of Borgia's attitude. Undeniably, he felt an
inclination to the contemplative life, but he sacrificed it on the altar of
obedience and fidelity to the spirit of the Society.

Borgia did retreat now and then to his beloved novitiate at Simancas. A
glance at his itinerary as sketched above shows how often he visited this
Castilian town.

In addition to his administrative duties, Borgia gave himself occasionally
to his favorite apostolate, preaching. He also wrote several spiritual tracts,
some of which date from this period, for example, his study on prayer and
his commentary on the Lamentations of Jeremiah.

Wherever he went he edified all, Jesuits and laypersons alike. Father
Diego Carillo wrote from Alcalá that "by his teaching he attracts people's
admiration and by his example he puts all to shame."[16] Tales of the glory he
renounced and examples of his humility and poverty fascinated the ordinary
people, while bishops, nobles, gentlemen, and ladies of quality flocked to
him, seeking advice or requesting a college of the Society in their respective
cities. Nadal confirmed that he was highly esteemed by the leading people
throughout the country and that he was well accepted by Jesuits.[17] In his
letters St. Ignatius attested that he was satisfied with what Borgia was doing,
and he praised the abnegation and zeal with which he carried out his office.[18]
As the founder's faithful son and disciple, Borgia endeavored to put a high
priority on obedience and religious observance, in conformity with the
directions he had been given.[19] In every matter he endeavored to conduct
himself according to the Constitutions.[20]

The results he obtained rewarded his endeavors: the Society witnessed
remarkable growth in Spain during these years. Not only did new foundations multiply but there was also a veritable efflorescence of vocations; many
a university graduate and many a holder of public office made application
to enter the Society. Borgia's example had motivated large numbers of young
men to imitate what he himself had done.

The foundations

The commissary general received requests to found colleges of the
Society in a number of different towns; some accused him of being too
generous in heeding these requests. But in deference to the truth, it should
be noted that he always insisted that the necessary stipulations be adhered
to; namely, that the Society be given a house or the guarantee of sufficient

funds to set one up, together with a pledge of adequate endowment to maintain the house and an agreed-upon number of Jesuits. The gravest problem was a shortage of personnel. Vocations abounded, as we have already stated, but the number was not always sufficient to assure qualified professors for every college. St. Ignatius placed no obstacle in the path of the commissary general, telling him that, provided requirements for the endowment and personnel were met, "the multiplication of colleges is the right way to proceed."[21] Another recommendation, particularly in the early days, was that more colleges than professed houses were be established. It should be noted here that the raison d'être for colleges of the Society was the formation of young Jesuits.[22] Ignatius called to Borgia's attention "the policy that no college be accepted where there was not a house with a church and an income sufficient to support at least fourteen or fifteen men."[23] Once these stipulations were guaranteed, the college could open its doors to lay students. Naturally, in no time at all the number of lay students surpassed that of Jesuits.

It is not our intention to sketch the history of each establishment that was founded in Spain during this span of time. Apart from those details that characterize a particular foundation, the history of all of them follows the same general design. A benefactor—bishop, noble, or gentleman—requested the foundation of a college in his city. He would offer a house and sufficient endowment, or he would promise to provide these eventually. Naturally, founders were always in a hurry, so they exerted pressure to open up a college even before the required conditions had actually been met. It was at this juncture that the superior had to weigh what he could do against the importance of the offer that was being made. However, Ignatius always insisted on one point touching upon poverty, namely, that theology professors, preachers, and confessors were not to be included in contract negotiations with benefactors. This was because the Society was committed to exercise gratuitously all ministries involving spiritual matters.

Our bird's eye view here prevents us from considering Spanish colleges founded before Borgia was appointed commissary general. By exception one or another of these colleges is singled out because of its importance or because its founder somehow merits comment. For example, we should not overlook the college of Córdoba, supported as it was by the marquise of Priego, mother of Father Antonio de Córdoba, and founded by Juan de Córdoba, dean of the cathedral, who in 1554 donated one of his houses to make possible the establishment of a college there.[24]

On August 24, 1554, Bustamante catalogued for St. Ignatius the names of cities where future colleges of the Society were being established. They include Seville, Granada, Sanlúcar, Baeza, Montilla, Almagro, Murcia, Cuenca, Avila, Plasencia, and Simancas; but not all these places saw institutions opened during this same year.[25] The college at Plasencia deserves special mention here because of the munificence with which the diocesan bishop, Gutierre Vargas de Carvajal, endowed it. St. Ignatius showed special interest in the college at Seville because of the importance of the city and of his great hope that it would produce abundant vocations. He recommended that a college and a house of the Society be founded there; the college was opened in 1554 and the professed house in 1580. The college at Granada should be singled out because of the kind benefactions of the local archbishop, Pedro Guerrero, while the one at Sanlúcar de Barrameda is notable only because it remained in operation for a very few years.

In 1555 colleges in Murcia, Monterrey in Galicia, and Zaragoza opened their doors. No establishment, however, met with so many obstacles as that of Zaragoza, where the religious from a number of different orders voiced opposition to a Jesuit foundation, arguing that, according to the privilege of seniority, a new religious house could be opened only if it was located some distance away from an existing one. Zaragoza's archbishop, Hernando de Aragón, sided with those opposed to the Jesuits; similarly opposed was the vicar general, Lope Marco, who was also the abbot of the Cistercian monastery of Veruela. As a result, the Jesuits had to abandon Zaragoza for Pedrola, where they were welcomed by the gracious Doña Luisa de Borja, countess of Ribagorza and sister of the commissary general. Then Philip II's energetic sister entered the fray. Spurred into action by the entreaties of Father Francis, Princess Juana dispatched a number of missives to the archbishop and his vicar. The fact that the opposition melted away and that in no time a solution to the problem quickly materialized is proof that her aim was accurate. The upshot of all this was the return of the Jesuits to the Aragonese capital on September 9, 1555.

In 1557 the death of Archbishop Siliceo of Toledo, always a hostile foe of the Society, removed the chief obstacle to the Jesuits' reception into that city. His successor, the Dominican Bartolomé de Carranza, wished to see a Jesuit establishment in the city, but he preferred a professed house rather than a college. Fathers Bustamante and Estrada, accompanied by two lay brothers, came to Toledo in October 1558; and on the 25th Borgia wrote from Valladolid to Laínez:

> [Carranza] says that he is very happy that the Society will
> come to Toledo and that he will befriend it in every way
> possible; however, it was a professed house he wanted, since

there was already a university in Toledo and another in Alcalá, etc., and also because studies somewhat impede working with souls. Then he gave his blessing to having the house set up, after which Father Bustamante left for Toledo with Father Estrada; the other men will be following them soon.[26]

In 1558 the colleges of Ocaña, Belmonte, and Montilla were ready to open. Plans to establish the last of these had been agreed upon as early as 1555, but it was not until 1557 that the Jesuits were able to take possession of the house given to them by the marquise of Priego. The Fathers began their apostolate there on January 1, 1558, to the great joy of the saintly Master John of Avila, who preached a sermon at the inaugural ceremony.

The year 1559 witnessed the setting up of three more colleges, Segovia, Logroño, and Palencia. The establishment of Palencia had been enthusiastically supported by Suero de Vega, son of Juan de Vega, the former viceroy of Sicily and great benefactor of the Society. This year can also be considered the founding date of the college at Madrid, a city that speculation had already marked out as the eventual capital of Castile. Doña Leonor Mascarenhas had purchased a house there with the intention of founding a college, and on August 2, 1560, she turned this residence over to the Society.

Novitiates

Father Francis in a very short time realized the advantage of having a separate novitiate in each of the Jesuit provinces. He recommended this plan to St. Ignatius on October 1554, suggesting that one novitiate be opened either in Gandía or in Valencia for the province of Aragón, another in Plasencia for Andalucía, and a third in Simancas for Castile. Ignatius approved this proposal, but stipulated that each house had to maintain a sufficient number of men.[27] Plans went ahead to open a novitiate in Valencia, but they came to nothing; a novitiate was begun in Córdoba for Andalucía in 1555, but it moved to Granada the following year. Of the three novitiates specifically named in Borgia's proposal, therefore, the one at Simancas was the most successful. Juan Mosquera, a knight of Santiago (one of the three military orders) and a highly respected gentleman in Valladolid, had presented the Society with a house in this small town, some eight miles from Valladolid. He had been an enemy of the Jesuits; but after being impressed by the example of the former duke of Gandía, he became a fast friend of the Fathers and offered them his Simancas property. Borgia judged the place to be ideal for the novitiate. Depriving himself of the assistance of his companion, Father Bustamante, he made him the master of novices there, and ordered that all candidates to the Society from the Castile colleges be sent to Simancas. In 1555 the commissary gave Ignatius an excellent report of the novitiate's progress, dwelling upon the number of novices—there were thirty at the time—and the religious spirit that prevailed among them.[28] He himself gave the novices frequent exhortations. Despite these auspicious beginnings, however, the Simancas novitiate did not remain where it was very long. In 1559, it moved to El Villar, a place not far from Astorga; then four years later, it relocated once again, this time in Medina del Campo; and from there it settled down in Villagarcía de Campos, where it became famous in the history of the Society as a model novitiate. The actual house at Simancas served as the villa for the college at Valladolid and the "refuge" for the commissary and for the provincial when the court was residing in the city.

The Roman College

St. Ignatius always showed the greatest interest in the college which he had founded in Rome in 1551. His clear-sighted vision of reality enabled him to see the role this house was destined to play; later endowed and enlarged by Pope Gregory XIII, this institution, now known as the Gregorian University, still continues to play the same role. It was to this college that young men from a number of different nations would come to receive their formation and, their studies once completed, would disperse to various parts of the world as ministers of the Lord. But such an enterprise entailed one huge problem—adequate funding. Professors and students were presenting themselves in increasing numbers each year; but where could Ignatius find the resources to feed and keep them? In 1553 the number of students reached sixty; the following year it had gone beyond a hundred. Because of the shortage of food in Rome, 1555 was a really harrowing year, yet the number of professors and students at the college had risen to 130. In 1557 it was 145; in 1558 the students alone numbered 150; and in 1561 their number had gone up to 180.

Pope Julius III took an active part in helping the college, setting up a commission for this purpose. Much was expected from his successor; however, the pontificate of Marcellus II lasted but a few days. The next pope was Paul IV, who very soon after his election became embroiled in a war with Spain. What he would do for the college could only be a matter for speculation.

Ever since 1550, when St. Ignatius had the opportunity to discuss his projects with Borgia face-to-face, he regarded Borgia as very likely the solution to his Roman College problems. Given the fact that he was person-ally wealthy, influential, and well-connected with the people that mattered, Borgia was in a position to help. In chapter four we saw what financial ar-rangements Borgia made before leaving Rome in early 1551; however, most of this money was earmarked for building the new church of the Gesù.

Borgia's enthusiasm for the college increased from the moment he was named commissary general in Spain; he now considered it of top priority, not merely because the obedience he owed his superiors demanded it, but also because he understood the importance of this apostolate. So indebted to him was the college that on more than one occasion it was referred to as "the Borgia college" or "the Borgia college of Jesus." Ignatius spoke about it to him as "Your Reverence's college," but Borgia preferred the appellation "the universal college" because it was "the seminary of the universal good." Ignatius realized that Father Francis alone was the key to the college's well-being. "God our Lord has used almost no other material means for this great work than Your Reverence, and without material means, the spiritual could not proceed."[29]

There was scarcely a letter of Borgia's to the general in which he does not speak of the ways he had scrounged for money. He went so far as to assert that, had he known what the universal college in Rome would become at the time when he endowed the college of Gandía, he would have given the amount to it rather than to the one in his native city.[30] But his earnest wishes clashed with the real world; it was not easy to find a bene-factor. "I am anxious to come to your help," he wrote to Ignatius; however, "I don't have a single cent."[31] Added to this predicament was the problem of transferring money to Rome. At the time when he renounced his estate, he imposed upon his son and heir, Carlos, the obligation of contributing five hundred ducats per annum to the Roman College. But the new duke was forever coming up with excuses that created a hitch in the agreement; but his father did not give in, even threatening to take his son to court over it.

Moreover, when Francis made his renunciation, Charles V agreed that an annuity of 400,000 maravedís, which was more than one thousand ducats, would be paid as a fixed per annum sum to the college.[32] Philip II extended this payment for a period of five years, but Borgia was aware that this infusion of capital would one day dry up and that other means of funding had to be found.

A glance at Borgia's correspondence during this period reveals, among other things, the following pertinent details concerning the Roman College. In July 1555 he recorded that he had sent some eight hundred ducats through Brother Antonio Gou. In February 1556 he sent on four thousand,

and in March 1558 he wrote that, in addition to the thousand ducats he had already collected, another five hundred were to follow; then in June 1559, he had another three thousand ducats to send on for the Roman College. A manuscript account of the college's early stages shows that Borgia endowed it with more than thirty thousand *escudos*, not counting the sums of money he continued to obtain from various benefactors.[33]

St. Ignatius believed that it would worthwhile to have a procurator expressly commissioned to raise money for the Roman College; Borgia gave him three. Here were other solutions proposed by Borgia to remedy the Roman College problem: (1) whenever a scholastic made his renunciation, the inheritance money should be channeled to the college; (2) every college should assume responsibility for supporting one, two, or three students in the Roman College; (3) this policy should be implemented by each of the provinces throughout the Society.

Ignatius and Borgia were united in this enterprise. But both were saints, and they realized that, once they had brought all human resources into play, in the last analysis they had to place all their trust in God. On one occasion, writing about this subject to Borgia, Ignatius observed: "To accomplish all the things we hope to do, any sum of money is too little. But God, who inspires these hopes in us, will not let them come to naught."[34]

St. Teresa of Avila consults Father Francis

In her *Spiritual Relations* St. Teresa of Avila enumerates the "spiritual persons of the Society of Jesus" with whom she spoke concerning matters of her soul. It is here that she mentions "Father Francis, formerly duke of Gandía, with whom I consulted twice." The first encounter between the saintly Carmelite and "the great contemplative," as she referred to Borgia in her *Way of Perfection*, must have occurred in 1555, when she began to speak with the young Jesuit Diego de Cetina about her spiritual life. The second meeting between the two saints took place in 1557, while Borgia was in Avila during Holy Week and Easter. During those years Teresa was torment- ed with difficulties in prayer, so this was the subject that she brought up to Father Francis. "[My prayer] confused me so much that I asked Father if it could be a delusion, but he told me that it often happened." Or, as she quoted him as saying in her *Way of Perfection*, "It was quite possible; . . . it had happened to him."[35] In the twenty-fourth chapter of her *Life*, Teresa was more explicit.

> At this time Father Francis, who had been the duke of Gan- día before he left all behind and entered the Society of Jesus

some years ago, came to our place. My confessor [probably Father Juan de Prádanos] and the gentleman about whom I have spoken [Francisco de Salcedo] arranged for him to pay me a visit so that I could talk with him and tell him about my experiences in prayer, because they knew him to be an expert in such matters, having himself been the recipient of great favors and blessings from God, as the rewards in this life for what he had given up for Him. After listening to all that I explained to him, he told me I was being led by the Spirit of God and that it seemed to him that I would be doing wrong to resist this Spirit in the future. He further told me that what I had done was right, but that I should from now on always begin my prayer with some scene from the Passion as a point of departure, and then, if the Lord should lift up my spirit, I should not resist Him, but rather that I should allow His Majesty to take my spirit and not to make any effort to hold it back. He prescribed this medicine and this advice as one who had himself considerable experience in such matters. He said that it would be wrong for me to resist further. Both I and the gentleman were greatly consoled; he was greatly relieved that [Father Francis] said that what was happening to me was from God.

As we see, it was Borgia's assurance, based on his own experience in the matter of prayer, that brought peace to St. Teresa. Incidentally, we have here an extraordinary testimony to the depth of Borgia's prayer and to his discretion in spiritual matters.

Dealings with the Hapsburgs

Princess Juana — Father Francis had to concern himself with the direction of Princess Juana, who, as we have already seen, was the daughter of Charles V and the sister of Philip II. Antonio Moro painted the beautiful portrait of her that hangs today in Madrid's Prado Museum. She was an altogether extraordinary woman. When her young husband, Prince John Manuel, heir to the throne of Portugal, died on January 2, 1554, she was nineteen years of age. Eighteen days later Princess Juana gave birth to the royal couple's only child, the ill-fated Prince Sebastian. However, she had to turn him over to the care of his grandmother, Queen Catherine, and his nurses when she was summoned to Castile to take over the government during the absence of her father and her brother Philip. On July 12 that same year, Philip embarked from La Coruña bound for England, where his new bride, Queen Mary Tudor, awaited him.

We recall that the princess had already discussed her spiritual life with Francis in Toro in 1552 and in Lisbon in 1553. She was fond of him and had recourse to him now during this very critical and difficult time of her life. Even before leaving Lisbon she wrote to him, asking that he wait for her at Tordesillas, where she intended to go to visit her grandmother, Queen Juana "la Loca."

Juana arrived in Tordesillas on June 9, 1554, and on that very same day she sent for Father Francis, with whom she spoke for more than an hour and a half. On the following day she held him in conversation for an additional two hours, "treating of the matters of her conscience and of the means Her Highness had to take so that in her preoccupation with governance she would not forget what belonged to our Lord."[36] There is no doubt that Francis had to give her spiritual direction; this was a great responsibility and "a return to Egypt" for him. Without question, this is the matter he alluded to ten years later when he inserted the following notation in his spiritual diary for June 10, 1564: "On this day ten [years] have passed since I was given the cross at Tordesillas."[37] His doubts about the propriety of his role persisted. To quiet them Borgia had recourse to Ignatius, who answered his queries on May 28, 1555, writing, "In virtue of holy obedience, I order you to accept this charge, knowing that you will carry it out with so much more devotion for having been ordered to do so."[38] The Lord would inspire him to fulfill this priestly ministry in a most efficacious manner.

It did not take long for the results of this spiritual direction to become evident. On August 24, 1554, Father Bustamante wrote to Ignatius, "We all see in the princess so many good effects of her colloquies, for she has edified the entire kingdom by her good example in the few days since she came from Portugal to her position as governor." Besides dedicating herself to works of mercy and leading a secluded life in the privacy of her home, she dedicated herself with so much energy to the affairs of state that "neither her age nor her sex seems to be a hindrance."[39]

The princess's confidence in her spiritual director's advice led her to desire to take vows in the Society and actually to make a formal petition to do so. The situation was delicate, especially considering that some six years earlier St. Ignatius had had a bitter experience with a lady from Barcelona named Isabel Roser and her two companions, who had wrested permission from the pope to make solemn profession in the Society. His experience in this affair is what led Ignatius to petition that the Society be free from the care of female subjects; on May 20, 1547, he obtained a favorable reply. In the princess's case, there were further complications. At an uncertain date, probably right after her husband's death, Juana pronounced vows in the Order of St. Francis; before she could take vows in the Society, she had either to be dispensed from her former vows or be granted a commutation from these vows by the pope. Because Ignatius had serious doubts about asking for the necessary permission, he submitted the case to five specialists. But how could he possibly refuse the request of a personage such as the princess-governor of Spain? At last, "although there were no small obstacles in this matter," Juana was granted what she had petitioned. On January 1, 1555, Ignatius wrote to Borgia that "we have received from the pope the commutation of vows requested by you in your letter regarding the affair, which you commended to me so earnestly, of Mateo Sánchez [the alias used to designate the princess]."[40] To guarantee secrecy, no record of what had taken place was kept anywhere. The princess's name had not been mentioned in the request for dispensation addressed to the Holy See, and the writ granting the dispensation was in the possession of the general himself. The vows that Juana was to take were to be those pronounced by scholastics in the Society, that is, perpetual on the part of the person who takes them but dispensable as far as the superior is concerned. This was, among other things, a safety measure in case reasons of state should ever require the princess to marry again.[41]

Because of the cloak of secrecy that covered this whole business, we do not how it transpired. One thing is certain: from this moment on Juana regarded the affairs and the houses of the Society as her own. At the time of her grandmother, Juana "la Loca's," death, she passed through Simancas, where she expressed her desire to stay in the house of the Society rather than take up lodging in the local castle. Here in the novitiate she requested to see the room where Father Francis had stayed.[42] Meanwhile, she continued her religious exercises and was "quite determined that, when her brother and her father returned, she would preach to them, so that through her instrumentality they would be saved and would straighten out some aspects of their conduct."[43] For his part, Borgia advised Laínez: "Señor Mateo Sánchez is also very devout and advanced, and I do believe that since my coming here [Simancas] our Lord has fostered many worthy desires in his soul." In 1588, he added in a letter, "Her Highness is, as ever, quite devoted to the Society," and a short time later: "Mateo Sánchez, with even increased devotion to the Society and with increased progress, is the same. All these deaths have taken their toll on him, and with good reason, but he supports them with great prudence and Christian spirit."[44] Borgia here was referring to the deaths of Charles and of his two sisters, Queen Eleanor and

Queen Mary, all three of whom died in the same year, 1558. Eleanor had been the third wife of King Manuel the Fortunate of Portugal before she became the second wife of Francis I of France; Mary had been the consort of King Louis II of Hungary and later Charles V's lieutenant governor in the Low Countries. Both died in Spain, where they were living in retirement, Eleanor in Talavera and Mary in Cigales, near Valladolid.

In addition to the "great love and trust"[45] for Borgia that she demonstrated, Juana gave concrete proofs of her attachment to the Society. She did what she could to help it grow in Spain; she gave financial aid to the Roman College; and, as we have seen, she intervened effectively in the Zaragoza tussle, where the Society had found itself at odds with the archbishop and religious orders. She assisted Borgia in his efforts to evade the cardinal's hat; she was given a share in the spiritual goods of the Society and through its aid received special permission to read the Bible in the vernacular.

But this relationship was not without its detracters. Juana's frequent dealings with Father Francis encouraged the evil-minded to detect therein irregularities which in reality did not exist. These suspicions collapsed of their own weight.

On the other hand, the good example given by the princess influenced the ladies of her court. Father Juan de Valderrábano wrote to Ignatius from Valladolid, "They go to confession so often that they seem to be more like religious than laywomen."[46] And they did not wish to confess to anyone except to the Fathers of the Society.

In chapter eight we shall have occasion to see how Princess Juana comported herself with her spiritual director during the most critical period of his life.

Spiritual Aid to Queen Juana "la Loca" — Responding to the wishes of Princess Juana and her brother Prince Philip, Borgia went several times to visit Doña Juana "la Loca" at her castle in Tordesillas. The principal reason for these trips was to attend to the spiritual well-being of this famous shut-in, whose mental disequilibrium had caused her to neglect her religious duties. We should recall that Borgia had already visited Tordesillas in 1552. He returned there in 1554, when Prince Philip, then making preparations to embark for England, asked Father Francis to visit his grandmother again. Borgia complied with the prince's request in April of that year, remaining with the queen for two months. Thanks to three letters he dispatched to Philip in May, we know what transpired during this visitation. His correspondence reveals that the queen graciously welcomed Borgia and allowed him to undertake the mission entrusted to him. He began it by reminding the queen of her duty to give good example to her subjects, who could be scandalized at seeing her living "without Mass, images, or sacraments." Juana opened up her heart to Borgia, explaining her problem to him. She asserted that the *dueñas*, who remained with her at the time of prayer, would grab her book from her hands, scold her, and make fun of the way she was praying. Evidently this was an example of one of her hallucinations. We should recall that one of these *dueñas* was Isabel, Borgia's daughter and wife of the count of Lerma, who also served as an official in the palace at a salary of seventy thousand *maravedís* yearly.[47] Borgia soothed the queen, assuring her that, if her *dueñas* were guilty of such actions, they would be condemned of heresy by the Inquisition and thrown into prison. He exhorted her to renew her profession of faith. She did so, adding that she would indeed like to confess and receive Holy Communion, provided the *dueñas* were dismissed.

This was done. The order was given to the *dueñas* not to attend upon Her Highness. Borgia then took a further step: he exhorted her to renew her resolution to live and die in the Catholic faith and to hear Mass. Just at this juncture a Franciscan, Fray Luis de la Cruz, made his appearance in Tordesillas. This man was the grandson of Count Juan Velásquez de Cuéllar, in whose household at Arévalo St. Ignatius had lived as a young page. It was the Franciscan's opinion that the queen was not in the proper state to receive the sacraments because of her mental condition. We do not know whether his opinion prevailed.

Father Francis departed from Tordesillas near the middle of May, leaving the mentally disturbed queen pretty much at peace. He returned in June, but this time it was chiefly to speak with Princess Juana, who had summoned him to meet her there on her return from Portugal, as we have already seen.

In March of the following year, 1555, the queen fell gravely ill. She suffered intense pain and screamed so loudly that she could be heard throughout the palace. She did not want to see anyone, not even her granddaughter; but, realizing that her grandmother's illness was the beginning of the end, Juana asked Father Francis to come. Francis's gentle, persuasive manner softened the queen little by little, until at last she was able to comply with his suggestions. She made an act of contrition and repeated after him the Apostles' Creed. There was some doubt that she could receive the last sacraments validly, so Salamanca's famous theologian, the Dominican Fray Domingo de Soto, was consulted. Arriving at Tordesillas on April 1, he acknowledged that the patient was well-disposed but judged that she was in no condition to receive viaticum, especially because of her vomiting spells.

On his advice that she receive the anointing of the sick, Father Francis administered the sacrament while the patient manifested the greatest devotion. He then placed the crucifix in her hand and she pressed it against her heart, uttering her last words, "Jesus Christ crucified, be with me."[48] She died at six in the morning of Good Friday, April 12, 1555, at the age of seventy-five. When Philip I ("the Handsome") died, leaving her a widow at the age of twenty-six, she had retired to Tordesillas, where she remained for the next forty-eight years. Borgia reported to Charles V on the last sickness and death of his mother, the daughter of Ferdinand and Isabella.

Charles V summons Father Francis – During the last days of his life Charles V gave his former lieutenant general of Catalonia proofs of his most sincere confidence and affection. The emperor had abdicated his throne in Brussels on September 28, 1556, and returned to Spain, disembarking at Laredo, intent on retiring to the Hieronymite monastery at Yuste in Extremadura. On November 11 he arrived in Jarandilla, lodging there until February 5 while his permanent living quarters were being prepared. In October he expressed the wish to have Father Francis at his side and asked Francisco Alvarez de Toledo, count of Oropesa, why Francis had not visited him. The count transmitted this query to Borgia, who on December 9 took the road from Alcalá to Jarandilla. Conveying this news to Laínez in a letter of the 13th of that month, Father Francisco de Villanueva added that in the opinion of many the Father Commissary General was in no position to refuse the wish of the emperor. "Although we have information that he is not very favorable to the Society, he is devoted to him personally, and so it seemed necessary for him to go."[49] In a letter to Laínez from Plasencia on December 28, Borgia recounted for him the details of the visit. The emperor, he said,

> [had] sent a request that Señor Rafael de Sa [the pseudonym of Father Francis] pay him a visit. Even though far away, Rafael obeyed the command and informed him in great detail of the affairs of the Society, concerning which he did not have a good opinion because of the perverse information he had received, but later he remained totally satisfied about everything, finding no cause to gainsay or refute anything that had now been proposed to him. I attribute this to the power God has given to truth and to genuine simplicity. Mateo Sánchez's father [recall that Mateo Sánchez was the alias for Princess Juana] showed himself satisfied, and he was

astonished at those who had dared tell him tales impugning the Society. He welcomed the one who had gone to visit him with more love than ever before, and the two of them remained conversing for three hours about matters pertaining to the service of our Lord.

Apparently, accusations hurled against the Society in Spain, particularly by the Dominican theologian Melchor Cano and the archbishop of Toledo, Juan Martinez Guigeño, better known under the Latinized form of his name, Siliceo, had reached the ears of Charles V. After discussing these matters, Charles then spoke with Father Francis about "his own plans, his condition, his household, his relatives, his lawsuits, and the peace he sought from our Lord in all things."[50] This meeting took place on December 19; and, when the majordomo, Luis de Quijada, gave his report of it to the secretary, Juan Vázquez, he added, "His Majesty says that [Father Francis] has changed very much from the days when he was the marquis of Llombai."[51] When the time came to bid Father Francis farewell, Charles V requested that he write often, promising that he would call for him again. As a matter of fact, he did exactly this toward the middle of the following year, this time not to chat with him about his affairs and the Society, but to confer on him an important mission.

In his *Life of Father Francis Borgia*, book 2, chapter 18, Father Ribadeneira recounts that on one of Father Francis's visits to the emperor at Yuste — "I do not know which one" — the latter proposed to him a case of conscience:

> Did he think it was a mark of vanity for a man to write about his own accomplishments? The reason for this was because the emperor told him that he had written about all his campaigns, together with his reasons and motives in undertaking them, but that he had been prompted to do this not out of vanity or a desire for personal glory but so that the truth might be known. For the contemporary historians he had read had obscured the facts, either out of ignorance or because of their own passions and prejudices.

These words of Borgia were considered an authentic testimony to the fact that Charles V had composed his memoirs. For many years these were considered lost, leading some to conjecture that they had been ordered destroyed by Philip II. In 1862, however, a Portuguese translation of these memoirs was discovered, which since then has gone through a number of editions and commentaries. It is generally agreed that Charles V dictated these reminiscences in 1555, describing events between 1517 and 1547.[52]

Father Francis is sent to Portugal – The mission Charles V entrusted to Father Francis in 1557 was both important and delicate: it dealt with nothing less momentous than the succession to the Portuguese throne. King John III died on June 11, 1557, his son and heir John Manuel having preceded him to the grave early in 1554. Sebastian, the only child of John Manuel and Princess Juana, was left as the heir apparent to the throne of Portugal. The first question that posed itself now was, Who would assume the regency until the child came of age? King John had set up the machinery that would enable his wife, Queen Catherine, to step into this role; however, Juana, the child's mother, believed herself better qualified to fill the post. But Charles V's concerns reached far beyond this detail. In an age when infant mortality was so high, it was imperative to assure the succession to the Portuguese throne, and Sebastian, only three years old, was weak and sickly. Moreover, because Charles was toying with the idea of uniting the crowns of Castile and Portugal, his candidate for the succession was Don Carlos, son of Philip II and his first wife, María of Portugal; he also, like Sebastian, was the grandson of King John III and Queen Catherine of Portugal. Charles V wanted to probe the mind of this sister of his, over whom he had exerted such great influence, hoping to gain her support for his plan. Accordingly, he summoned Father Francis to Yuste and asked him to go to Portugal to confer with Queen Catherine. We can easily imagine the impression, not to say the shock, that such a request made upon Borgia. This indeed was something that invited him to "go back to Egypt," the expression he used referring to the things of the world that he had once and for all renounced. But how could be refuse the emperor's request? He accepted it less reluctantly only because his mission was to be merely investigative. It was understood that his mission was to be carried out in the utmost secrecy. Borgia observed this stipulation, even when describing the situation to his superior, Father Diego Laínez, who was at that time vicar-general of the Society. In a letter from Simancas on July 27, 1557, Borgia said:

> The father of the same Mateo Sánchez [that is, the emperor] is again using our friend Rafael [that is, Borgia himself] in a matter that clearly shows that the old friendship has not been lost, for he is sending him on a highly important assignment; and so Rafael must go now, as it is believed, to Sant Roque [Portugal] where Father Doctor Torres is. Even though his trip right now is so secret that nothing more

about it can be told to Your Reverence, nor will anyone here know about it until the proper time, Your Reverence should entrust the matter to God because that is what we are doing here too. God willing, he will leave here in three days, that is, on the 30th of this month.[53]

Thus, his departure was set for July 30. On August 22, he was in Jarandilla, from where he addressed a letter to Peter of Alcántara, indicating that haste prevented his visiting El Pedroso but that his plans were to see him on the trip home.[54] We know that he fulfilled this promise.[55] We know about the success of his mission through his letters to Charles V from Lisbon on October 6 and 12, letters in which he made use of aliases in speaking of persons and places. There has been some debate about what the queen's reactions were to her brother's proposals. But even if we have no other circumstantial evidence, when we read the following sentences in Borgia's correspondence, we are presented with indisputable proof that Catherine was in agreement with Charles V's plan: "In the meanwhile, Messer Agustino [Charles V] can be very much reassured that all goes well; . . . I repeat that this matter is altogether certain and is in every respect satisfactory, and that Catalina Díez [Queen Catherine] is quite willing to do what Juan Díez [John III] ordered, which is exactly what Messer Agustino wants done."[56] Modern research confirms that Catherine was indeed in agreement with her brother's wishes.

We may conjecture that, his mission completed, Borgia retired to his ordinary duties, giving little thought to what the eventual outcome in Portugal would be. In the meanwhile, life continued on its accustomed course. Don Sebastian did finally become king of Portugal; but, when he met his tragic death at Alcazarquivir in 1578—the same year that his grandmother Queen Catherine breathed her last—Philip II was at last in a position to effect the union of the crowns of Castile and Portugal, a union which lasted from 1580 to 1640.

The final summons – The last time that Charles V called Borgia to come to his side was in December of that same year, 1557; on that occasion Francis remained in Yuste for two days. The emperor "ordered that Father Dionisio [Vázquez] and I be given lodgings, and this was a favor and concession he granted to no one else, not even to those closest to him." Besides showing his love in words, "he sent me an alms out of his own poverty with the stipulation that I should by all means accept it, adding that when he owned more he had given me more, and so now that he was poor he was giving this little to another poor man as a token of the love he bears me and of his desire to show it in deeds and in outward signs."[57] Writing in detail about these events to Laínez, Borgia asked him to commend Charles to God, so that he might realize his strong desire to find solitude and spiritual help, to the edification of all.

Borgia did not assist the emperor in his last hours, but we know that the latter asked for him. Borgia gave an account of Charles's Christian death to Laínez in a letter of October 25, 1558. "Kissing the crucifix and continuously speaking about God, and taking great pleasure in listening to the things of the Lord, he breathed his last."[58] He added in this letter that Charles had made him executor of his will; and even though he tried to excuse himself from accepting this charge, the emperor ordered him with the greatest insistence to accept it. It seemed to Borgia that he was in no position to refuse, "since he always loved me so much, and because of the gifts that he had lavished upon me." He believed that Father General would have no objections to what he had done, but rather would approve of it. But to be more certain, he consulted six Fathers, "some of them doctors and senior men," and they all advised that he accept the responsibility even before receiving approval from the general.

Philip II — Philip II was scarcely a year old when in 1528 Borgia began serving at the court. During his bitter years wrestling with the Inquisition, Borgia could remind the king that he had on many occasions held him in his arms when Philip was a small child. We have already seen how Charles V had planned to appoint Borgia as majordomo for his son and heir and how these plans went awry. Then in 1559, when Philip was getting ready to take over the reins of governing Spain, he addressed Borgia a letter, asking him his opinion about those best qualified to hold the highest offices in the government. Father Francis answered him in a memo on May 5 of that same year.[59] I am not totally convinced of the authenticity of this document, published by Cienfuegos and subsequently accepted by many historians. If it is trustworthy, however, it unquestionably testifies not only to the degree of confidence the king had in the commissary general of the Society but also to the latter's knowledge about matters of state and men of rank in the Spain of that day.

Over all, however, occurrences during this period of history indicate that Philip did not, in fact, show the same esteem and trust his father had demonstrated toward Francis. Borgia's clash with the Inquisition, which we shall describe in chapter eight, implanted a suspicious attitude in Philip's mind which was not soon rooted out.

The First General Congregation (1558)

The news of St. Ignatius's death on July 31, 1556, did not reach Borgia until September 17, when he received Father Ribadeneira's letter of the 6th of that month from Belgium. He expressed his feelings on learning this news when he wrote Father Diego Carrillo that the "sense of alienation and the grief felt" at the death of so good a father was tempered by "the firm hope that the Society will begin anew to expand," thanks to the prayers of so powerful an advocate in heaven.[60] Subsequent events demonstrate how well-founded that hope was.

Now a general congregation had to be called to elect Ignatius's successor and at the same time give official approval to the Constitutions of the Society, which Ignatius out of humility had not submitted for final approbation during his lifetime. But assembling a general congregation, which at first blush would appear to be quite simple given the small number of those who were to take part in it, was from the very beginning beset with obstacles. Almost two whole years had to pass before it could be convened. Why the delay? Diego Laínez, elected vicar-general on August 4, 1556, four days after the founder's death, announced that a congregation would convene at Rome or, if that should prove impossible, at Loreto or Genoa in December of that same year.

Formidable obstacles stood in the way of this proposed meeting, at least for the priests who had to come from Portugal or Spain. The ordinary difficulties encountered while traveling long distances in those days were aggravated by the delicate health of some of the delegates. Added to these complications was the war then raging between Pope Paul IV and King Philip II. In view of this conflict, Borgia believed, if the pope ordered that the congregation take place in Rome, then "we cannot argue about it." Otherwise, he proposed that the congregation should be convened in a city equidistant from the places the delegates had to travel. His first choice was Avignon, but later he opted for either Barcelona or Perpignan, "which are at the very limits of our Spain and the closest points for someone coming by sea from France or Italy."[61] While these alternatives were being debated, the commissary general continued to take steps that would enable the delegates from Spain and Portugal to set out for the place selected. There was a time when the trip to Rome did not seem to offer many difficulties, for a truce had been declared between the two parties. Nadal believed he had to take advantage of this opportunity, so he departed immediately for Rome, arriving there on December 2, 1556. Later, after he had had the opportunity to examine the situation on the spot, he strongly ("vehementer") favored

Spain as the place where the congregation should meet.

Meanwhile, the first postponement was made; the congregation would now convene in April 1557. Borgia continued his preparations and proposed a schedule that would permit the Spanish and Portuguese Fathers to return to their work promptly. They would leave Spain at the beginning of February and so be able to return home before the summer.

Yet another exasperating development arose. Valladolid issued an order prohibiting any Spaniard, priest or layman, from going to Rome and bidding those presently living in the Eternal City to leave it within three months. Borgia communicated this news to Laínez in a letter of February 9, and in successive letters he sought further instructions from the vicar-general. Seeking to make sure that his correspondence would arrive safely at its destination, he sent Juan Bautista Rivera, a scholastic not yet ordained, to Rome with a document explaining the reasons for holding the congregation in Spain. The papal nuncio in Spain, Leonardo Marini, likewise showed himself favorable to this solution and conveyed his recommendation to the pope.

Meanwhile, Fathers coming from various provinces were arriving in Rome, where they were apprised of the impasse. Reasons for convening the congregation in Rome were obvious, yet they appreciated the difficulties facing the Spaniards, whose presence they by no means wanted to exclude from the forthcoming congregation. Finally, they agreed to request the pope to accede to the Spanish recommendation, but Paul IV curtly rejected any proposal that the congregation be held in Spain. "Do you want to aid and abet Philip II's schism and heresy?" In the face of this stance the Fathers could only wait and see if matters would improve.

But by June the situation had become even more sticky. Laínez went to the Vatican, requesting an audience with the pope, but he was not received. A short time later Cardinal Scotti paid him a visit and in the name of Paul IV specifically ordered him to hand over three sets of documents: the Constitutions of the Society, all the bulls and rescripts granted to it by previous popes, and a list of all the Jesuits living in Rome. He absolutely forbade any of these Jesuits to leave the city; furthermore, he added that the pope wished to review everything that pertained to the Society and had entrusted this task to Cardinals Scotti and Giovanni Reumano.

What had happened? Hard as it is to believe, there is no denying the fact: Father Nicolás de Bobadilla, one of the oldest and most respected of St. Ignatius's first companions, had launched a bitter attack against the Institute of the Society. He had not reacted well to Laínez's appointment as vicar-general; moreover, he resented the fact that Laínez had taken into his counsel two workers hired at the second hour, Fathers Nadal and Polanco. He argued that the Constitutions had not been approved and that there were many items in them that should be amended; under the circumstances, he held, everything should revert to the status quo before the confirmation of the Society. In other words, all authority should be placed in the hands of "the founders" of the Society. At first, four of the most respected priests agreed with him; but, when they realized the consequences of his argument, they withdrew their initial support. Only one persisted in his adherence to Bobadilla, the Frenchman Ponce Cogordan; he it was who addressed a memorandum to the pope, asserting that plans to convoke the congregation in Spain were designed solely to escape papal surveillance. One can well understand the impression such an accusation made on a pope so jealous of his own prerogatives and so poorly disposed toward Spain. And the situation becomes even more understandable when we remember that Paul IV had already been warned before this incident about certain practices in the Society's legislation. This fact explains why he decided to have everything concerning the Society turned over to him for examination. On an earlier occasion he had told Laínez that Jesuits should not place too much confidence in what his predecessors had conferred, because what one pope grants another can change or abrogate.

Nadal fended off Bobadilla's and Cogordan's assaults while Laínez proposed that the entire matter be submitted to the judgment of some cardinal. The pope accepted this suggestion, appointing Cardinal Michele Ghislieri, the future Pope St. Pius V, as investigator of the case. The upshot was that all the written documents pertaining to the Society were returned unaltered. Bobadilla began to back off. At the invitation of Cardinal Guido Ascanio Sforza di Santa Fiora, he went to Foligno to work there on reforming some monasteries of the Sylvestrine Benedictines. Once he had left Rome he did not return to press his case. Ponce Cogordan also abandoned his crusade.

The external political situation was changed too. The French army under the command of the duke of Guise withdrew its support, leaving the pope no other alternative than to begin negotiations for peace with Philip II. The principal obstacle for the congregation's meeting at Rome was thus removed.

But what remained a problem for Borgia and the other Spanish Fathers was the difficulty of traveling to Rome, a difficulty aggravated by health problems. Despite the fact that he was ill, however, Borgia declared himself ready to take to the road, as he said in a letter to Laínez. "And so, making a sacrifice of myself, I declare, dear Father, that even if the journey were farther than Rome, I for my part would be ready to go." We get some idea of the actual state of his health when we recall that the trip he had made to Portugal in 1557 at the behest of Charles V almost cost him his life. After this episode his health worsened because of hemorrhages which caused him to lose a considerable quantity of blood and because of "a new infirmity in the urinary tract."[62] So the doctors absolutely forbade him to undertake another trip, thereby forcing him to give up his plans to go to Rome.

Poor health also kept at home in Spain Bustamante, provincial of Andalucía, and Estrada, provincial of Aragón. Father Bautista de Barma served as a substitute for the latter. It is more difficult to account for the absence from the congregation of the provincial of Castile, Antonio de Araoz. We do not know the precise reason why he chose to make the journey by land instead of joining his confreres as they embarked at the port of Rosas. Then, immediately after arriving at the French frontier, he retraced his steps, claiming he had not been allowed to cross into French territory.

There were two solutions proposed to make up for the dearth of professed Fathers at this approaching congregation: either immediately admit to the profession those whom St. Ignatius had already selected for it, or have each province send to Rome some nonprofessed among its three delegates; the congregation itself could then raise them to the profession. Borgia inclined toward the first alternative. So, with Rome's consent, he admitted to the ranks of the professed Father Juan Plaza, master of novices for Andalucía, and sent him to the congregation as his substitute.

Now at last, after so many unexpected complications and sudden reversals of plans, the Fathers were ready to convene the Society's first general congregation, which they did on June 17, 1558. The first item of business was the election of a general. July 2 was the day selected for the voting. On this day, at that time the feast of the Visitation, the twenty electors met under the presidency of Cardinal Pedro Pacheco and chose Father Diego Laínez on the first ballot. One vote was cast for the absent Borgia.

Borgia's memorandum to the General Congregation

Because he was not able to be present in person at the congregation, Father Francis sent it two written statements. The first bore his signature and those of Fathers Miguel de Torres, Antonio de Araoz, Luis Gonçalves da Câmara, and Gonzalo Vaz, all of whom had convened at Valladolid on March 12, 1558, just before the anticipated departure of everyone except Borgia for Rome. This document was a kind of petition in which the signatories requested that once the new general of the Society had been elected the first decision taken should be "not to discuss removing, changing, or altering anything in our Constitutions."[63] As we can see, this supplication was a solemn attestation of fidelity to the text of St. Ignatius; it was based both on the happy results that observing the Constitutions had produced and on the conviction that these Constitutions had been the work of "an instrument endowed with prudence and with knowledge so holy and so Catholic."

The second document was a memorandum in which Borgia proposed a number of issues which he believed the Congregation had to treat in detail.[64] Borgia had entrusted this document to Father de Araoz, who, as we have already seen, did not reach Rome, with the result that the memorandum did not arrive at its intended destination in time for consideration. However, after the Congregation had adjourned in September 1558, the new general and his assistants gave a written answer to each of the points Borgia had raised.[65]

A brief summary of this document shows us which matters Borgia considered to be of greatest importance for the Society at that juncture.

After recommending that thanks be given to the Lord for the increase granted to the Society, he urged the following:

1) "To keep the Rules and Constitutions with all solicitude and due care." Experience had shown him that "at those times when these have been kept with greater strictness there has been more fruit, and when they have been neglected more have been the stresses and storms."

2) That the exercise of the spiritual ministries of the Society, such as teaching Christian doctrine, visiting those in prisons, and assisting the dying, be encouraged.

3) That, in accordance with the prescriptions of Part VI of the Constitutions, secular businesses be avoided.

4) That poverty be fostered; and to facilitate this matter professed houses should be established, at least one in each of the provinces of the Society. He suggested that such houses be set up in the Spanish cities of Seville, Toledo and Valencia. Laínez wrote in his response that this idea sounded good to him, provided the professed houses did not compromise colleges already established and that future colleges would not be adversely affected.

5) That prayer be fostered "as a house of refuge which preserves the spirit of the Society." He added that "any help given to promoting prayer will be help given to the Society." As for specific points, such as whether Jesuits should make their prayer as a community assembled in the church or each one should make it privately in his own room, Borgia saw advantages in both alternatives, even though his personal preference was for each one's praying in his own room. In the response he received, he was informed that the congregation did not want to change anything concerning times for

prayer as outlined in the Constitutions. The ninety-seventh decree stated as much, but this same decree also enjoined superiors to deal with anyone who did not proceed according to the spirit of the Constitutions. Superiors could determine the length of time a man was to dedicate to prayer, lengthening or shortening it for a professed and commuting it for a formed coadjutor. As can be seen, in matters regarding prayer the congregation followed the Ignatian criterion of not imposing rigid rules on formed Jesuits; but, when the situation called for it, it directed the superior to intervene in order to assist the subject with his prayer.

6) That the provincials visit the colleges frequently, and that they confer from time to time with the commissary general in order "to deal with serious matters." It would be profitable to appoint visitors to the provinces to deal with other matters and, by exercising "the office of angels of peace," to foster union between superiors and subjects.

We can appreciate Borgia's preoccupation with trying, on the one hand, to keep the Constitutions and the traditional procedures of the Society intact and, on the other, attempting to respond to the criticisms of some and the expectations of others regarding "external matters." It was with the utmost prudence that he proposed solutions. For example, he recommended two answers to the problem of sung Masses in the churches of the Society. These high Masses were popular with many people, particularly on important feast days. Borgia suggested either that some parts of the Mass be sung, but without the participation of the professed, confessors, and preachers, or that singing at Mass be entrusted to priests who were not Jesuits. Father Laínez answered that the pope had already by that date imposed the obligation of choir on the Society.

As a response to critics who blamed the Society for not having imposed penances by rule, he recommended that "without putting aside its manner of proceeding," the Society ought to prescribe some penances, although they should not bind under sin. In this way, what was already done in the Society would become normative. Laínez answered the commissary that the ninety-sixth decree of the Congregation upheld the principle of not imposing penances by rule.

One of the most delicate subjects Borgia brought up in this memo-randum concerned the vows scholastics take in the Society, specifically, the vow of chastity. This was a simple vow which forbade but did not invalidate a subsequent marriage. In Borgia's opinion, an opinion that was shared by others, the vow lent itself to a lack of seriousness as far as a vocation was concerned. He and another Spanish procurator proposed that, to remove this danger, the vow taken by scholastics "should have the force of the solemn vow, although as far as the Society is concerned, it should be dispensable." Otherwise, they would have to ordain scholastics subdeacons, since this order implicitly placed a man under the obligation of celibacy. It should be noted that Borgia's apprehensions in this matter were real and that Father Nadal had already recognized the feasibility of giving scholastics solemn vows in certain circumstances. In its ninety-fourth decree the congregation showed it did not want to touch any aspect of the nature of the simple vows as they were described in the Constitutions. A solution to the problem of chastity that Borgia had raised was given in 1584 by Pope Gregory XIII in the bull *Ascendente Domino*, which provided that, like the solemn vow, the simple vow of chastity not only constituted an impediment to a subsequent marriage but nullified it as well.

Once the general had been elected, the congregation focused its attention on examining and approving the Constitutions. It solemnly declared that as to their contents they should be respected and observed just as they stood in the original text left by St. Ignatius, and that as a whole as well as in their essential components they were not to be submitted to the body for discussion. After some details had been tidied up, the Latin text of the Constitutions went to press in August. Everything indicated that the Congregation was grinding down to a smooth conclusion when Cardinal Alfonso Carafa of Naples appeared in the hall during the session of September 8. Speaking in the name of the pope he asked that two points be incorporated into the Constitutions: that the tenure of office for the general not be for life, but only for three years with the possibility of confirmation or re-election; and that the Society have choir, as do other religious orders. Clearly, these two regulations did away with two of the most important innovations Ignatius had introduced in the concept of religious life. The Society obeyed the pope's order. However, since Paul IV had not revoked the concessions granted by his predecessors and since his command was transmitted orally and by no other instrument, the Society considered that this command had the force of a particular precept whose binding power ceased with the death of the one who imposed it. Such was the interpretation of the most distinguished canon lawyer of the day, the Majorcan Jaime del Pozzo, an opinion shared by four other jurists. At that date Paul IV was eighty-four and on the following August 18, 1559, he died. So it happened that his order continued in effect for less than a year.

The final session of the general congregation was held on September 10, 1558.

The newly elected general, Diego Laínez, renewed Borgia in his office as commissary general of Spain and Portugal.[66] On February 9, 1560, he explained the reasons for his decision to Father Antonio de Araoz in a letter responding to difficulties raised by Father Juan Bautista de Ribera.

> As for Father Bautista's comments about removing Father Francis from office, or about his not trusting him: I have always known Father Francis to be a servant of the Lord, and one who for His love he left the world as he did; and inasmuch as our Father gave him this office, it did not seem that I had any grounds for removing him from it, nor did the thought of doing so cross my mind. It is enough that he perform his job and let the provincials do theirs, as he was instructed to do; and I believe that from the time he was so instructed he has done this. I shall write to him again to tell him to carry on until I find some reason why I should make a change in this matter.[67]

The letter to Borgia to which the general referred was written on the same day as the preceding, that is, on February 9, 1560. The general was aware of the fact that his commissary general was at the time in Portugal; so he told him that his trip, among other things, should give him the opportunity

> to look over the province [of Portugal], and not to isolate yourself or forget your responsibilities. You should realize that you may not lay down your cross without permission, and I have never had any intention of granting such a permission to you; nor shall I, providing there is no reason for it. It has seemed to me that it is better that you, as their superior, should have the superintendence of the provincials so that, recognizing your supervisory position, they might have recourse to you at all times, take advantage of your office, and not fail to help and serve the Society in the Lord.[68]

In chapter eight we shall see the circumstances in which this letter was written as well as what the general meant when he called upon Francis "not to isolate" himself but to fulfill his office.

7. The Ascetical Writer

Borgia is entitled to a place among the Spanish spiritual writers of the sixteenth century. He can be numbered as well among the classical authors of the Castilian language because of the precision of his style. His opuscules, many of which he entitled "treatises," have deservedly been included in the Espirituales Españoles series, which continues to print hitherto unpublished or rare works, chiefly those of the writers during the Golden Age of Spanish literature.[1] These publications, along with modern studies of the spiritual currents of this period, enable us to place Borgia's writings in their proper mise-en-scène.

Significant though Borgia's writings are in themselves, they are noteworthy in a biography of the saint because of the grief he experienced when they were included in the catalogue of forbidden books published in 1559 by the Spanish Inquisition. In the next chapter we shall deal with this condemnation and study its momentous consequences in the author's life.

It is significant that Borgia began writing and publishing short spiritual works when he was still the duke of Gandía, and he did not stop until the end of his life. A list of his works comprises seventy titles, in addition to a few more which are not merely repetitions or adaptations of these seventy.[2] Father Nieremberg included some of these works "which had not been published before"[3] in his life of Borgia published in 1644. Many of these works were translated into various languages. A comprehensive Latin edition of Borgia's *Opera omnia* was published in Brussels in 1675.[4]

The writings

Borgia wrote six treatises while he was in Gandía, in addition to an opuscule on the method for saying the rosary, reflecting a devotion going back to his Barcelona days, and a 1546 sermon on humility. The principal themes in these treatises are self-knowledge and confusion, that is, a sense of shame for not corresponding properly to God's gifts. It seems that he was alluding to these works in a letter of December 15, 1545, in which he confided to Peter Faber that he was thankful to God for having allowed him "to finish these little works that I had begun." In a letter to St. Ignatius on January 26, 1547, Father Oviedo had this to say: "The booklet that His Lordship wrote has already been printed and it is very useful because it deals with humility and self-confusion, matters in which His Lordship is practiced and proficient." He was referring to Borgia's earliest published opuscule that we know of, *Spiritual Eye Salve*, which came out in 1546. This was subsequently included as the third treatise in the book *Seys tratados muy deuotos y vtiles para qualquier fiel Christiano, compuestos por el illustriss. S. don Francisco de Borja Duque de Gandia y Marques de Lombay, etc.* Including treatises 2 to 7, this edition "was printed in Valencia at the house of Ioan de Mey in the month of September of the year 1548."[5]

There is only one known extant copy of this volume, preserved at Louvain. This is the work which, as we shall see, stirred up the imbroglio with the Inquisition that caused Borgia so much trouble. We shall deal with the subject matter of these six treatises below, under "themes."

In 1549, while he was studying theology in Gandía, Borgia composed in Latin a series of six litanies presenting in prayer form the theological subjects he was studying "according to the scholastic teachings of St. Thomas." He published these in 1550.[6] To this same period belongs the *Short Treatise on Confusion* (treatise 9), written, it seems, in obedience to Father Andrés de Oviedo, rector at Gandía. The Alcalá de Henares printer Juan de Brocar included it in his clandestine 1550 edition of the *Segunda parte de las obras del Ilustrísimo señor duque de Gandía*. Indeed, it was the only treatise in this volume actually by Borgia.

The periods during which Borgia produced the greatest number of spiritual tracts proved to be between 1551 and 1553, while he was leading a relatively quiet life at Oñate, and from 1554 to 1559, while he served as commissary of the Society in Spain and Portugal. These works are simply the meditations, conferences, or sermons Borgia gave in the different cities he visited.

Treatise 10, his *Instruction for the Good Government of a Lord in His Estates* which he addressed to Carlos, his son and successor to the duchy of Gandía, belongs to this same period. Its prologue is dated January 22, 1552; but it is evident from a letter of Francis to Ignatius on April 29, 1553, that it was not finished by that date. In his letter Borgia stated that he was unable to comply with the request for this treatise by Pedro Fernández de Velasco, duke of Frías and constable of Castile, because he was still working on it. It is a treatise on the education of princes, after the pattern of similar treatises that appeared in Spain during the course of the sixteenth and seventeenth centuries. Unquestionably, Borgia put everything into it that he had learned in the course of his four years as viceroy of Catalonia. Taking inspiration from such ancient philosophers as Aristotle, Plato, Cicero, and Seneca and from saints such as Augustine and Thomas Aquinas, he first describes the qualities all good rulers should possess. He proposes as a model King David, a man "after God's own heart." In the second part, making use of the question-and-answer system, he attempts to solve the most difficult cases a good ruler may have to face.

The *Very Helpful Pattern of the Soul of Christ* (treatise 11) was written at Oñate in August 1553 for the Jesuits at Coimbra. He encourages them not to be satisfied with an external imitation of Christ's actions but to clothe themselves with His sentiments. Composed in Portugal were two *amonestaciones* or admonitions for the worthy reception of the sacrament of the Eucharist (treatises 12 and 13). One was dedicated to Princess Juana, daughter of Charles V, the other to the infantas Doña María and Doña Isabel of Portugal.

Also extant are several prayers, considerations, and exercises devoted to the subject of self-knowledge, topics so dear to Borgia's heart (treatises 12 and 13).

While at Simancas in 1556 he wrote his *Exposition on the Lamentations of Jeremiah,* sermons which he had preached in Valladolid and in Alcalá during the course of the previous year. Father Nieremberg published the preface and the first chapter of this work. The other three chapters were not published in the Spanish original, although a Latin translation was included in the Brussels edition of the *Opera omnia.*

In his 1557 work *Spiritual Treatise on Prayer* (treatise 20), Borgia explicitly dealt with the matter of prayer. We shall treat this subject below under "themes."

Between 1554 and 1559 he wrote the *Meditation on the Three Powers of Christ our Redeemer* (treatise 21), designed to be used by the Poor Clares in Madrid during the final three weeks of Advent. Dating from this same period is an *Exercise for Seeking the Presence of God throughout the Day* (treatise 22), as well as another *Exercise on the Three Powers of the Soul, Treating How We Should Prepare Them to Be a True Dwelling-Place of the Three Divine Persoas* (treatise 23). A number of "exercises" or "counsels" appear here; they are of unspecified dates, but they were written before Borgia moved on to Rome in 1561 (treatises 24-34, 36).

During his Roman sojourn between 1561 and 1572, it is only natural that Borgia's writings to Jesuits should be abundant. Here we have exhortations —with those addressed to the novices being of particular interest—meditations, and brief commentaries on the Constitutions of the Society. On the latter subject he wrote some *Notes Drawn from the Constitutions for the Greater Perfecting of the Society in the Observance of our Institute, Carrying It Out with Delight and Vigor.*[7] In these notes he deals with points regarding the Examen and the rest of the Constitutions, up to Part II, Chapter 4. He also wrote a brief treatise entitled *Examples and Teachings from the Evangelists Particularly Pertinent to our Institute.*[8] He thus explains the purpose of this work: "On the 15th of September of the year 1570, I began doing what I had intended to do at various times, namely, taking examples and teachings from the Evangelists that are especially pertinent to our Institute and concentrating on these in the light of what is written in the Rules and Constitutions of the Society of Jesus." He applied forty-five considerations from different parts of the Gospel to the Society's Institute.

Sermons — Borgia dedicated himself to the ministry of preaching during the whole period between his ordination in 1551 and his departure for Rome in 1561, producing edification and much fruit both in Spain and Portugal. But his accomplishments in this field of the ministry went beyond mere preaching. Quite a number of these sermons survive in manuscript form, from the one in Latin on humility which he delivered in 1546[9] to the one he preached on September 16, 1571, in the Valencia cathedral at the request of John de Ribera.[10] However, the most complete surviving series of religious discourses consists of the forty-three sermons he delivered in Portugal during the years 1560 and 1561.[11] Borgia moved his hearers both by his eloquence and by his suave manner, but most of all by the force of his example. Here is the testimony of another great preacher, Father Francisco Estrada, given in a letter to St. Ignatius dated May 1, 1553: "He preaches with great ease and little artificiality, and moves more people in one sermon than other famous preachers in many because people are astonished to see a duke poor and preaching; in and through him they give glory to God and confound themselves."[12]

The fruit of his experience was the *Brief Treatise on How to Preach the Holy Gospel* (treatise 35), as it was called by Nieremberg. The advice he gives here to preachers is both prudent and practical. First of all, the preacher must have a high regard for his apostolate. He should trust in God, who will not fail to help him with His grace. Next he suggests how the preacher should prepare the sermon and deliver it, and offers recommendations on how he should act afterwards. Gospel texts should be the preferred subject of the sermon. "He ought to proclaim Scripture with Scripture itself," and with commentaries both ancient and modern. "Familiarity with the writings of the holy Fathers Augustine, Jerome, Gregory, and Chrysostom will be especially useful to him." Once he has studied the subject the preacher should bring it to his prayer and meditate on it. He should then make an outline of the sermon. Considering that writing it out in full was for beginners, he recommended as sufficient making notes "on half a sheet of paper." The sermon should not go beyond one hour—not an excessive length in those days. While delivering the sermon the preacher should maintain his self-control. Although aware of controversial theological questions, he should not bring them up in the pulpit, because "it is better not to touch on them, not even to refute them." Alone in his room after the delivery, "he will give much thanks to the Lord for having been pleased to make use of him in so exalted a ministry and so preeminent an end." He should be on guard against the praises he may hear. On the other hand, if he sees that the sermon did not produce the expected results, he should remain at peace in the assurance that he did what obedience commanded him to do. He should persuade himself that "the humbler he is, the greater will be the fruit he will gather, and the more he will please the Lord."

This treatise on the art of preaching was one of several similar ones published in Spain during the fifteenth and sixteenth centuries. It was reprinted more often and in more languages than any other of Borgia's treatises.

Meditations — While he was general Borgia wrote several series of meditations, some on the religious vows, some on the vocation to the Society, some on mortification, and so on. But his best-known meditations are those for Sunday and weekday Masses and saints' feasts found in the Roman missal of the time.[13] In the preface of the first series, he begins considering "the profit that comes from meditating on the Holy Gospel." Hence it is that the edition published in 1912 was aptly entitled *El Evangelio meditado*.[14] These meditations were composed between 1563 and 1568, although as early as 1562 Father Nadal had urged Borgia to put his reflections down in writing because "I think it will be something of great profit."[15] Borgia mentions these meditations a number of times in his spiritual diary. On March 25, 1567, he proposes "to finish up these meditations."[16] In 1568 he decided to give them to the delegates gathered in Rome for the congregation of procurators and "let the finishing touches be put to them."[17]

These meditations are particularly valuable because they follow the liturgical year, a novel practice in those times.[18] They begin with the first Sunday in Advent and end with the twenty-fourth and last Sunday after Pentecost. As counterparts to these meditations Francis composed others for the saints' feast days.[19]

The structure of these meditations is clearly Ignatian. It embodies the following parts: preparatory prayer; the history, containing the Gospel text of the day as found in the missal; a petition, which was the prayer or collect of the Mass; a number of points; and a final colloquy. The considerations proposed in the points were reflections on the chosen Gospel passage, followed, true to Borgia's style, by an acknowledgement of how poorly one has acted in response to God's benefits and how unfaithful he had been to the examples and teachings of the Gospel. The colloquies are expressions of ardent love for God.

Borgia got the idea of having some of the Gospel scenes engraved and printed along with these meditations to help the person meditating concentrate his imagination on the subject of his prayer. Father Nadal volunteered to find an engraver in Flanders to do the pictures, but the project did not see the light of day during Borgia's lifetime. Father Nadal then personally took up the project and had his own *Evangelicae historiae imagines* printed in Antwerp in 1593. This was the edition that made the work so famous.

His spiritual diary, belonging to the last days of his life, and his letters form a part of Borgia's literary production. In chapter twelve we shall investigate his spiritual diary, a jewel of Christian spirituality that gives us a point of departure for discovering the interior life of the third general of the Society of Jesus.

Borgia's letters, some of which have been published in the Monumenta Historica Societatis Iesu, are mostly administrative, but his principles of the spiritual life are never entirely absent from them.

In particular, his letter to the whole Society in 1569 deserves special mention. It can be considered his policy statement as far as the spiritual lives of his subjects were concerned. At the meeting of the congregation of procurators the previous year, the delegates submitted to Borgia a detailed panorama of the state of the Society. He saw it as a newly planted vineyard, with its tendrils already extended to the sea (Ps. 80:12). Before it could produce fruit it required care. The letter can be divided into two parts. The first is intended for Jesuits in formation. It deals with such important subjects as the selection of candidates, the solid formation of novices, and the formation program for scholastics. According to Borgia, novices should not be in a hurry to leave the house of formation. Scholastics should combine virtue with learning because "to be a good scholastic one has to be a good novice, and to be a good professed one first has to have been a good novice and a good scholastic."[20]

In the second part Borgia stresses the principles he believes are paramount for maintaining the spirit of the Society, namely, love of prayer, mindfulness of poverty, fidelity to obedience, mortification of the will, and love of Christ's cross. His conclusion is "Look to your vocation" (1 Cor. 1:26). The Jesuit should look at what he must do and how he measures up to what God wants from him. In all that he says or does he must "look at whether these things are worthy of being said or done by one who is a member of the Society. With this measure let him measure all else."[21]

The themes

After this overall view of Borgia's writings, we are ready to look at the major themes he developed. This will in effect be to map out the salient features of the saint's spirituality.

When reading these writings one gets the clear impression that their common element is the antithesis between God's gifts and the shabby way the Christian receives them. In one form or another all his considerations revolve around these two questions: What has God done for us and what are we doing for Him? God, the creator, the redeemer, the compassionate, is contrasted with the creature, sinful and ungrateful. "What was I before I was created? What has God done for me? What should I do? What have I done? What should God do to me? What has He done for me? What should I do for Him?"[22]

Since God's benefits were evident, the person meditating should focus his efforts on self-knowledge. Borgia's first biographer, Father Dionisio Vázquez, tells us that "from the moment he devoted himself to long mental prayer, he dedicated the first two hours of prayer each day to self-knowledge, with contempt for self and confusion over his past deeds and life; and from everything he saw, heard, or read he drew forth humility and confusion."[23] Self-knowledge was the subject of the first, third, and fifth of his 1548 *Seys tratados;* and he devoted later compositions, for example, treatises 16 and 17, to the same subject. Borgia was convinced that "the greatest strength we have is in knowing our weakness and misery."[24] From this comes humility, "the foundation of the [spiritual] edifice." We should not fall prey to the illusion that we can go directly to God without this foundation of humility. "If you wish to live intimately in God, my soul, first try to live intimately in yourself."[25] The holy fear of God, which is the beginning of wisdom, is born from self-knowledge; it is not merely a subservient and unformed fear, but one which is filial and reverential.[26] After all is said and done, fear is the way to arrive at the love of God. "If you want to acquire His love, strive to acquire self-detestation."[27]

From self-knowledge springs confusion, the sentiment that is most characteristic of Borgia's spirituality, at least during the earlier period of his life. For the philologist, "to confound" is synonymous with "to shame, to humiliate, to debase; it is a term employed especially by the mystics to denote the humiliation that comes from self-knowledge."[28] St. Teresa considered it a favor from God. "It is one of those great graces which our Lord wrought in me, and one of those which put me to the greatest shame and confusion whenever I called to mind the sins I have committed."[29]

Borgia dedicated the whole of treatise 9 to the subject of confusion, and he returns to this topic with great persistence in his other works. Later we shall see how he applied it to the exercise of mental prayer. What he taught others merely reflected what he himself felt and experienced in his intimate colloquies with God. For a brief period, between 1551 and 1552, he signed a number of letters "Francis sinner." This action was not the fervent outburst of a newly converted man, but the expression of a deeply rooted, profoundly felt conviction. Such humility surprises a person who studies his life because he would not be able to find any period when it could be said that Borgia led a life of sin. But the feeling of being a sinner, even the greatest sinner in the world, is a sentiment that God inspired in other great saints, for example, Paul and Francis of Assisi, and in more ordinary people who have led innocent lives.

Borgia's feelings of confusion take on intensity when the saint is brought face to face with the sufferings of Christ. Seeing Christ covered with wounds while he himself is unscathed, he bursts out with an exclamation which he repeats in one form or another on the pages of his spiritual diary: "Christ covered with wounds for me and I without them!" Sometimes there are only the last words, "and I without wounds." This sentiment, however, is not merely the fruit of his spiritual maturity; we find it already in his first treatises, for example, in *Spiritual Eye Salve.*

> Look at your head, and as you see it without thorns, be ashamed; and likewise . . . without nails in your hands and feet; and finally consider that, although none of your limbs move without God's power which actuates them, you will find your feet have moved with haste to persecute Christ; with your hands and works you have wounded Him and with your tongue you have bruised Him.[30]

Perhaps no other statement expresses better this sentiment than the one we find in a Latin piece that belongs to the saint's final years: "Lord, seeing You so wounded, I do not want to live without wounds."[31]

Borgia did not go on and on considering his own wretchedness. Soaring to a contemplation of the Trinity, he dedicated one of his 1550 litanies to this sublime mystery. He composed an *Exercise of the Three Powers of the Soul, Treating of How We Should Prepare Them So That They Can Be a True Dwelling-Place of the Three Divine Persons* (treatise 23). He dedicated the three powers of the soul to the three divine Persons: memory to the Father, understanding to the Son, will to the Holy Spirit. He gave suggestions on how to prepare for the indwelling of the Trinity in one's soul, but in so intimate a matter he deferred to the personal experience of each individual. "I leave the rest, which can be neither felt nor expressed, to those who practice this exercise with humility. Hoping in the Lord, they will find spiritual peace and joy in it."[32]

Having implanted humility and self-abasement so deeply in himself, he exhorted souls to the purest love of God. Man must "turn from being man to being God by participation, . . . which is wrought by being one spirit with God through conformity of love and charity."[33]

He recommended that the works undertaken during the morning be offered to the Father, those in the afternoon to the Son, and those in the evening to the Holy Spirit.

As the years progressed his sentiments became more and more purified. Around the year 1568 he took the parable of the wicked husbandmen and the allegory of the vine and branches as a point of departure to address the Father and Son with feelings of ardent emotion; and he concluded that God had done so much for him, yet he had done so little for God in return.[34]

A constantly recurring theme in Borgia's writings is Jesus Christ; even as early as 1548 in treatise 3, entitled *Mirror of a Christian's Works*, he proposes that one enter the way of perfection by imitating the example of Christ and putting on his sentiments. Jesus for him is the door leading to the Godhead; anyone "who does not enter through this door" is to be considered a thief. "In order to contemplate His divinity, one must first contemplate His humanity."[35] Here we see how alien to him was the tendency of some of his contemporaries who discouraged the contemplation of Christ, alleging that it was more perfect to go directly to the Godhead. We should recall what St. Teresa had to suffer because of this teaching. As we have already indicated when we examined the themes of his meditations, the Gospels invariably provide the subject matter for Borgia's writings.

There is an original subject that he develops in the *Pattern of the Soul of Christ* (treatise 11). We should not limit ourselves to a purely external imitation of what Christ did, but we should assimilate the sentiments of his soul in order to make these our own. From the moment of its creation the soul of Christ was a wonderful instrument of the Godhead. The Christian should try to be the same, through the proper use of his faculties and senses becoming a tractable instrument of God. Borgia, who was so taken up with music, proposes for consideration the image of an organ or of any other musical instrument which responds faithfully to the touch of the one who plays it. "Let the sound of your organ be in accord with what God wants of you." "Allow yourself to be played and touched by the hands of your artificer. The soul of Christ judged the troubles of the present life to be of little importance. You should do the same. You suffer very little compared to what you deserve. The soul of Christ continuously offered the cup of His passion to the Father; we likewise should offer our daily sacrifices to the Lord because, "just as to serve You is to reign, so to suffer for You is to rejoice." The soul of Christ enjoyed the beatific vision, yet He allowed His lower nature to suffer the torments of the Passion. We too should embrace sufferings. "The moment you see you are not suffering, judge it as time lost and no less dangerous; and let the fact of seeing yourself without suffering be a suffering to you."[37] The closer the soul of Christ was to the Word, the more it obeyed Him. It is by exercising the presence of God that we live in union with Him.

Borgia's devotion to the passion of Christ and to the Eucharist appears clearly in a number of these opuscules. The visage of the crucified Christ is ever present in them; and from this encounter, as we have already pointed out, he draws forth sentiments of confusion. One more example: "Your negligence caused the wounds in His feet and your disobedience opened up His side; your tongue put the bitterness in the gall and, finally, your pride crowned Him with thorns."[38]

The Blood of Christ provides him with themes for meditation. He used to contemplate the seven occasions when Christ shed His blood, and he wrote a meditation upon each of them. These seven themes were the circumcision, the bloody sweat in the garden, the scourging at the pillar, the crowning of thorns, the stripping away of His garments, the crucifixion, and the wounding of His side.[39] One of his daily devotions was to consider these bloodlettings, comparing them to corresponding vices, virtues, and gifts of the Holy Spirit.[40] Christ's wounds offered him the opportunity to pray for those intentions that were closest to his heart at any given time.[41]

Borgia may justly be considered one of those strongly attracted to the Sacred Heart. He considers Christ's side a place where the devout soul can find an everlasting abode. The aperture in His side opens up Christ's heart to us. He had already written in the 1548 treatises, "One must ask every-thing from the same Host and Lord who is to come, requesting He supply our poverty from the bountiful storeroom of His divine heart into which each soul may enter to take therefrom what she finds she lacks."[42] It is in the treatise on prayer (treatise 20) that he develops this theme more extensively. "To enter into the heart of Christ, which is our dwelling, our house of refuge, and our shelter, one will first pass through the material and then through the spiritual."[43]

A number of Borgia's works are exhortations on the worthy reception of the Eucharist (treatises 5, 12, 13, and 14). Whoever receives weekly Communion—which was as often as one could receive in those days—should divide the week into two parts, dedicating the first three days before Communion to preparations for receiving it worthily and the three following days to giving thanks for so great a gift. This is the theme he develops in the fourth of the *Seys tratados* of 1548 (treatise 5). The person should spend the mornings of these days asking the Lord to grant him the grace he desires, and during the afternoons he should concentrate on making the same prayer to the Blessed Virgin.

One interesting note: Borgia regarded sacramental Communion as a door leading to prayer. "In general we usually see that those who receive the sacrament with greater frequency find greater facility in their prayer, and in contrast, those who receive it less often find greater difficulty."[44]

A man as attached to prayer as Borgia could not help but lay open to his readers his ideas on the subject. This he did in several of his works, but in particular in his *Spiritual Treatise on Prayer* (treatise 20) of 1557. To prove the necessity of prayer, he takes as his point of departure St. Luke's account of Jesus' exhortation on "the need to pray continually and never lose heart" (Luke 18:1). Rather than teaching the methods of prayer in this treatise, he analyzes the problems that make it difficult. Such hindrances are excessive fear about one's worthiness, a lack of humility and mortification, excessive intellectualizing, distractions and useless thoughts, lack of consolation, sadness and melancholy, and infrequent reception of the sacrament of the Eucharist. He devotes a chapter in this treatise to each one of these impediments.

Chapter four, which deals with intellectualizing, deserves special mention. Some do not pray because they tire of "all the thinking and they weary the mind by dragging it by force through the steps and meditations they are accustomed to make." But, in fact, one should find prayer a refreshment for the spirit, "like the farmhand who gets back home, feet tired from working and hands weary from digging, and his whole body worn out from the day's labor." Thus, "the one who enters into prayer should arrive there in a relaxed state, deeming it a great relief not to have to work at harvesting, and in this way he will receive consolation and repose, and he will not be afraid to enter into prayer, but rather will find ease therein."[45]

In the seventh chapter he criticizes the conduct of those who "at the beginning of their prayer have recourse solely to acts of the intellect and then later work on acts of their will," in spite of the fact that "there is no doubt that the acts of the will are more excellent because they embrace the acts of the intellect, and therefore they include all." Just as he who gives away his possessions all at once gives more than the one who gives them away piecemeal, "so also the principal act our spirit can make is one, that is, to yield and surrender itself to God with all its possessions—blood, life, soul; and once this act is made, we have nothing else to do but persevere in it, and not undo it or take it back,"[46]

The final chapter of this treatise is dedicated to vocal prayer. Even though mental prayer is superior to vocal prayer, as the spirit is superior to the tongue, vocal prayer is highly recommended. Borgia suggests that one pray little with devotion rather than much without it. "Let him value more a sigh and a groan that come from a contrite and broken heart than many words lukewarmly and dryly said." Thus, "if he says the rosary let him raise his mind to the mysteries of the Redeemer's life, and at each Hail Mary let him recall one of these mysteries."[47]

On two occasions Borgia focuses on the holy rosary as a subject of meditation: in his *Method for Reciting the Holy Rosary* (treatise 1), where he reflects on the method he used while he was viceroy in Catalonia, and in the *Points of the Holy Rosary* (treatise 19), which he composed sometime prior to 1557. In both of these treatises he proposes the mysteries of the rosary as subjects of meditative vocal prayer. The meditation is divided into several points.

The methods

Following a very common custom of that era, Borgia divides the matter he proposes for meditation according to the days of the week. We see him using this practice in the *Method for Reciting the Holy Rosary* (treatise 1), the *Spiritual Exercise* (treatise 6), the second part of the *Pattern of the Soul of Christ* (treatise 11), in some of the *Meditations* (treatise 28), and in the *Seven Meditations on the Seven Fonts of Blood* (treatise 30).

Although he wants each day of the week sanctified by these meditations, Borgia also proposes matter for prayer, petition, or offering to God that is to be used during the several hours of the day. For example, he offers an *Exercise for Seeking the Presence of God Throughout the Day* (treatise 22), in which he suggests that we "try to transform into the purest gold your getting dressed, your eating, and your sleeping."[48] Every one of our daily actions, from the time we wake up in the morning until the moment we go to bed at night, should be accompanied by a spiritual reflection raising them to the level of prayer. In proposing these considerations for the twenty-four hours of the day, he was teaching others what he himself practiced.

In general, the themes he suggested for meditation were developed along a practical and simple system. Regarding the rosary he proposed the following: First, pause for a while to consider each mystery. Second, call to mind the gift of God in this mystery and give Him thanks for it. Third, draw confusion for having drawn so little profit from it. Fourth, request some particular grace according to the mystery.[49] At other times he recommended three things—consideration, prayer, and reminder, by which he meant some text from Holy Scripture that could recall the subject matter of the meditation. We see, therefore, that the methods set out by Borgia clearly follow the lines of formal prayer, balancing harmoniously the operations of the intellect, the will, and the affections. We find this method, with its characteristic precision, in the meditations for ferial and holy days of the liturgical year and for Masses said on feast days of the saints.

8. Conflict with the Inquisition (1559-1561)

"While in Segovia I learned the news about the list of forbidden books the Council of the General Inquisition had published; among the books proscribed was an *Obras del cristiano*, a book which they claim that I had written."[1] So wrote Borgia to Father General Diego Laínez from Medina del Campo on September 8, 1559. He had come to Segovia sometime between the 15th and 22nd of August, and the Inquisition had published its catalogue of forbidden books in Valladolid on the 17th of the same month. Immediately upon receipt of this shocking news he left Medina for Valladolid to consult with Father Provincial Araoz and others about what course of action to take.

We can imagine his dismay. Given the prestige he enjoyed in Spain, to say nothing of the integrity of his faith, he had been dealt an earthshaking blow. His life was now entering an exceedingly painful phase which was to last two years; at the conclusion of this period it would head off in a new direction.

Until this time the Spanish Inquisition had shown the greatest confidence in him. Around mid-April 1558 he had raised an alarm that Lutheran doctrines had made their way into several cities of Castile and Andalucía, placing at the disposal of the Holy Office his own loyal assistance and that of the whole Society in order to put a halt to this infiltration. "It brings tears to one's eyes," he wrote on the 25th of the month, "to see what they are beginning to uncover in Castile."[2] It was because this surge of Protestant teachings coincided with the campaign to disgrace the Society that he became more and more preoccupied with the problem. On May 26 of that year Father Juan Bautista Ribera wrote Laínez from Valladolid, telling him that "the father of lies has been unleashed: some claim we are arrested, others that we are exiled or burned at the stake, others that the Theatines (for so they call us in this Babel) are at the root of these Lutheran errors," whereas in fact they should be saying "that they are the cause of these errors' having been brought to light."[3]

From the very outset, as we said, Borgia showed himself willing to work for the defense of the faith. His proffered services were readily accepted; he was asked to remain in Valladolid for the express purpose of aiding the accused who had to face a scheduled auto-da-fé. After a number of post-ponements, this grim spectacle was finally held in the main square of Castile's capital city on Trinity Sunday, May 21, 1559. Borgia and other Jesuits gave spiritual assistance to the defendants at this somber ceremony, presided over by Princess Juana in the absence of her brother, Philip II. Specifically, Borgia was given the difficult job of communicating the sentence meted out to the young and beautiful Señora Ana Enríquez, daughter of the marquises of Alcañices and daughter-in-law of his own daughter, Juana de Borja. He consoled her at that critical, terrible moment, hearing her confess that she would have preferred a secret death to the public ignominy specified in the sentence. Ana had given clear indications of repenting, so she was condemned to walk to the scaffold wearing a sanbenito and carrying a candle. Then she had to return to prison, from which she was released after a three-day fast.[4]

As if predicting the storm that was to break, Borgia confided to Laínez, in a letter on June 29 of that year, that he did not feel that he had the strength to go to the Indies or the talent to "teach young children in a classroom"; however, "I will not manifest anything else beyond the desire I have had for the last few months, that is, to die by shedding my blood for the Catholic truth of the Roman Church." He asked his superior to pray that the Lord would accept this sacrifice "if this would please Him, but if not, then at least, He would see me dying without actually shedding blood and this would be another type of death for Him."[5]

God was not going to ask him to make a bloody sacrifice of his life, but rather He would ask for the bloodless sacrifice of his reputation.

The Catalogue of Forbidden Books

What is the background for the publication of the Catalogue or the Index of Forbidden Books in 1559? We have already seen that as early as 1558 pockets of Protestantism were appearing in Spain. Toward the middle of that year machinery for repressing Protestant teaching was set in motion, primarily to combat the clandestine importation into Spain of books by heretics. The Inquisition had already uncovered two boxes of this literature smuggled in from Geneva by Juan Pérez de Pineda, a convert to Calvinism.[6] On January 2, 1558, an auto-da-fé of books was held in Valladolid, and on the following September 13 legislation was passed threatening capital punishment to anyone who would bring into Spain books printed outside the kingdom and without due authorization from the king. Two factors speeded up this process: the publication in 1559 of the Roman *Index*, ordered by Paul IV, and suspicions on the part of the Inquisition based on the publication of a catechism by Archbishop Bartolomé de Carranza of Toledo. The Inquisition may have had as its principal purpose the condemnation of this catechism and included other works simply as an excuse to publish its catalogue.[7] In addition to various theological books and a number of editions of the Bible, there were other spiritual works besides those attributed to the duke of Gandía that the Inquisition singled out for condemnation. Among these were the *Book of Prayer and Meditation* and *Guide of Sinners* by Fray Luis de Granada and the *Audi filia* of Master Juan de Avila. Borgia was obviously in good company. It was clear that the Inquisition cast a prejudiced eye on books in Spanish. As Araoz wrote to Laínez, "These times are such that one has to be very careful about writing books."[8] The devout had to get used to doing without them because "spiritual books are not to be published in the vernacular."[9] Father Pedro Navarro wrote from Granada that "we are living at a time when we preach that women should keep their hands on their distaff and on their rosary and not get involved in any other devotions."[10] St. Teresa keenly felt the effects of these measures, and she grieved about being deprived of books that nourished her devotion.

In Borgia's case a clear irregularity had been committed. He had never written a book bearing the title *Obras del cristiano*. This was the title of a clandestine edition of his treatises that appeared in 1550 at Baeza.[11] That same year a printer in Alcalá named Juan de Brocar published without Borgia's authorization two books entitled *Primera de las obras . . . compuestas por el Ilustrísimo señor don Francisco de Borja, duque de Gandía*, and *Segunda parte de las obras del Ilustrísimo señor don Francisco de Borja, con otras muy devotas*. The first of these books contains his authentic *Seys tratados*, plus three works by three other authors. There was nothing in the second book by Borgia except his *Treatise on Confusion*."[12] Brocar believed he could make a greater profit by taking advantage of the duke of Gandía's name, "increas-[ing] the size of the book so that it would be worth more money" and thus "make a better sale."[13] The Inquisition did not take these facts into account; it gave no explanation for its condemnation, nor did it point out in Borgia's authentic writings anything that smacked of heterodoxy or could be interpreted as being heterodox. In the face of appeals the Inquisition responded, "What was decided was well decided."[14]

Since the enactment dealt with an anthology of various works, one had to determine first of all which pieces fell under the prohibition. The condemnation had been made "in bulk," as Araoz expressed it in a letter,[15] so no one knew if the writings incriminated were really Borgia's or were from a different hand. Second, one had to ascertain which pieces were really Borgia's and which were not. When asked about this point, the Holy Office responded that it was not its responsibility to undertake such an investigation;[16] the burden of proving his innocence rested with the interested party. Accordingly, Borgia gave power of attorney to Father Pedro de Saavedra, who in turn petitioned the mayor of Alcalá for a formal declaration on the authenticity of the writings in question. On September 27 and 28 the mayor cited as witnesses four booksellers of Alcalá to testify which were the authentic writings of the duke of Gandía and which were not. The mayor "interposed his authority and juridical decree according to the law," but "evidence" of such a nature was of no use to anyone.[17] Meanwhile, "the scandal which comes from all this," as Araoz wrote, "is great and greatly harms the Society."[18]

The suspense continued. Borgia was never able to learn why his books had been condemned; nor was he able to discover whether any actual error had been detected in them or whether they had been proscribed merely because they were in the vernacular. This second interpretation was the one which prevailed. Hence some, both in Spain and at Rome, felt that the solution to the problem lay in translating them into Latin, a task which was entrusted to Father Ribadeneira. Tullio Crispolti translated some of them into Italian.

A present-day reader can find no proposition in these tracts that deviates in the slightest way from pure orthodoxy. The suspicion is that the inquisitors never even read the works or, if they did, they did so in a superficial way. However, it is true that what may seem perfectly orthodox today may have created problems in that atmosphere of religious tensions. For example, extolling faith in Jesus Christ may have under those circumstances been enough to stir up suspicion.

It is also possible that in Borgia's writings, or at least in those attributed to him, some traces could be found of the theory of the "benefit of Christ" expounded in a tract of that title by the Italian Benedictine Benedetto da Mantova. These ideas were discovered in the first edition of St. John of Avila's *Audi filia*, and were corrected by the author in the subsequent editions.

Both Borgia and Father Provincial Araoz informed Father Laínez immediately about what was taking place. Laínez was already familiar with the problem because of the accusations launched against the Society by Melchor Cano and the Franciscan Bernardo de Fresneda, Philip II's confessor. Despite the fear that all this could have an effect on the king's attitude,

Laínez received the complaints against Borgia "calmly and equably."[19] He exhorted him to take "this affair with all interior and exterior peace and tranquility, and with proper respect for the Holy Office, especially during these times when the Enemy tries in so many ways to sow tares among the wheat of Catholic teaching." All this notwithstanding, however, he also believed that, in addition to entrusting the matter to the Lord, he ought to "employ all the licit means that He wants us to use."[20]

Laínez wrote a letter to Araoz on September 26, giving him the following guidelines: Initiate no lawsuits, but rather "keep complete calm and gentleness, both interior and exterior, and total goodwill and respect toward the Holy Office . . . especially during these times." Araoz was to do everything possible to prove that Borgia was not the author of the greater part of the works attributed to him. Since he had composed and published the essays "before he entered the Society, when he was a beginner, and at a time when there was no heresy in this province," the offensive propositions ought to be examined so that they could be once and for all expunged or explained and the booklets could be reprinted. If the problem arose from the fact that they had been written in Spanish, they should be translated into Latin. Laínez was confident that the ordeal would have a happy outcome because "that which is without foundation in truth soon falls of itself."[21]

But in Spain the situation was viewed more realistically. Here they were certain that permission would never be granted to reprint Borgia's works either in Spanish or in Latin, either with or without emendations, because once it gave a judgment the Inquisition usually remained inflexible. Araoz consulted with the grand inquisitor, Don Fernando de Valdés, who told him that he accepted Borgia for what they said he was; nonetheless, he was not going to change his position. Meanwhile, panic was spreading among ordinary good people because in a general way the *Index* had put a blanket proscription on all sermons, tracts, hymns, and prayers which had Scripture or the sacraments of the Church as their subject matter. In Seville they even feared that this ruling applied to the *Spiritual Exercises* of St. Ignatius, so the rector of the college there made haste to round up all the copies in Spanish that he could find and turned them over to the Inquisition.[22] Alarm signals sounded also in other cities, such as Barcelona.

Departure for Portugal

So matters stood when, on November 11 of that year, 1559, the cardinal infante, Enrique of Portugal, wrote to Borgia, inviting him to visit the College of the Holy Spirit, which he had founded in Evora and which now granted academic degrees by virtue of the university status bestowed on it by Pope Paul IV.[23] Realizing that Borgia was not far from Evora, the cardinal believed he could make the journey without too great a hardship; he was also confident that his presence among them there would give himself and the professors much consolation. Borgia accepted this invitation and went from Montilla to Evora, where he promptly fell ill. When she learned about this, Queen Catherine sent a sedan chair and servants to move him to Lisbon, where he could receive better care. The commissary general accepted the offer, but with the intention of returning to Evora as soon as possible so that he might free himself "from the inconvenience of the court." He arrived in Lisbon January 26, 1560.

Whether Borgia made the trip primarily to satisfy the wishes of the cardinal infante or whether he accepted the invitation as a pretext to get out of Spain, the fact is that he never again set foot permanently on Spanish soil. In the eyes of many it looked as if he had fled. And indeed he did, and it may well be that this flight saved him from falling into the hands of the Inquisition, as did Archbishop Carranza! We do not know if he was aware of that possibility; but, thanks to a letter of Araoz to Laínez on May 20, 1560, we do know that "it has been leaked out that there was a vote and consultation about arresting him while he was still in Valladolid, and it was decided that there were insufficient grounds. It is by conjecture we believe all this; since these proceedings are secret, as they should be, we do not know for sure."[24] Conjecture it may have been; it is enough to know that at the time it was considered quite possible that the Inquisition would order Borgia's arrest.

As for the date of his departure from Spain, it seems that we should not take literally what Borgia wrote in his spiritual diary for October 25, 1566: "Thanksgiving for departing Egypt seven years ago."[25] October 25 could not have been the day of his departure, seeing that he was still in Orgaz on the road to Montilla on November 3. What is certain is that he left for Portugal in November of 1559.

When Laínez learned of his action he was surprised, not knowing if his motive was "to inspect the province" of Portugal in his capacity as commissary general or "to live in seclusion and completely forget his office." Though wishing him to "continue supervising the provincials as their superior," Laínez suspended judgment until he learned for certain the reasons for his trip.[26]

There is no doubt about the fact that Borgia wanted to get away from Castile, not so much because he feared for his personal safety—we have already seen that he was ready even for martyrdom—as for a certain disenchantment that made him yearn to pull away, at least temporarily, from public life. Within his spirit the longings for a secluded, though not necessarily solitary, life revived. He selected the house of San Fins in which to satisfy these desires. This was a former Benedictine monastery on the banks of the Rio Miño, the border between Portugal and Galicia, which Paul IV had attached to the Jesuit college of Coimbra in 1548. Reasons of health also entered into Borgia's decision.

With gentle insistence Laínez wrote to him, saying that if it was because of his health that he went into seclusion, it seemed to be a good idea; otherwise, "I have my many doubts."[27] He noted that "to retreat so often seems to me that you want to make another Magdalena in Portugal,"[28] alluding to La Magdalena, the hermitage near Oñate where Borgia had retired after his ordination to the priesthood.

As a matter of fact, Borgia had no intention of evading his duties. After leaving San Fins he planned to visit, at the very least, the houses of the Society in Portugal and to exercise his ministry in the neighboring towns. Then from Portugal he could go to visit Castile and later take the sea route to Andalucía for the same purpose. Such was his determination, but his natural inclination was to retire into seclusion. "Were it not for the fact that Your Paternity orders me not to forget Martha," he wrote to Laínez on June 5, 1560, "I would bid her farewell." But then he wrote concerning San Fins that, since "there is almost an entire house here,"—there were six priests and two Brothers—he proposed setting up a professed house in Oporto. "That is what I ask Your Paternity to grant for my peace of mind because the Lord gives me ardent desires to die in a house of poverty and not in a college; in Rome and in Lisbon there is a court, and therefore I could not reach my goal except in this manner." But in Oporto he could combine Martha and Mary, that is, the active and the contemplative lives.[29]

Laínez, Araoz, their advisers, and even Francis himself asked themselves the same question: Should he or should he not return to Spain? Seeing everything from a distance, Laínez always opted for the affirmative, among other reasons not wishing to offend Philip II. In Spain Princess Juana, Ruy Gómez de Silva, and the marquis of Mondéjar, president of the Consejo and friend of the Society, also thought he should return. Araoz was undecided because "not to come back brings disgrace and to come back is dangerous."[30]

We have already seen that Borgia's arrest had been contemplated on account of his writings. But there was another factor which made his position difficult in that inquisitional atmosphere, namely, his good relations with Archbishop Carranza. One particular incident illustrates the problem he faced. Diego de Córdoba, the counselor to the Inquisition and bishop-elect of Avila, had left some very important papers of Carranza's in Borgia's keeping, papers which from that time on were untraceable. True, Borgia affirmed that he had returned them the same day he had received them, but some wondered if indeed he might still have them.

Laínez confessed he could never put this whole business aside and that it had more than once robbed him of sleep; he offered Masses and prayers for its resolution. If there was no other solution, he was ready to send Nadal to Spain to intervene or even go there himself. As it turned out, he did dispatch Nadal to Spain. After disembarking near Rosas, Nadal arrived in Barcelona on January 1, 1561; later meeting with Borgia in Oporto at the beginning of April, he sounded him out.

Seeing the turn that events were taking, Laínez hit upon a radical solution: He would call Borgia to Rome and make him assistant general of the Society; he could replace Father Luis Gonçalves da Câmara, who was to go to Portugal to become the tutor of the infante and future king, Don Sebastian. If Borgia would not accept this post, it would go to Father Paschase Broët; if he did accept it, he would be asked to plan to be in Rome in September 1560.[31]

In June 1560 Laínez formally appointed Borgia to the office of assistant. He could not allow the damage that was being done to the Church, "to which a grave affront is being made by disgracing it and depriving it of ministers like this, and rendering them useless for its ministry."[32] But Laínez's decision was not the equivalent of issuing Borgia an order in the strict sense of the term, not even under these circumstances. Employing that same delicacy that St. Ignatius had used with him, Laínez left it up to Borgia to make the final decision. To head off cries of foul play, he devised an expedient: Pope Pius IV would call Borgia to Rome and have him take care of some church business. Easily acceding to this plan, on October 10, 1560, Pius IV sent a brief ordering Borgia to come to Rome because the pope's pastoral solicitude encouraged him to seek out good and faithful ministers to be near him.[33]

Now the old question was put into a new light. Would Borgia's going to Rome be the better thing? If so, should he first notify Philip II? What effect would an unannounced departure have on the attitude of the king and the inquisitors? Among those who gave their opinion, Father Antonio de Córdoba was against his leaving, declaring that this departure "would confirm those who say he is running away." Such an accusation would be against his good reputation, about which he was insufficiently concerned. In Spain "displeasure" with him is running high, Córdova continued, adding: "Such is the Lord's love for him that—to our sore cost—since He denies him the martyrdom of his person that he so earnestly prays for, He must grant him the martyrdom of his reputation." [34]

Philip II's attitude

Philip II's attitude in this conflict, reveals clearly the monarch's personality and style of governance.[35] He attached little importance to the close ties that had united the former duke of Gandía with his family, particularly with his father, Charles V, and his sister, Princess Juana. In religious matters he always gave unconditional support to the Inquisition. Every attempt made to persuade him to see that Borgia received fair treatment was useless "because the door is shut," as Araoz wrote to Laínez on February 7, 1561. In this same letter dealing with Philip's attitude toward Borgia, Araoz reported "that he takes him for what they say he is, but that he does not want to become involved in such cases because these are judicial matters. This is his ordinary characteristic answer."[36] Once again Philip II showed himself "a great concealer and dissembler of unpleasantnesses."[37] People who knew the monarch well and who had an influence on him, such as Ruy Gómez de Silva, thought it better not to apply pressure to him.

All this shows why Borgia, who knew Philip II well, always refused to meet with him and why he disregarded the entreaties of those who advised him not to leave Spain without at least presenting his devoir to the king.

Borgia decides to leave for Rome

In early 1561 there were still misgivings about Borgia's going to Rome. Nadal called Fathers Araoz and Saavedra to Alcalá for a consultation about the matter. The consensus was that, for the five reasons which they enumerated, it would be better to postpone Borgia's journey. To Nadal in particular it seemed a "shame that a man like Rafael [Father Francis] should steal off like a man who had a wicked reason to do so." This is what he wrote to Borgia himself in February or March 1561.[38]

But Borgia had made a prior decision, the gist of which he communicated to the general in a letter of November 25, 1560.[39] He proposed three solutions for his case:

1) That he be left where he was in Oporto and that when all assignments were to be renewed in the following July he be removed from his position as commissary general.

2) If he did not deserve this, that he be allowed to move to Lisbon, "for the desire he has of dying in a professed house." There, with the help of Fathers Miguel Torres and Luís Gonçalves da Câmara, he would be able to do his work, and at the first opportunity he would make a tour of Spain.

3) If despite these arguments the superior believes he should accept the pope's brief, then the general should impose it upon him in virtue of holy obedience, "because otherwise he will go with doubts, so far as he can see, and less consoled with regard what he has determined and even offered to the Lord, namely, to get away as far as possible from Egypt and its stench." Interiorly he felt at peace, because "I believe I say truthfully that I delight in the cross of the book."[40]

Father Laínez did not wish to impose that command. He had his secretary Polanco write to him in his name on March 2, 1561. "Although he himself [Laínez] will not decide about Rafael's [Francis's] coming, Your Reverence can discuss the matter with Father Nadal, for our Father has judged it preferable to refer the matter rather than to give a decision from here."[41]

Meanwhile, Laínez had recourse to a relative and friend of Borgia's, Cardinal Ippolito d'Este of Ferrara (whose mother was the famous Lucrezia Borgia, the daughter of Pope Alexander VI), beseeching him to arrange for a new brief from the pope. Since Borgia did not want to set out until he knew the pope was informed about everything, it would be well if the order were renewed. The pope could summon him "on the pretext of the Council [of Trent] or for any other cause that might occur to His Holiness."[42] As it turned out, Pius IV issued another brief, bearing the date June 20, 1561.[43] In it he told Borgia that, since the Church had need of subjects endowed with gifts of integrity of life, doctrine, and other qualities, the pope exhorted him to take the road to Rome, where he would utilize his services "either for the Council or for other affairs."

But Borgia did not await the arrival of this second brief. The more deeply he reflected, the more clearly he saw that the first papal brief had for him the force of an order which he was obliged to obey because of the fourth vow taken by the professed in the Society binding them to special obedience to the pope regarding missions or appointments.

On June 7, 1561, Borgia and Nadal met at Coimbra, where each wrote his own declaration of intent, to which the other attached his signature. Borgia's explanation of his decision has a moving grandeur about it.[44] He declared that by virtue of his fourth vow of special obedience to the pope, and given the fact that in Part VI, Chapter 1, of the Constitutions of the Society a singular importance is given to obedience towards the pope;

moreover, notwithstanding the fact that, according to the advice of Father Nadal and of the general himself, even after receiving the pontifical brief "I remain free . . . to decide one way or the other, and that whatever option I make, he [Laínez] would consider good, and he would judge it to be the better; therefore, with the support of the Lord's grace, I decide in favor of going." He intended to take advantage of the opportunity to make the journey by sea because his many infirmities would make it most difficult to go by land. He hoped that "this will be an act of 'rational service'"[45] and that God will give him the strength to carry it out. Borgia and Nadal signed this document. This much is clear, therefore: Despite his poor health and despite the fact that Father Nadal and Father General Laínez would have considered no a good answer, Borgia made his decision, heroic under the circumstances, on the basis of his fourth vow of special obedience to the pope. His attitude should not surprise us. On a previous occasion he had written that "I would consider it a blessing if the 'old man' in me remained paralyzed."[46] And of him it was written, "Everything he did, he did strictly under obedience."[47]

In his statement Nadal declared that, with regard to the projected trip to Rome, "I have always been against it"; nevertheless, in view of the papal brief he had told Borgia "that he was free to decide whatever seemed best to him in the Lord," and that should he decide he ought to go, "I would would consider that to be for the best and for the greatest service for God our Lord; thus, since he has decided to go, I fully concur and pray God our Lord that everything will turn out for the greater glory of His Divine Majesty."[48] This document was signed by Nadal and Borgia.

The die was cast. Responding to Queen Catherine de' Medici's meddlesome insistence, the pope had asked Laínez to accompany Cardinal Ippolito d'Este to the Colloquy of Poissy; so the general was already on his way to France to dialogue with Calvinist theologians when he communicated to Borgia that the second, by now unnecessary, brief had been sent. He added that he had informed the Sovereign Pontiff about everything.

Remaining undecided was whether it would be better for Borgia to make the trip through Castile. Secretary Polanco advised the trip "to remove the occasion for important people to talk." If Borgia believed that this trip could not be made "without danger to his person," then Father Córdoba should go ahead to see "if there was really any danger."[49] Everything should be done to prevent the king from losing esteem for the Society, to dissipate his prejudices against the Society, and, above all, to disabuse him of the notion that the Society was siphoning money out of Spain.

Beginning in September, Father Alfonso Salmerón would take the place of the absent Father Laínez, and Father Cristóbal de Madrid would attend to the day-to-day business at the curia. It was Father Madrid who advised the general in a letter of July 4 that a courier would leave in fifteen days, carrying the second brief addressed to Borgia.

But, as we have already seen, Borgia did not wait for the arrival of this brief. One month after signing his declaration, he began his journey, as we can deduce from a note jotted in his spiritual diary for July 12, 1568: "Thanksgiving for this day seven years ago."[50] Taking Fathers Pedro de Saavedra, Gaspar Hernández, and the faithful Brother Marcos as companions, he set off on his journey.

The journey ensued as follows. On July 12, 1561, he set sail from Pontevedra in northwest Spain headed toward Bayona, a small Galician port near Vigo; but a fierce storm forced him to reverse course and return to Pontevedra, where he disembarked. Once again in San Fins, he wrote to Nadal, indicating that he was sticking to his plans despite this initial setback. In a final attempt to detain him, Nadal sent a messenger, urging him to pass through Castile to pay his farewell to the Court. But when the messenger arrived at San Fins, Borgia had already left overland without leaving a trace of his whereabouts. Soon after reaching Villalpando in Zamora, he came down with a fever and was forced to remain there. Learning of this stopover, Nadal lamented that Borgia had passed so close to Valladolid without presenting himself at court, where nothing would have happened to him. On August 1 Borgia wrote that he had arrived at Avignon; on the 16th he left Genoa in the direction of Bologna, and from there he took the road to Loreto on the 23rd. Finally, on September 7, the day before the Nativity of the Blessed Virgin, he arrived in Rome in much better condition than when he had left Portugal. On November 9 he addressed a letter to Cardinal Ippolito d'Este's brother, the duke of Ferrara, explaining to this friend and relative of his that, notwithstanding his ordinary poor health and the hardships of so long a journey undertaken at the height of summer, he had come to Rome in obedience to the pope, who wanted to confer with him about certain matters that pertained to the Catholic religion.[51]

In Rome he found a completely different atmosphere from the one he had left behind. No sooner had he set foot in the Eternal City than Pope Pius IV sent his welcome through a private chamberlain. Three days later the pope granted him an audience, at which Father Ribadeneira was present. In his life of Borgia, Ribadeneira recounts that the pope offered him an apartment in the papal palace, but that the saint declined this offer. Borgia himself confirmed this in the letter to the duke of Ferrara. These were the words of the pope: "We will take care of your person and your affairs, as we are obliged to you because of the rare example you have given to the world in our days."

There was an enormous uproar in the Spanish court when the news of Borgia's departure from Spain became known; the impression there was that he had fled on Laínez's orders. Together with the latter, Nadal bore the brunt of the blame, and he had to excuse himself by writing that "Rafael [Borgia] made the decision himself and against his own advice." Araoz, who transmitted the news of the Spanish court's reaction to Rome, voiced his fear that the Society would have to suffer the consequences, and that Nadal's apostolate in Spain would be compromised. In fact, Araoz had to intervene before the Consejo Real to ensure the continuance of Nadal's mission.

As is usually the case in instances such as these, those implicated tried to justify their conduct after the fact. Araoz, who often enough reiterated that he had done everything possible, wrote to Father Salmerón, now substituting for the absent Laínez, lamenting his own tribulations, and adding: "My conscience does not accuse me of having intentionally done any harm to the Society or to its Institute."[52] He was alluding to his activities at court. Nadal's behavior was stranger yet. He wrote to the inquisitor Valdés placing Borgia in a rather bad light and offering to assist the Holy Office "without any regard for Father Francis," whom "we shall throw out of the Society" if he proves to be guilty.[53] In another letter to Laínez he said that they should make sure that the displeasure that existed at court because of Father Francis's conduct not envelop the whole Society. He believed that "until matters are clarified" Borgia should not be assigned any office in the Society.[54] And to Father Ribadeneira he wrote, "The tempest which has been raging here on account of Father Francis's departure is great, and the sea is rough, so it will not be easy for us to fend off the cold wind, as I trust in the Lord we shall be able to do."[55]

Off in France, Laínez believed it his duty to come to the defense of his subject and of the Society, and this he did in a letter to Francisco de Vargas, the Spanish ambassador in Rome, written from Saint-Germain and posted November 25, 1561. Skirting the topic of Philip II's complaint that both subjects and funds were being taken out of Spain to help the Roman College, he focused on Borgia, asserting, "What I know, before our Lord, to be absolutely certain is that, as far as his faith is concerned (apart from his other good habits), he is as untarnished as the purest gold, and he was one of the first to assist the Holy Office in discovering the errors that are multiplying rapidly in Spain."[56] At the beginning of this chapter we saw that this was indeed the case. Laínez concluded his letter to the ambassador by explaining the reasons for Father Francis's departure, first to Portugal and later to Rome.

Thus ended this sad episode. As we continue our narrative we shall see how Borgia's life in Rome unfolded; meanwhile, in Spain spirits quieted down. On December 27, 1562, the feast of St. John the Evangelist, the disciple who laid his head on Christ's bosom at the Last Supper, Father Francis wrote a letter to Father Ribadeneira. He was in a mellower mood as he shared with Ribadeneira his sentiments regarding the events which had taken place a full year before. "Since we are not worthy to be among those caressed upon His chest, let us be His companions upon His cross. Oh, how easy it is to write and say this! But how dreadful appears the cross when it comes through our door; yet this cross frees us from the other crosses upon which we are already crucified, crosses all the more cruel for being less recognized."[57]

As far as public opinion in Spain was concerned, Nadal was able to report in a letter to Salmerón on March 23, 1562, that "the rumors that erupted over Father Francis's departure have already died away, and the subject is not mentioned any more, or is mentioned seldom."[58] As far as Borgia was concerned, Nadal, forgetting past differences of opinion between the two, now rejoiced that "the good Father was no longer in danger"; commenting on the turn of events, he saw in them the hand of Providence, "as if the departure of Father Francis to Rome had been arranged by God's hands . . . for he would perhaps never have gone there except for what happened, events all but compelling him to go."[59]

Actually, the misfortune suffered by Borgia opened up to him the road to the destiny that God had marked out for him.

His works were not removed from the Catalogue; it was not the ordinary policy of the Inquisition so to act. But to remedy the situation, when Cardinal Quiroga published the 1583 edition of the *Index*, he wrote that, if in the Catalogue the reader found listed names of authors

> of great Christianity and very well known throughout the world, such as John Fisher, Thomas More, Jerónimo Osorio, Francis Borgia, and Juan de Avila, it was not because these writers had separated themselves from the Roman Church or from its teachings. Rather, it was either because the pro-scribed works were falsely attributed to them; or because in these works there were words or phrases fraudulently insert-ed; or because it did not seem right that these works should be published in the vernacular; or because in these works there were some propositions which the authors interpreted

correctly in the sound, Catholic sense but which the wickedness of the heretics caused to be misinterpreted.[60]

Later on, during the process of Borgia's canonization, the Congregation of Rites subjected his works to an examination and approved them on November 21, 1648.[61]

9. Assistant, Vicar, and Superior General

Borgia, assistant general

Although he did not take over the office of assistant until 1564, Borgia had been summoned to Rome in 1561 to fill this post when the incumbent, Father Luis Gonçalves da Câmara, was assigned to Portugal. In July of that same year, Cardinal Ippolito d'Este, accompanied by his theologian, Father General Diego Laínez, left Rome bound for Queen Catherine de' Medici's abortive Colloquy of Poissy. Father Juan de Polanco, secretary of the Society, accompanied Laínez on this journey to France. These circumstances explain the delay in Borgia's assuming the office of assistant. Meanwhile, the provincial of Naples, Alonso Salmerón, stayed on in Rome as assistant general, while Pedro Ribadeneira, provincial of Tuscany, filled in as secretary and Juan Bautista Ribera assumed the office of procurator.

In 1562 another series of changes took place. The sessions of the Council of Trent resumed in January of that year, and Laínez left France to take part in them. Then in May Salmerón also went up to Trent as a papal theologian, leaving Borgia as the acting general and commissary general for Italy. In December 1563 the final session of the Council was adjourned and Laínez began his homeward trek. He arrived in Rome on February 12, 1564, and four days later appointed Borgia assistant, at the same time placing him in charge of the colleges of Amelia, Tivoli, and Frascati.

These are the unadorned historical facts. As far as these events related to his personal life, from the time he came to Rome in September 1561 until May 1562, Father Francis enjoyed a peace-filled period, which he put to good use, regaining his strength and devoting himself to prayer. A man as well known as he, however, was not really able to live a hidden life; for, besides attending to his own correspondence, he had to receive visitors and maintain contact with the Roman curia, especially with a number of prelates. One of these, Cardinal Bartolomé de la Cueva, called him to his side as he lay on his deathbed in June of 1562. Moreover, he kept in close touch with Cardinal Alessandro Farnese, discussing with him the construction of the

Society's new church in Rome; and he kept the lines of communication open with the secretary of state, Charles Borromeo, who during this period was undergoing a spiritual metamorphosis. Father Juan Bautista Ribera played an important role in this transformation, because as procurator he had opportunities to converse with Borromeo. Furthermore, Borgia did not neglect his favorite apostolate of preaching. During the Lent of 1563 he delivered biweekly sermons in the national church of St. James of the Spaniards in the Piazza Navona, where the elite of the nobility and some seven or eight cardinals crowded together to hear him, joined by a great number of the faithful.

Between May 1562 and February 1564 he was able to gain firsthand experience in dealing with the everyday business of the Society. Even though Laínez governed personally from Trent, of necessity many matters passed through the hands of the commissary for Italy. For example, in 1563 he had extensive dealings with the priests soon leaving for Milan to found a college there. At the same time, he finalized arrangements to found the college at Chambéry and negotiated the terms for opening the college at Mantua, endowed by Ercole Gonzaga as he lay dying. One of the most delicate matters he had to face was the direction of the Roman Seminary, entrusted by Pius IV to the care of the Society. This plan had provoked a counterreaction on the part of the local clergy, as did the announcement that Jesuits would examine candidates to the priesthood and visit the parishes of Rome.

Right after Laínez's return from Trent, Borgia's chief task was to assist the general, whose health had been weakened by his many journeys and by his labors at the Council. The two of them spent some time together at Frascati, where Father Francis resided during a good part of 1564. Between May and October of that year the many illnesses which had made war on the general declared a truce, so he made plans to take over the preaching in the Roman church of the Society during the approaching Advent. Even though he did begin this series of sermons, he was not able to finish them. On January 1, 1565, the titular feast day of the Society, Father General dined in the refectory for the last time with the community; then on the 7th he celebrated his last Mass. On the 17th his condition became so serious as to cause alarm. He sent for the pope's blessing and received the anointing of the sick, after requesting that Father Francis be present. During these rites he fixed a meaningful look on Borgia, as the latter recounted in a letter to Salmerón. "After the anointing with the holy oils, he looked squarely at me, and then raising his eyes he invited all of us to depart, for he too was departing with a most joyful expression on his face and with his eyes fixed on me in a contented way, and then looking up once more, he again focused his gaze on me."[1] We see here a sign of Laínez's unmistakable love for the former duke of Gandía, as well as a premonition that it was Borgia who would succeed him. Father Laínez died on January 19, 1565.

The Second General Congregation (1565)

Imitating St. Ignatius, Laínez had decided not to appoint a vicar to lead the Society at the time of his death. Following the provisions outlined in the Constitutions, therefore, all the professed Fathers who were currently in Rome had to elect a vicar. This election took place on January 20, the day following the general's death, and the man chosen for that office was Father Francis Borgia. Wasting no time, the new vicar announced on the 21st that he was convening a general congregation on the coming 20th of June.

During the five months of his term as vicar—months that seemed to him like years, as he wrote to the noble lady Leonor Mascarenhas—there was no lack of work to keep him busy. As would be expected, those matters which did not require immediate decisions were put aside for the attention of the future general. But there was one problem that could not be postponed: finding the wherewithal to house and feed the Fathers who would be coming for the congregation. Counting electors and "procurators," those attending would number some fifty-two in all—a considerable group to add to the three hundred Jesuits usually resident in Rome. Borgia had literally to beg for alms by writing personal letters to people with whom he himself and the whole Society had maintained good relations. His efforts paid off well. For example, the count of Oropesa sent him 150 ducats to cover expenses incurred by the congregation.

Fortunately, vicissitudes similar to the ones that had caused delays in convening the first general congregation did not interfere with the second one. After the provincial congregations had been held to elect the two professed who would attend along with the provincials, the Fathers of the congregation held their opening session in Rome on June 21, 1565. By this date the majority of electors were already present in the city. Before dealing with any other matter, the congregation designated Father Salmerón to accompany Father Vicar Borgia as he went to request Pope Pius IV's blessing. The Fathers then resolved to begin the business of the congregation immediately, without awaiting the arrival of those electors who had been delayed. A number of these were expected to arrive in time for the feast of the Visitation of the Blessed Virgin Mary, July 2 at that time, the day scheduled for the election of the new general. As it turned out, Everard Mercurian, provincial of Lower Germany; Ponce Cogordan, an elector from

France; and Pedro Ribadeneira, sent from Sicily, did get there in time; but the electors from the province of Andalucía did not. This delegation, composed of Father Provincial Juan Plaza and Fathers Bartolomé de Bustamante and Juan Bautista Sánchez, did not arrive in Rome until July 20. That very day these delegates joined the working sessions of the congregation.

Two of the first companions of St. Ignatius were among the electors, Father Nicolás Bobadilla and Alonso Salmerón. Father Simão Rodrigues had excused himself because of poor health. Besides Father Francis, the vicar, and his assistants, Jerome Nadal, Cristóbal de Madrid, and Juan de Polanco, the congregation included such distinguished members as Peter Canisius, provincial of Upper Germany; Edmond Auger, provincial of Aquitaine; Antonio Cordeses, provincial of Aragón; Diego Miró, provincial of Portugal; Jerónimo Demènech, provincial of Sicily; and, finally, Benedetto Palmio, provincial of Lombardy, who had been designated to preach the sermon on the day of the election of the new general.

Everything was carried out in conformity with the directives of the Constitutions and the First General Congregation. An allocution given by the vicar on June 28 introduced a four-day period of preparation for the election. In his address Father Francis limited himself to an explanation of the norms established by the Constitutions for the election of a general. The general should embody in the highest degree the qualities of virtue, wisdom, and prudence so necessary for the fulfillment of his office. He ought, moreover, to possess the ability to govern, be able to command with gentleness and firmness. Borgia then exhorted the electors to devote to prayer and reflection the three days that were to follow, but bade them not to reveal their preferences until all had assembled for the balloting. A good part of his exhortation was aimed at putting the delegates on their guard against allowing themselves to be motivated by ambition or personal and human designs.[2]

Borgia had toyed with the idea of informing the electors in his allocution that he had excluded himself as a candidate; but heeding the advice of Fathers Ribadeneira and Salmerón, he held back. They had argued that such a gesture could be interpreted in a sense contrary to what he intended.

On July 2, 1565, the thirty-nine Fathers present at the congregation attended a Mass celebrated by the vicar and received Holy Communion from his hands. Then hearing a Latin sermon preached by Father Palmio and after spending some time collecting their thoughts, they proceeded to cast their ballots. Father Francis was elected on the first balloting with thirty-one votes; immediately thereafter those electors who had voted for other candidates cast their votes with the majority. Then kneeling before him each one of them kissed the hands of the new general. Afterwards, they sang a Te Deum in the church of the Society, after which all the other Jesuits in Rome came forward to kiss the general's hands. Coincidentally, the third general of the Society was elected on July 2, the same day as the second general seven years earlier.

At this time the new general was fifty-four years old.

After the midday meal that same day, all the Fathers who had participated in the congregation went to the nearby convent of Ara Coeli, where the pope was staying. Pius IV did not hide his delight when he learned the results of the election; and, as Polanco informed the provincials in writing, the pope said many things "which showed the esteem he bears for our Father General. And in addition to other statements he said there could be no other choice that could possibly be more pleasing to him, or any other man from whom greater service of God and exaltation of the Society could come." Addressing himself to the Portuguese ambassador who had accompanied the Fathers to this audience, Pius IV attested: "These are good men; these are our soldiers, etc."[3]

Borgia's election was well received in Rome and elsewhere. The news was not, however, greeted with enthusiasm at the Spanish court, a fact which can be understood, given the series of events already described in chapter eight.

But what were the feelings of Borgia himself? There is no question that he would have preferred to live in obscurity, obeying rather than commanding. In his spiritual diary, in which he continued making notations even in the midst of the pressures of the congregation, he marked off July 2, 1565, as "dies meae crucis," the day of my cross.[4] Four days later he jotted down this prayer to the Lord which he had been repeating in one form or another continuously: "May the Lord either take me or remove this office from me or give me the grace to govern." On July 6, he added, "I offer myself for the Society, my blood and my life."[5] And then on the following July 23, he noted, "Hope that the Lord will help the affairs of the Society and me as well as I deal with them."[6]

The election completed, the delegates got down to work on July 3. The general announced as the first item of business his appointment of Father Juan de Polanco as secretary of the Society, a position that he had held under the first two generals.

Then the congregation decided to delay the election of the four assistants until July 25, feast of St. James the Apostle but in fact this election was put off another three days to give the delegates more time to reflect and to make inquiries. Before taking the vote on July 25, the delegates approved the motion that, as far as it was possible, assistants were to be selected by electors from these four groups of nations: Italy and Sicily, France and Germany, Portugal and India, and Spain. Those elected were Antonio Araoz for the Spanish provinces; Everard Mercurian for those of France and Germany; Benedetto Palmio for Italy and Sicily; and Diego Miró for Portugal, India, and Brazil. In the evening of that same day Father Polanco was elected the general's admonitor.

Father Araoz, who had received forty-one out of forty-two votes cast by the Spanish group, was once again a cause of grief for Borgia because he would not move to Rome to do his job. He gave as an excuse his poor health, as well as his need to dispel the suspicion that the sole reason he had been elected to this office was to remove him from the Spanish court. A struggle ensued between the general and those who supported Araoz, namely, Ruy Gómez de Silva and Philip II himself. Faced with such opposition, Borgia was forced to yield and grant Araoz permission to remain temporarily in Spain; as a matter of fact, however, he stayed on there for good.

The decrees of the Second General Congregation

It is not within the scope of this biography to present a detailed account of the decrees and precepts approved by this congregation. Suffice it to sketch them broadest outline in order to show how they would give direction to the policy pursued by the new general. The first impression one gets when reading these decrees and canons is that they were intended to regulate the Society's growth. The emphasis was now on consolidation rather than on expansion; especially was this the case when it came to the colleges. One decree called for curbing the unrestrained mushrooming of colleges. Only those colleges that had adequate endowment and sufficient personnel to guarantee proper functioning were to be accepted. It was more important to bolster the colleges that already existed than to open new ones. Some of these institutions were singled out by name and brought up for discussion, but in almost every instance the ultimate decision was left to the discretion of the general. As far as Spain was concerned, we should merely point out that the survival of the colleges in Zaragoza and Mallorca was put into jeopardy.

The city and *jurados* of Valencia had offered their university to the care of the Society; but the congregation did not think the offer should be accepted, despite a guarantee of three thousand ducats per annum included in the offer. The Society did not think it had sufficient resources to undertake a work of such magnitude.

The congregation also decided against administering and teaching in diocesan seminaries, called into existence by the Council of Trent. It made an exception for seminaries to which colleges of the Society were annexed, provided the personnel available warranted undertaking such a work.

The congregation decreed that each province should have its own novitiate and, insofar as possible, its own seminary or house of studies. Most important, novices should devote themselves to spiritual formation and not concentrate on studies, although they could be allowed to study during their second year of novitiate.

Naturally, special attention was given to matters dealing with the Institute of the Society and to its internal organization. The delegates insisted that they were unable to touch any matters that they considered essentials of the Institute. A commission was set up to examine some doubtful points in the Constitutions. One problem in particular that demanded considerable work was harmonizing three passages from the book of the *Examen* and from the *Constitutions* that dealt with the distribution of the possessions of Jesuits making their renunciation.

The delegates decided to suppress the office of commissary, who had exercised jurisdiction over a number of provinces, substituting for it the office of visitor, who could be sent when circumstances called for it.

They also waived the concession that the Council of Trent had granted to religious orders, allowing them to possess real property in common.

The delegates stipulated that the so-called Rules of the Summary of the Constitutions were to remain intact, but they instructed the general to revise and abbreviate the so-called Common Rules and the rules that pertained to various offices. The general was also to set up a commission whose mandate it was to compare the Latin translation of the *Constitutions* with the original Spanish and make needed emendations where discrepancies were found.

On the question of how often a general congregation should be convened, the delegates voted to summon a congregation every seven years or, in case there was no need for one to be called at that time, every nine years. However, some members requested that this vote be reconsidered; as a result there came into being what we know as the "congregation of procurators." Henceforth, procurators, or representatives sent by their respective provinces, would convene in Rome every three years to decide whether or not a general congregation should be convoked.

The forty-first decree, which in the edition of the *Institutum Societatis Iesu* became number 29, deals with increasing the time of prayer in the Society. Since this is a subject which has been discussed so often, the actual text of the decree merits translation in its entirety. It reads as follows: "For some days there was talk and discussion about increasing the time of prayer, which had been defined in Part IV, Chapter 4, of the *Constitutions* [342]; and finally it was approved that the general could, according to his discretion, increase the time of prayer, as it would seem fitting to him in the Lord, taking into account persons, places, etc."

In chapter ten we shall have the opportunity to discuss how St. Francis Borgia implemented this decree.

The delegates also left to the general's discretion the decision to introduce the sung mass and vespers into those places where these did not already exist. In those places where it was found that the sung Mass and vespers did not serve the final purpose of the Institute and the edification of the neighbor, or in case there were not enough priests present to sing masses and vespers, the general could suppress the practice.

Finally, we should mention that the Congregation decided that the quarterly letters, in which the different houses and colleges throughout the Society recorded the news of significant events, were from now on to become annual letters. So was born the celebrated *litterae annuae* so well-known in the history of the Society. All this correspondence that came from the houses and colleges between 1581 and 1654 was published year after year, making up a total of thirty-six volumes.

The original enumeration of the directives and canons of the Second General Congregation is different from that found in Volume 1 of the Florentine edition of the *Institutum Societatis Iesu.*[7]

By mid-August it seemed that the Fathers at the congregation were running out of subjects to talk about; for adequate reasons a number of delegates had already been given permission to return to their respective provinces. In his own name and speaking for a number of other delegates, therefore, Peter Canisius moved that the congregation adjourn before the end of that month. The final decision was to complete all business by September 3, and that indeed is what happened. We should note that the congregation took place during the intense summer heat, when it was considered injurious to the health to be in Rome.

An allocution from the general put the finishing touches on the proceedings.[8] As he bade them farewell, perhaps for the last time, Father Francis reminded the assembled delegates of their duties toward God, toward the neighbor, toward themselves, and toward the general. He reminded them that the Lord had entrusted them with the care of a vineyard to which they should dedicate themselves with fidelity. As far as the neighbor was concerned, he reminded them that they had to fulfill the role of the Good

Samaritan, seeing that so many in Italy and Spain lived their lives submerged in vice, and so many others in France and Germany lay wounded because of the heresies of Calvin and Luther. He expressed some fears for the delegates themselves: the fear they might not forget the discussions and struggles that had arisen during the congregation, the fear that the ties of obedience might be loosened, and the fear that divisions might arise within the Society.

The most moving passage of the exhortation referred to Francis himself. He asked the Fathers to treat him like a beast of burden. People try not to load the beast with more than his strength will allow. If he falls they try to lift him to his feet; if he falters they goad him on. "I am your beast of burden; you loaded this job on me. Treat me as they treat one of these beasts." To engrave his request on their hearts and carry out in practice the sentiments that he had uttered so openly to them, he announced that he was about to kiss humbly the feet of each one of them. Thus ended the congregation and thus began the six years of Borgia's generalate.

10. Administrative Policies and Decisions

Such are the responsibilities placed upon the general by the Constitutions that the history of his private life becomes intertwined with that of the order. Still, it is possible to disentangle what any given general did from the developments of the Society itself. As a biographer, I shall endeavor as best I can to restrict myself to sketching out what Borgia personally did, placing his activities within the framework of the Society of his time.

One preliminary observation: As one reads his letters and instructions, one comes to the conclusion that the cardinal point in Borgia's administrative policy was to implement the decrees of the general congregation that had elected him to office. In chapter nine we gave a résumé of these decrees. Borgia's fidelity in carrying out the mandate given him by the congregation is evident in essential matters, for instance, revising the rules of the Society and drawing up regulations for novitiates and colleges; it is evident as well in matters of lesser importance, for instance, prohibiting Fathers of the Society from accepting permanent assignments with princes or prelates and being at their disposition as members of their entourage, a practice proscribed by decree 40 of the Second General Congregation.

Here we shall treat the following matters entrusted to the new general by the congregation: the revision of the rules, time assigned for prayer, regulations affecting novitiates, and an educational curriculum for the colleges. We shall also consider two administrative techniques of which Borgia made use: the congregation of procurators and visitors sent to the various provinces. Since Borgia's generalate paralleled Pius V's pontificate, we shall also study the relations between these two saints and the influence the pope's decisions had on the Society between 1565 and 1572.

The revision and publication of the Rules of the Society

In the mind of St. Ignatius the Constitutions of the Society were to have two characteristics, immutability and universality. In addition to this unchanging document there were to be ordinations and rules that could be modified and adapted to the circumstances of time and place.[1] When St. Ignatius and his collaborators first began to edit the rules at the beginning of 1548, this was the objective they had in mind.[2] The resulting rules can be divided into three groupings. First, there is the summary of the Constitutions that would be accessible to all Jesuits, even to those who did not have access to the complete text of the *Constitutions*. In the first Spanish edition these bore the title *Regulas generales sacadas de las constituciones*[3] and contained the basic principles of the Society's spirituality. They were selected from the book of the *Examen*, as well as from the Preamble and Part III of the *Constitutions*. Laínez had ordered them printed for the first time in 1560 under the title *Quaedam ex Constitutionibus excerpta*.[4] Because they began with the words "Summa Sapientia" or "The Supreme Wisdom" (the opening words of the Preamble to the *Constitutions*), they were called the *Summa Sapientia* rules until the time of Father Mercurian, when they were given the name *Summary of the Constitutions*, the title they retained until modern times. In the second grouping we have the Common Rules for all Jesuits. These contained detailed regulations for the spiritual life and house discipline. The first redaction of these was made in 1549, and the next in 1553/54.[5] Laínez also edited them in 1560.[6] In the third classification are the rules for Fathers and Brothers assigned to perform specific jobs.

In its decree 57, the Second General Congregation resolved that

> the general rules which begin "Summa Sapientia" are to remain intact; the others shall be revised and, as far as possible, amended, paying special attention to those rules which it is certain emanated from our Reverend Father Ignatius; it should be determined whether they should be adapted to the present times and whether they are useful to the general good. Rules for offices of provincial, rector, and other officials should especially be revised and amended.[7]

Once elected general, Borgia undertook the work the congregation had entrusted to him. He set up a commission composed of Fathers Everard Mercurian, Cristóbal de Madrid, Bartolomé de Bustamante, and Juan de Polanco to revise and abbreviate these rules.[8] Writing to Nadal on March 22, 1567, he informed him that

> We are also at work revising and correcting job descriptions
> and rules as was ordered by the congregation; and at this
> date we have finished those of provincial, visitor, rector,
> minister, procurator general, treasurer, prefect of the church,
> and priests, and also the common rules; the rest will be dealt
> with and, with the help of the Lord, promptly sent out.[9]

They finished their task in June of that year and began sending the rules to
the provinces.[10] On July 2, 1567, the general promulgated them in an allocution he gave at the Roman College.[11]

Two editions of the rules he had drawn up were published during his
generalate. The first was issued in Rome that same year, 1567; it did not
appear as a book but in brochure or pamphlet form.[12] The Rules of the
Summary were published as they existed in the 1560 edition. As for the
Common Rules, there were sixty-four in Laínez's time, which were now
whittled down to forty. The second edition, now in book form, though
without pagination, was published in Naples in 1568.[13] Missing from this
edition were the rules for provincials, visitors, rectors, and ministers, which
remained in manuscript form.[14]

After Borgia's term of office, the Rules were revised by Father General
Everard Mercurian in the 1580 edition that became all but definitive. In 1582
Father General Claudio Acquaviva, followed in 1615/16 by the Seventh
General Congregation, gave them the form which they retained until the
Twenty-seventh General Congregation of 1923 ordered them revised. This
revision was published in the 1932 edition.

The time for and manner of prayer in the Society

We have already seen in chapter nine that decree 29 of the Second
General Congregation authorized Borgia to lengthen the time of daily prayer
in the Society. We shall later show how the new general implemented this
mandate; but, because his legislation has been understood as differing from
what St. Ignatius had prescribed, we must first of all examine the latter's
thinking in respect to prayer.

It should be noted that Ignatius was always a man of prayer. Nevertheless, when it came to laying down rules for prayer in the Society, he was
moderate to an extreme. In Parts IV and VI of the Constitutions he com-
ments on this subject, particularly in [342] and [582].

Ignatius made an important distinction between formed Jesuits, both
professed and coadjutors, and Jesuits still in formation, particularly the
scholastics. For the former, as "men who are spiritual and sufficiently

advanced to run in the way of Christ our Lord, to the extent that their bodily strength and exterior occupations undertaken through charity and obedience will allow," he imposed no prescriptive rule other than that each should be guided by what "discrete charity" dictated, that is, spiritual discernment directed by the supreme rule of the love of God.[15] As we read in a variant text that was not incorporated into the final version of the Constitutions, Ignatius took for granted that formed Jesuits "needed no spurs."[16] He wanted them to give themselves to the essentially apostolic goals of the Society, eliminating everything that could distract them or deflect their energies from this objective. But also in the same paragraph of the Constitutions cited above ([582]), he recommended that "on the other hand they should keep themselves alert [in the usage of spiritual practices] that these practices may not be relaxed to such an extent that the spirit grows cold and the human and lower passions grow warm." Another basic criterion was that the Jesuit should know how to find God even in the midst of his occupations or, according to the classical definition formulated by Father Jerome Nadal, that the Jesuit should be a "contemplative in action."

As far as those Jesuits in formation who have completed a period of trials and undergone a number of experiments, the Constitutions limit themselves to prescribing the following: one hour of daily prayer, excluding Mass but including the Little Office of the Blessed Virgin, and two examinations of conscience, one at midday and one at night.[17]

Note the term "one hour," which is cited twice in the short paragraph to which we have referred. From the time of St. Ignatius until our own days, there has consistently been discussion about "the hour" of prayer in the Society. Discrepancies have arisen over how this "hour" should be understood. The Fathers at the Thirty-first Congregation in 1965/66 defended the notion of "the hour" in decree 14, explaining how it should be interpreted and how it should apply in each individual case.

One more basic ingredient in Ignatian spirituality is the role the spiritual father and, ultimately, the superior should play. Even the formed Jesuit is expected to consult with the superior about the time he gives to prayer. "Even if [the superior] thinks it expedient to give some determined time to keep [the subjects] from being either excessive or deficient in their spiritual exercises, he will have the authority to do this" ([583]). The role of the superior is evident: When Jesuits are face-to-face with the danger of erring either by excess or by deficiency, the superior is the referee. This same principle was also reiterated by the Thirty-first General Congregation.

Here, then, we see the general outline of Ignatius's rules on prayer in the Society. There is no doubt that his great moderation in this matter can be traced to two events in his life. First, his fear of deviations in the matter of prayer, examples of which he himself had witnessed in Spain, where men and women who had spent long hours in prayer ended up falling victims to the most unfortunate aberrations. For this reason he stressed mortification over prayer.[18] Second, when he himself was a student he saw that spending long hours in prayer was detrimental to his studies. Nadal tells us that, when Ignatius founded the Society, he set limits to the prayer of the scholastics precisely because of this experience, convinced that studies "in a certain way demand the entire man."[19] It should be added that the scholastics had made a whole month of the Exercises and had undergone a number of experiments and probations before they began their studies. This fact explains his great principle that "a truly mortified man needs only a quarter of an hour to unite himself with God in prayer."[20] For reasons of human frailty or because of temptations from the enemy, should a scholastic be in need of more prayer, the superior could determine how much to allow.

Having briefly considered St. Ignatius's thinking about prayer in the Society, we now turn to examining how his second successor viewed this same subject. It should not be surprising that Borgia leaned toward lengthening the time of prescribed prayer; both his own personal inclinations and the Spanish zeitgeist of which he was a product inclined him to this. The question of prayer in the Society was one of the points he raised in the memorandum he sent to Rome in 1558 when he realized he would be unable to attend the First General Congregation in person. As we have seen, this document failed to arrive in time for the Congregation's consideration. Nevertheless, the subject itself was discussed and the results encapsulated in decree 97, which rejected any changes in what had already been spelled out in the Constitutions. Father General Diego Laínez followed this line of thinking, as we see in a letter of December 31, 1560, to Father Antonio de Quadros, provincial of India.

> The sense of the Constitutions in this matter of the hour of prayer is that [Jesuits] should not go beyond the limits already set without permission; nor should they fail to employ a full hour in prayer without permission. It is up to the discretion of the superior to see for whom, when, and under what circumstances he should contract or expand these limits.[21]

After the election of Borgia the Second General Congregation took up this matter once again. Deliberations pro and con went on for several days, a clear indication that there was no uniformity of opinion among the delegates. It is reasonable to suppose that the new general lined up with those on the side of increasing the time of prayer. This opinion was advanced by the early seventeenth-century Jesuit historian of the Society, Father Francesco Sacchini,[22] who wrote that Borgia was inclined to believe that the shortcomings he saw beginning to crop up in the Society could be traced to a lack of prayer on the part of its members. Borgia wrote about this problem to Peter Canisius on December 3, 1566, insofar as it pertained to the Upper German province.[23] At the Second General Congregation in 1565, Father Alonso Salmerón, provincial of Naples, and Fathers Jerome Nadal and Juan Alonso de Polanco were probably in the general's corner, whereas opposing him were the voting members from Germany and France.

As Father Pedro de Leturia so well observed, the result was a compromise.[24] Instead of imposing a longer period for prayer, the congregation authorized the general to initiate such changes "as seemed to him best in the Lord, taking into account persons, places, etc."[25]

On November 5, 1565, two months after the congregation had ended, the new general made use of the power delegated to him by

> also ordering that the time of prayer be extended, and that in the Spanish provinces there be, according to the prevailing custom, one hour of prayer in the morning; in the other provinces there be three quarters of an hour in the morning, and in the evening one half hour, divided between prayer and the examen, in addition to the examen made before the noon meal.[26]

From this directive it is easy to deduce that the two examinations of conscience made each day were definitively excluded from "the hour of prayer." The difference between the various provinces of the Society is obviously not great, but it does show that Borgia put to use the flexibility prescribed by the congregation.

As far as Spain was concerned, the case can be made that as a matter of fact this new regulation brought no change whatsoever. The phrase "according to the prevailing custom" meant either that by this time the custom of morning prayer was already an accepted tradition or, at the very least, that it had been the accepted practice for some time. A directive to Father Juan de Valderrábano, provincial of Toledo, on October 9, 1565, confirms this fact. This order required that

> in addition to the two examinations of conscience, scholastics, confessors, preachers, coadjutors, and professed should ordinarily make the one hour of prayer each day, according

to the custom of these provinces; along with this the superior should be solicitous for the state of health and ability of his subjects, and that those who showed any cause could and should be dispensed from this ruling. The examinations of conscience made before the noon meal and before going to bed at night should not be changed, and priests also should make these examinations of conscience.[27]

Here we see that the hour of prayer was imposed on all, the formed as well as those in formation. If priests had been expected as the very minimum to do everything that the Constitutions had legislated for the scholastics, now they were expected to comply with legislation that extended the time of prayer to a whole hour. We shall soon see how this regulation was understood in the other provinces of the Society.

Dividing the time for prayer between morning and night, an innovation for the non-Spanish provinces, should be seen as a tentative measure, binding those provinces under the new obligation in the least way possible.

Borgia may well have been unaware of the fact that his new directive was in practice the same as that prescribed in the *Constituciones de los colegios,* composed in 1549 or 1550. Even though Polanco was the author of these basic regulations for operating the colleges, they must have reflected St. Ignatius's thinking, just as did the *Industrias con que uno de la Compañía de Jesus mejor consiguirá sus fines,* likewise written by Polanco just about this time or shortly before the *Constituciones de los colegios.* This latter work was never sent out to the colleges, possibly because it made its appearance at the same time as the final touches were being put to the last part of the Constitutions, scheduled to be published around 1550.

The *Constituciones de los colegios* required that scholastics, in addition to their daily Mass, the Little Office of the Blessed Virgin, and one or two examinations of conscience each day, should "devote some time to meditation and mental prayer, if they are able to do so; each one should remain in his room spending three fourths of an hour, or at the most one hour, praying in the way that suits him best, after having discussed the matter with his confessor." He could divide the three quarters of an hour into two parts, spending one half hour at prayer in the morning and a quarter of an hour or one half hour in the afternoon, before the night meal.[28]

This evening half hour of prayer and the examination of conscience proved to be the practical stumbling block in this Borgian legislation. A number of provinces sent back reports that by the late afternoon the scholastics were exhausted after the labors of the day and so were prone to fall asleep. The fifteen minutes that had been added to the evening examen was shifted about in different ways. Nadal proposed that in Germany the fifteen-minute period be placed before the night meal; but it gradually became clear that the practical solution was to attach it to the forty-five-minute morning period, as was already the Spanish practice and was little by little becoming the Roman custom, as well. Borgia himself had described this change in a letter to Nadal written on June 28, 1567, indicating that in Rome "we are well pleased with this arrangement."[29] So the custom that would finally be sanctioned by the Fourth General Congregation in 1581 was gradually becoming accepted.

Up until now we have confined ourselves to the time of prayer. Borgia was more open when it came to the types of prayer to be employed during the allotted time. He did not impose mental prayer, preferring to allow each one to choose whatever form of prayer seemed most suitable; however, we should not be surprised that, when all was said and done, his preference lay with mental prayer, as both Nadal and Mercurian understood. This was a matter that should be left to the spiritual father, Nadal reported, or to the particular initiative of each one. But Borgia adamantly opposed having a bell rung to indicate when one should move from vocal to mental prayer.

We should not place too much importance on the distinction between "prayer" and "meditation." We see that in Ignatian terminology the two were used indiscriminately and at times both were applied in the same context.

Borgia did not want to impose one method of mental prayer in prefer-ence to another. When he learned that the provincial of Aragón had ordered his subjects to spend the time of prayer making acts of the love of God, he wrote to him that, although in itself this was the best form of prayer, not all were capable of it, adding that, to direct Jesuits in the way of prayer, the Lord had left them the Spiritual Exercises of their founder. All methods of prayer were good, he said; just as the motions of the Holy Spirit were diverse, diverse too were individuals. So each one ought to have the freedom to choose the way of praying that would help him most.[30]

There were a number of practical rules given, particularly to those who were obliged to recite the breviary. In June 1566 Nadal left an instruction at the college of Ingolstadt to the effect that those who were obliged to say the breviary should not use the time of prayer to do so unless a half hour of mental prayer had preceded their beginning it.[31] It was Nadal who also had instructed the priests in Antwerp that, in addition to praying the breviary, they should make an hour and a half of mental prayer, as was the custom for priests to do in Italy.[32] Included, no doubt, in this period of time was the time for the two examens; and here the rule was that the quarter of an hour should not necessarily be spent on the examen properly so called, but that some of this time should be spent in prayer.

After Borgia's death the prayer question continued to be debated, but it was the Fourth General Congregation that finally settled the matter once and for all. Without any prior discussion that we know of, the congregation passed decree 5 on February 27, 1581. This decree provided that "the custom of the whole hour of prayer, in addition to the two daily examinations of conscience, should, as a pious and salutary custom, be maintained in its entirety [*omnino*], exactly as it was introduced by Reverend Father Borgia."[33] As we can see, the decree speaks of a custom, not of a previously decreed law. On the other hand, the Fathers at this congregation did not comment on whether this prayer should be made in the morning or whether it should be mental prayer; but the newly elected general, Claudio Acquaviva, officially interpreted the congregation's decrees and by the power invested in him by the congregation declared that the prayer should both be mental and take place in the morning. Those unable to make mental prayer were to follow the directions of the superior or the spiritual father, according to what was prescribed in Part IV of the Constitutions. Peter Canisius enthusiastically supported this piece of legislation as it applied to Germany, from which, as we have already seen, most of the opposition had come. Both Father Giulio Negrone, in his commentary on the Common Rules of the Society,[34] and Father Francis Suárez, in his treatise on the Society,[35] recognize that the practice of mental prayer was introduced gradually by custom into the order, and that this custom eventually became the law.

In conclusion, if we take stock of the changes Borgia initiated in this matter of prayer, we can sum them up in this way:

1) The third general of the Society acted in conformity with a decree of the congregation that elected him.

2) As far as the time of prayer was concerned, the change was moderate and flexible. In those days one hour of prayer was considered the minimum for both religious and laity who made efforts to be people of prayer. This does not take into account the time spent listening to the interminable sermons preached in the churches and the extremely long office the priests were required to recite daily. As far as the method of prayer was concerned, we have seen that Borgia maintained balance between vocal and mental prayer.

3) Even nine years after Borgia's death the question was still being discussed, and during the intervening time individual Jesuits and the various provinces were able to express their opinions freely. If Borgia's decision to lengthen the time of prayer had been somehow against the Ignatian spirit, could this have gone unchallenged and uncorrected in an era when so many illustrious contemporaries of the founder were still alive? On the contrary, the passage of time consolidated the custom, a sign that the Society absorbed the change without trauma.

4) It was possible that times changed as the years rolled on after Ignatius had formulated his policy on prayer. One difference lay in numbers. The thousand-member Society of St. Ignatius's time had grown to four thousand in Borgia's era. Moreover, St. Ignatius had always assumed that his sons were committed to a high degree of spirituality, particularly in regard to mortification of the senses, which as a rule would have made lengthy prayer unnecessary. But whenever there was a certain slackening of fervor—a contingency that was ever present—Ignatius wanted superiors to order the time of prayer lengthened. We have an inkling that this could have been the case during the generalate of Borgia from as distinguished a man as Father Gil González Dávila, assistant for Spain during the administration of Father Everard Mercurian (1573-81); former provincial in Castile, Toledo, and Andalucía; and visitor to the provinces of Aragón, Castile, and Toledo. He asked in one of the conferences on the Rules of the Society that he gave while provincial of Andalucía (1585-88), "Why is it that there is so little time of prayer in the Society?" And he answered that Ignatius

> took for granted that the novices would leave [the novitiate] so mortified that they would need a bridle and not spurs. If we do not ordinarily see the novices end their training with a hunger that is so fervent and desirous for prayer, the fault belongs to them or to the superior or to both. I always divide the blame between them. Seeing that this was the case, the Society, using the authority given by our Father in the place mentioned [Constitutions [341f]], has lengthened the time for prayer, as it did in the Fourth General Congregation, and thereby confirmed the directive of Father Francis that besides the examens there be one hour of prayer.[36]

The novitiates

Borgia always had a predilection for novitiates, regarding them as the "source of sanctity"[37] or "Bethlehem, which means the house of bread,"[38] because here provision was made for the bread of virtues so essential for walking along the way of perfection. In the novitiate the foundations of the spiritual life were laid; without such foundations the edifice could never stand firm. Convinced that "from the good novice comes the good scholastic,"[39] he condemned the practice of rushing out of the novitiate to begin studies.

In its decree 14 the Second General Congregation legislated two policies concerning the novitiate. First, in each province there should be a house of probation either apart from or annexed to a college. If attached to a college, however, a special place was to be set up for novices away from scholastics in their studies. Second, the two years of novitiate prescribed by the Constitutions ([16, 336]) should be dedicated entirely to spiritual matters. Studies could be allowed in the second year, but then only with permission from the provincial, after prior authorization from the general.

Even St. Ignatius had long expressed the wish that the novitiate be a separate house,[40] but the problems he encountered in the early years prevented the implementation of his wishes. Added to these problems, however, was the occasional premature assignment of novices either to study in the colleges or to be involved in the running of the house.

In Borgia's time an *Ordo domus probationis* was drawn up,[41] a document which gave minute directions on how each hour of the novice's day was to be spent, in order to ensure the proper functioning of houses of probation. In the morning the novices were to spend an hour of meditation or prayer, either vocal or mental according to each one's ability, following the directives each one received from the novice master. They were to attend daily Mass. The attended conferences on the book of the *Examen* and on Part III of the *Constitutions*, after which they were to separate into small groups and discuss what they had just heard in the conference. The remaining hours of the morning were to be dedicated to various household chores or to manual labor. They were to make another half hour of prayer in the afternoon, recite vespers or the rosary, study the catechism, and do some physical work. This was the schedule to be followed except during those times when the novices were making the experiments prescribed by the Constitutions. One of the experiments that was considered of particular importance was the month-long Exercises that each one made.

Among the novitiates existing during the time of Borgia, three deserve special mention: the one located in Rome and the two established in Spain, at Medina del Campo and Villarejo de Fuentes.

Borgia had a special place in his heart for the Roman novitiate of Sant' Andrea al Quirinale, which he founded on November 30, 1566,[42] aided by the generosity of the family of Andrea Croce, bishop of Tivoli, and of Doña Juana de Aragón, duchess of Tagliacozzo, who had endowed it. St. Ignatius had directed the spiritual life of this lady; her son Marc Antonio Colonna was present at the ground-breaking ceremonies and received the title of Founder. Sant'Andrea's first master of novices was Father Alfonso Ruiz, a native of Córdoba, whom Laínez had summoned to take over this office in 1564. Under his direction were formed men of the stamp of Claudio Acquaviva, who was to become the fifth general of the Society, and Stanislaus Kostka, a young Pole who entered the novitiate in 1567 and died a holy death the following year at the age of eighteen, on the feast of the Assumption of our Lady. On June 6, 1569, the new novitiate building was inaugurated; Borgia used to come here to give conferences to the novices and to seek privacy for his prayer.

The novitiate at Medina del Campo was the successor of the earlier one at Simancas. In 1562 Nadal ordered the first novices to take up residence there; from that date until 1566 the novices were under the direction of a great master of the spiritual life, Father Baltasar Alvarez, who implanted in them a love of prayer, mortification, and religious virtues. Speaking of this novitiate Borgia said that "to a great extent the fruit our Lord gathered in that province [Castile] through the hands of the Society was contingent upon it."[43] In 1569 there were twenty novices and the house was being prepared to receive more. Father Luis de la Puente, who entered the novitiate in 1574, has described the atmosphere of this house of formation. In 1577 the novitiate and its master of novices moved to a new location not far from Valladolid, Villagarcía de Campos, destined to play such an important role in the history of the Society.

What the novitiate at Medina was for the province of Castile, the one at Villarejo de Fuentes in Cuenca was for the province of Toledo. In 1567 some twenty novices came here from Alcalá with their master of novices, Father Juan Manuel de León. This novitiate's founder, Don Juan Pacheco de Silva, was able to speak of it as "a mirror of Paradise," observing that those who lived there seemed more like angels than men.[44]

We are not going to draw up a list of all the novitiates founded during Borgia's time, but some should be singled out. For example, in Italy there were the novitiates at Loreto and Novarella in Reggio Emilia; the latter opened in 1570 with the famous Father Antonio Valentino as master of novices. The Portuguese novitiate was at Evora; in France there were two, at Tournon and at Avignon; Germany had its novitiate at Mainz; Belgium, at Tournai; Brazil, at São Salvador de Bahía.

The colleges and the first "Ratio Studiorum"

We shall speak in chapter twelve of the colleges founded during Borgia's tenure of office when we deal with the expansion of the Society. Suffice it to say at this point that the increase was remarkable. At the time of St. Ignatius's death in 1556, there were 50 colleges in Europe; in 1574 there were 163. In other words, the number of colleges had tripled in a space of merely eighteen years. Although the number of Jesuits grew in greater proportion, going from one thousand to four thousand during this same time frame, this increase was insufficient to supply all the colleges with adequately trained teachers. This situation was the problem of superiors in general and of Borgia in particular. On the one hand, it was not easy to say no to requests coming in from every side to open new colleges; on the other hand, there was simply a dearth of men prepared for classroom teaching. The greatest number of teachers in the colleges were young scholastics not yet out of formation.

As for what was being taught in the colleges, we can give the following brief summary. Ordinarily young boys did not learn to read and write in the colleges, although such teaching was not considered alien to the Institute of the Society. The majority of colleges offered classes in grammar and humanities spread over five courses, three of grammar and two of humanities and rhetoric. At that time there were few colleges of the Society which offered complete courses in philosophy and theology, in spite of decree 9 of the Second General Congregation requiring each province to have one college where such courses were available. In those colleges offering philosophy the students took logic, physics, and metaphysics for a period of three and one-half years. Three professors taught these subjects, following the same students from the first to the third year. As for theology, the Constitutions stipulated that Jesuits should follow a four-year curriculum ([476]) based on "the scholastic doctrine of St. Thomas" ([464]). But in those early decades Jesuits who received a complete theological training were few and far between; however, there were a number who entered the Society after they had already received this training.

The first "Ratio Studiorum" — Every historian of education recognizes the importance of the *Ratio studiorum* of the Society of Jesus, promulgated in 1599 in its final redaction by Father General Claudio Acquaviva. What few know, however, is how long a road this well thought-out educational code had to travel before reaching definitive form. St. Ignatius had long before recognized the need for a plan of studies, as he indicated in the Constitutions ([455]). But progress had to be made step by step.

From the outset the Society wanted to initiate the *modus parisiensis* in all its colleges, that is to say, the curriculum of studies and method of teaching in use at the University of Paris when Ignatius studied there. Father Jerome Nadal inaugurated this method at the college of Messina, founded in 1548; after 1551 it was adopted at the Roman College, the institution which had the reputation for setting the pace for all colleges in the Society. Father Nadal also brought the Paris method to the Spanish colleges in 1553 and 1554, when he was visitor to Spain.

During Father General Diego Laínez's term of office, specialists in various fields met on a number of occasions with a view to drawing up a curriculum of studies; and once the Council of Trent had ended, Father Laínez concentrated more of his energies upon completing the first part of this document, which dealt with grammar and the humanities. Though it lacked only the finishing touches by 1565, it was never sent out to the provinces for implementation.

This part of the project had to wait until 1569, when Borgia ordered that the norms regulating the curriculum of lower studies be sent out to the provinces. This was the first *Ratio studiorum*. Official in character, universal in scope, it remained in force for thirty years, being superseded in 1586 when Father Acquaviva promulgated the new *Ratio*.[45]

The part dealing with the higher studies of philosophy and theology was promised as a second stage, but requests came pouring in to Rome from a number of provinces requesting that this work be accelerated. Everything must have been ready for sending out by 1571; but Borgia's journeys to Spain, Portugal, and France, undertaken on June 30 that same year, and his death in September 1572 impeded the promulgation of this *Ratio* for higher studies.

Borgia did, however, issue a directive about the type of doctrine that was to be taught in the colleges. The Constitutions had limited themselves to giving only this guideline on the subject: "The doctrine which they ought to follow in each area of studies should be that which is safer and more approved, as also the authors who teach it. The rectors will take care of this, by conforming themselves to what is decided in the Society as a whole for the greater glory of God" ([358]). There were two possible ways of applying this policy. First, by issuing general guidelines and, second, by indicating that certain specific propositions were proscribed and that others must be taught. Father Nadal inclined toward the first alternative, whereas Father Diego Ledesma, prefect of studies at the Roman College, expressed his preference, as he always did, for spelling out the details. In 1564 he drafted a long list of propositions which should be defended in the colleges of the

Society and another long list of propositions which ought to be condemned. To a certain extent Borgia sided with Ledesma and in 1565 issued a decree citing a number of general principles and specifying sixteen "propositions which should be held and taught by Ours and which should be held as true."[46]

Let us finally say a few words about the spiritual formation of the students housed in the colleges of the Society. It is evident that this aspect of their training was given special attention. The sodalities of the Blessed Virgin Mary contributed in a unique way to the formation of a generation of young Christians. A young Belgian Jesuit named Jean Leunis, who taught grammar to the lowest grades, founded the first of these sodalities in the Roman College.

The visitors

The Constitutions of the Society mention superiors (provincials), visitors, and commissaries as men who hold a given office in the order's various provinces.[47] But it appears that in the beginning the precise job description of each of these positions of authority was not clearly defined. What was it that differentiated a visitor from a commissary? Perhaps this was the reason why it took some time to draw up rules that defined the function of each of these offices.

The provincial's job description presented few problems. It seems that as early as 1556 or 1558 rules were drawn up defining this position. At any rate, between 1558 and 1560 directives, including a section about the provincial's visitation to the houses and colleges, were drawn up and sent to the provinces.[48] Referring to commissaries and visitors, Nadal remarked in 1561 that "these are not ordinary superiors; the general gives them the power and authority he wants and for the length of time he wants. But even though they are not ordinary, it seems that in some nations, such as Spain, their position will be permanent."[49] These offices were extraordinary, then, and both their function and their duration were determined by the general. We have already seen in chapter six that in 1554 Borgia was named commissary for the Portuguese and Spanish provinces, a position he exercised, at least *de jure*, until he was summoned to Rome by Pope Pius IV in 1561. The commissary was a kind of delegate or representative of the general or, as the case may be, of the provincial, in whose stead he acted within a specifically defined territory. As the name "visitor" indicates, this official's function consisted in visiting the houses and colleges.

The Second General Congregation in its eleventh decree abolished the office of commissary as an ordinary and permanent office,[50] but it left the general with the right to name a commissary if he thought it necessary or useful. At the same time it mandated that a "commissary" be named to visit the provinces every three or four years, or whenever the general deemed such a visit advisable. As we see, the name "commissary" was applied to the function of visitor.

Borgia recognized at an early date how useful visitors could be. In the 1588 memorandum which he addressed to the First General Congregation upon realizing that he would not be able to attend its sessions, he requested that visitors be sent to the provinces. Less sympathetic to these officials, Laínez replied that this same function was in fact performed by the provincials and commissaries.[51] His supposition was, of course, that the office of commissary would continue to function. But what was to be done now that the Second General Congregation had abolished this office from the administrative organizational chart? The congregation adopted the only possible solution by distinguishing between the now-abolished office of permanent commissary and that of visitor.

When we dealt with the rules of the Society earlier in this chapter, we saw that the general congregation which had elected Borgia to the generalate also instructed him to revise the rules, paying particular attention to those that dealt with the various offices.[52] The new general set out immediately to accomplish this task. In 1566 he drew up a job description for the one who would make the visitation to the various houses, and the rules he designed applied both to the ordinary visitor—the provincial, that is—and to the extraordinary visitor, who was the visitor properly so-called.[53] During 1566 and 1567 he reviewed the rules of the provincial, reducing to only two those dealing with visitations. In 1567 he added two new rules to the office of the visitor properly so called. On March 22 of that same year he was able to write to Nadal that among the other rules he had already completed were those for the offices of provincial and visitor.[54] As a result of the postulates given to him by the congregation of postulators of 1568, he prepared a new edition of rules for visitors and published it in 1568/69.[55]

Convinced as he was of the importance of this office, he naturally lost little time in naming visitors for most of the provinces, not only for those in Europe but also for India and Brazil.[56]

He used to send a newly appointed visitor instructions on how he was to proceed in fulfilling his mission. These instructions testify to the prudence and the religious sensitivity of the one who drew them up. We see that he expected these visits to result in a better functioning of the province as regards both proper religious observance and apostolic progress. But the visitor was not viewed merely as a policeman. Although one of Borgia's instructions was addressed to Father Bustamante, it had a more universal scope, as its title indicated: "Avisos e instrucciones para los visitadores de las provincias" (Advice and instructions for visitors to the provinces). Here is the first paragraph:

> One of the chief aims of the visitation is to leave all Jesuits consoled and inspired, and the visitor should realize that this is what the general very much wants him to do. For this reason the visitor should make himself loved and appreciated rather than disliked by superiors and subjects. He should conduct his visitation with sincerity and simplicity in the way he writes and orders. He should not proceed in a juridical manner, using witnesses and notaries, because this is not the way our Lord has led the Society, but rather in a natural and simple manner.[57]

The visitor should praise the good he finds and should support it. If something needs changing, "it should not be done with severity or dissatisfaction." He should uphold and endorse the superiors' authority, approving as much as he can what they have commanded. Better it is to straighten what is crooked than to bring in something completely new. The implementation of what the visitor has ordered should be left to the provincial or to superiors; as far as possible, this implementation should be made after he left the college or house in question. All these dispositions are intended to protect the authority of the superiors. To avoid making decisions in haste, it is better to postpone action for a while, according to the circumstances.

Unfortunately such discreet directives were not always followed. It is generally accepted that a certain tendency toward rigorism prevailed during these times. Father Sacchini, a historian of the Society, described it, attributing it not so much to the general as to immediate superiors.[58] One of the most notable examples is Father Bartolomé Bustamante, who demonstrated more impressive qualities as an architect than as a superior. Borgia was forever correcting and warning him, but sometimes his corrections were not sufficient. As a consequence, one of the most serious complaints against the third general of the Society was that he placed his confidence in men who did not deserve it. Even though these had all the good will in the world, they lacked prudence and moderation in governing others.

The congregation of procurators of 1568

As we have already seen in chapter nine, decree 19 of the Second General Congregation provided for a congregation of procurators or delegates from the various provinces to convene every three years so that, along with the general and his assistants, they could decide by vote whether or not a general congregation should be convoked.

There was a precedent for these congregations of procurators in the Constitutions, which direct that one Father from each province come to Rome "at least every three years, but every four from the Indies, after being elected by the votes of the professed and rectors of the provinces, to inform the general about many things" ([679]). The Constitutions did not prescribe that these elected Fathers should all come at the same time, nor did they stipulate that together with the general and his assistants they should vote on whether or not a general congregation should be called. Yet these were the two functions that characterized the procurators' congregation. During such a congregation each procurator was to inform the general on the state of the province in light of the passage from the Constitutions cited above.

At the end of his first three years in office, Borgia called for a procurators' congregation to take place in 1568. As soon as a province received word of the convocation of this congregation, it prepared for its own congregation, following the procedures Borgia had formulated, published, and sent out in 1567 to all the provinces along with the revised rules of the Society. The rectors of the colleges and the professed of the four vows, whose number in those days was small, took part in these provincial congregations. According to the *acta*, which are still extant, the Roman province had twenty-two electors, the largest number of all the provinces. Castile had twenty and Aragón only eight.

Due to space limitations we cannot give the names of all the procurators elected to go to Rome; much less can we give even a partial listing of the items presented to the general for his consideration. We shall merely state that the provincial congregations voted unanimously not to convoke a general congregation.

This first congregation of procurators in the history of the Society held its initial session on October 2, 1568. Because of illness the general was not able to preside. Father Everard Mercurian, assistant for Germany, chaired the meeting in his name. Counting the general and the assistants, the participants at this congregation numbered eighteen. On the 6th of this same month the general called the second session to order; during this meeting the delegates cast a unanimous vote not to convoke a general congregation.

In addition to this main order of business, Borgia held a conversation with each of the procurators. We still have the responses he gave to the items their individual provinces had proposed for his consideration. Reading these over today one cannot but admire the general's discretion, as well as his fidelity to the Constitutions and to the first two general congregations, both qualities so evident in his decisions.

There is one matter that we cannot omit. The Spanish provinces asked that an assistant be named for Spain because Father Antonio de Araoz, though he had been elected to this office in the Second General Congregation, had asked for and received permission not to report to his post. Borgia promised to act in this matter; subsequently, on October 9 he appointed Father Jerome Nadal the Spanish assistant. Nadal had just returned to Rome on September 22 after visiting the provinces in Germany and France.

It was decided that the second congregation of procurators should be held in 1571; Borgia did convoke it, decreeing that the delegates should arrive in Rome toward the end of May or, at the very latest, in the first part of June, before the terrible heat descended upon the city. The plan was to spend the summer months indoors, thus completing work by the first part of September, allowing the Fathers time to get back to their provinces before winter closed in.

When the various provinces received news of the convocation, each one held its own congregation. By the first of June there were a good number of procurators in Rome. But this congregation was unable to conclude its work in a normal fashion, for on the first of the month Pope Pius V appointed the general to accompany Cardinal Michele Bonelli, the pope's nephew, on a mission to Spain and Portugal. However, since the retinue of the cardinal, known in history as Cardinal Alessandrino, was not ready to set out from Rome until the 30th, Borgia had the whole month of June to join the procurators in their work. We still have the postulates sent by the provinces and a record of the responses given to them, although some of these responses were handed down by the vicar, at that time Father Jerome Nadal.

Since we do not have the *acta* of this congregation, we do not know if any plenary sessions were held, nor do we know if a vote was taken regarding a general congregation. So there is some doubt whether this congregation of 1571 should be numbered among the congregations of procurators.

Borgia's plan to resign as general

Borgia was not successful in carrying out a project he had been working on for some time: relinquishing the generalate. We have already seen that he considered the day of his election to this office as "the day of my cross." From that moment on he felt the strongest urge to liberate himself from this burden. He was confident that he would be able to do this in October of 1568 while the congregation of procurators was in session.[59]

This wish became ever stronger as his life drew to a close. Not only was he convinced that, as Ribadeneira phrased it, "the government did not rest easy in his hands," but he also felt the burden of poor health and the weight of his years.[60] As he saw his life fading and his final days approaching, he also had the desire to dedicate himself more intensively to prayer. His biographers, Vázquez, Ribadeneira, and Sacchini, to cite a few of the earlier ones, claim that the example of his predecessors, Ignatius and Laínez, both of whom had also wanted to give up the generalate, fueled this desire.

Although both Ignatius and Laínez actually did wish to resign, the fact that Borgia, whose office was a lifetime commitment, wanted to renounce this office has been seen as a unique incident in the history of the Society. But this is not the case. In 1550 St. Ignatius called all the professed to Rome to present them with the finished text of the *Constitutions*; then, taking advantage of the opportunity afforded by their presence, he notified them of his intention to tender his resignation. The Fathers did not accept it.

The Laínez case was different. In 1558 Pope Paul IV had decreed that the general of the Society's tenure of office should be limited to three years. Despite the fact that canon lawyers argued that this restriction ceased to bind in 1559 with the death of the pope who had imposed it, Laínez wanted to observe it nonetheless. He made public his wish that a successor be appointed at the end of his first three years of office on July 2, 1561. The assistants thought otherwise. Still, he was not satisfied and requested that all the professed express in writing their opinion on this matter. Almost all the votes which arrived in Rome were negative. Following the advice of Borgia and ten other priests, he decided that the best solution would be to ask the new pope, Pius IV, to declare formally that Paul IV's decree was no longer in effect. This the pope did on June 22, 1561, and Laínez had to stay on at his post.

Now we return to Borgia's case. After commending the matter most earnestly to the Lord and after saying many Masses for this intention, he called the assistants together and laid before them his plan to summon a general congregation to receive his resignation and name his successor. The assistants rejected his proposal and encouraged him to carry on. He "resigned himself for the time being, seeing they had closed the door on his attempts," as Ribadeneira put it.[61] This contemporary biographer did not specify the date when all the activity outlined here took place; but immediately afterwards, in book 3, chapter 13, of his life, Ribadeneira gave the account of Borgia's trip with Cardinal Alessandrino to Spain and Portugal.

So we are inclined to believe that he had intended to submit his resignation at the congregation of procurators of 1571. Sacchini reported the event in two places, while dealing with the congregations of 1568 and 1571, both of which we have already described.

St. Pius V and the Society

Borgia's generalate ran concurrently with the pontificate of St. Pius V, who was pope from January 7, 1566, until May 1, 1572. To be more exact, Borgia became general six months before the election of Cardinal Michele Ghislieri and died six months after this pope. Two saints, both religious, had been called to govern at the same time—one, the universal Church; the other, a religious order which had been in existence no more than twenty-five years, but which was already giving clear signs of vitality. They shared not only sanctity of life but also a common zeal for souls and an ardent desire for reforming the Church.

In a letter dated January 15, 1566, and addressed to all the provincials of the Society, Borgia announced the results of the election, while singing the praises of the new pope. Because of the pope's reputation for inflexible austerity, "most people did not seem pleased, but those who want the reform and spiritual awakening of the Church were pleased" with this election.[62] From the very beginning Pius V gave clear indications of his affection for the general of the Society. For example, when he was on his way to be enthroned in the Basilica of St. John Lateran, he noticed Borgia standing with the Jesuits who were watching the papal cortege pass in front of the house of Santa Maria della Strada. The pope ordered the coachman to halt and, beckoning Borgia to approach, he embraced him and spent a few minutes conversing with him. In the first month after the election he twice received Borgia in audience. The first time was on January 14, when he came "to kiss the pope's foot and to receive his blessing"; on this occasion "His Holiness showed special love, and he asked that Borgia visit him often and report to him whenever it seemed fitting to do so, showing that he wanted the Society to assist him in the service of God and the Church."[63] The second audience, which lasted much longer, took place on the 21st. Here the general reminded the new pope how the Constitutions ([617]) obliged the professed of the Society through their fourth vow of special obedience to the pope. The pope "even with tears showed him how much this oblation pleased him" and then asked the general to draw up a list of Jesuits whom he could send to the Diet of Augsburg and to the apostolate in Germany. The general in turn petitioned him to confirm all the favors his predecessors had conferred on the Society, a request that the pope was pleased to grant.

We are able at this juncture to present a short list of instances demonstrating the kind of confidence Pius V had in the Society. He selected Fathers Nadal and Ledesma to take part in the Diet of Augsburg, then added the provincial of Germany, Peter Canisius, to their number. In 1569 he requested that two priests be assigned to a commission set up to revise the Latin Vulgate version of the Bible; accordingly, the general selected Father Manuel de Sá and Pedro Parra for this project.[64] Then, he wanted Jesuits to serve as examiners of candidates to the priesthood and to ecclesiastical benefices for the diocese of Rome, a responsibility that Borgia tried to escape, citing canon 57 of the Second General Congregation.

The Society was entrusted with performing works of corporal mercy, such as distributing public aid to the victims of the 1568 plague.

In this same year the pope set up two commissions, appointing four cardinals to each of them. The mandate for the first was to counter the heretics, that of second to convert the infidels.[65] Borgia communicated the pope's decision to Nadal in a letter of August 2, 1568.[66] According to testimony given by Polanco, it was Borgia who recommended that the pope create the second of these commissions, which was in time to become the Congregation *de Propaganda Fide*, instituted in 1622 by Gregory XV.[67]

Responding to rumors circulating in Spain that the pope entertained a certain disaffection for the Society, Borgia wrote a letter on March 7, 1568, declaring that "His Holiness loves the Society and he grants manifold graces and favors to it; he shows his love not only in words but in [giving it] assignments of the greatest importance."[68] It seems the pope made use of the Jesuits in many enterprises and ministries. He had appointed Polanco the apostolic preacher, a German Jesuit preached to the Swiss Guard in their native language, and another Jesuit preached in St. Peter's Basilica. All the Fathers who came to kiss the feet of His Holiness were very well received, and the pope spoke with them as if he were their own father, discussing the affairs he had entrusted to them. Each year he presented to the Society more than 1,200 ducats in alms.

Succeeding Polanco as apostolic preacher was Father Francisco de Toledo, who remained in this office until 1593, when Clement VIII elevated him to the cardinalate. He lived in the apostolic palace and was also the theologian to the Sacred Penitentiary.

Borgia offered Pius V priests to serve as chaplains to the soldiers who had gone to bring relief to Malta, then resisting the assaults of the Ottoman Turks, to those fighting in France during the wars of religion, and to those who were preparing to fight against the Turks. Six Jesuits participated in the naval battle of Lepanto; their leader was Father Cristóbal Rodríguez, whom

Don Juan of Austria stationed aboard his own galley.[69]

Finally, we should note that on July 7, 1571, Pius V declared the Society a mendicant order, with all the privileges this designation entailed.[70]

Penitentiaries of St. Peter's Basilica — In 1570 Pius V showed his trust in the Society by giving it the responsibility to select from among its members confessors or, as they were then designated, penitentiaries for St. Peter's Basilica in Rome. The pope had decided to restore the college of confessors to serve the faithful and also the pilgrims who would come to the three most important Roman basilicas. To the Dominicans he assigned the Basilica of St. Mary Major, to the Franciscans, that of St. John Lateran, and to the Jesuits, St. Peter's Basilica. He dispatched Cardinal Francesco Alciati and his associate, Monsignor Nicolá Ormaneto, to inform the general of the Society of his decision. The pope deemed insufficient all Borgia's arguments against this proposal and refused to change his mind. Among other considerations Borgia objected that this project would demand a great number of men from various nations, all of them possessing sufficient expertise in theological and moral matters to solve complex cases proposed by penitents coming from every corner of the world. But in the end Borgia had to obey the pope's command. On May 1, 1570, the Society assumed this responsibility for St. Peter's and assigned six priests to begin their ministry as confessors. By the following November the number in the community had grown to twenty, among whom were twelve priests from different linguistic backgrounds. They appealed to Cardinal Charles Borromeo, who had promoted the idea of entrusting the Society with this project, begging that he get them the furniture, books, and clothing necessary for their work. They had "their college next to the Sacred Palace," being housed in a building situated in the present St. Peter's Square; but after 1656 they moved to the palace of Cardinal Domenico della Rovere, which is on today's Via della Conciliazione. The Society served in this apostolate until its suppression in 1773, when Pope Clement XIV confided it to his brothers in religion, the Franciscan Conventuals, who have maintained it until the present time. We should note that one of the rectors of this "college" was the future St. Robert Bellarmine.

Pius V and the Society's Institute — The sincere esteem which Pius V manifested toward the Society from the very outset, however, was not enough to erase from his mind certain prejudices which were understandable in a pope who had been a member of one of the Church's oldest religious orders. He was never really able to accept two innovations introduced by St. Ignatius: exemption from choir offices and the simple vows taken by Jesuits in formation. As far as the vows were concerned, it seemed to him unjust that a man had to pledge himself in perpetuity, while the Society reserved the right to dismiss him should it later consider him unfit to remain. The pope expressed his opinions on these two points, and Borgia responded through the mediation of Cardinal Pacheco. He cited the solemn approbation granted the Society's Institute by previous popes and by the Council of Trent; he also asserted that an alteration in matters so essential would amount to a substantial change in the structure of the Society's Institute, in terms of which Jesuits pronounced their vows. As for choir, Borgia argued that its imposition would destroy the principle of mobility which the Society considered essential in pursuing its apostolic ministries.

The pope yielded in the matter of the simple vows, even though he introduced a modification that we shall describe below; but, as far as choir was concerned, he maintained his position "in order to insure mutual encouragement to devotion" among Jesuits. But even here he made some qualifications: Scholastics were exempt and during those hours when there were few people in our churches, the requirement would be fulfilled if a few priests, even only two, assisted at choir. When the divine office was not sung, the time spent in choir was, in fact, not very long; nonetheless, Borgia requested that the obligation of choir be put off until the new breviary was published, and the pope granted this extension.[71]

After this storm seemed to have blown itself out, another surprise appeared on the horizon. During the Christmas season of 1566, when some young candidates were scheduled for holy orders, the pope, speaking through his cardinal vicar, ordered that no religious was to be ordained until he had made his solemn profession. This regulation had a strong precedent, for the Council of Trent in the decrees of the twenty-first session specifically stated that diocesan priests were not to be ordained without either guaranteed prebends or hereditary goods to support them. The purpose of this regulation was to obviate the sad spectacle of priests having to beg for their living.

Borgia again represented to the pope the seriousness of this change, explaining that it flouted St. Ignatius's intention of admitting to solemn profession only those subjects who had given proof of their competency and had undergone long periods of testing. Furthermore, he argued, the grade of spiritual coadjutor would for all practical purposes be abolished in the Society. The consequences of all this would be that the Society would either have very few priests or would have to grant the solemn profession without regard for the rigorous selection so firmly desired by its founder. The general also cited the approbations extended by previous popes and by the

Council of Trent to the Society's Institute.

The pope would not accept these arguments and reaffirmed his stance through Cardinal Alciati on June 26, 1567. Borgia's disappointment is reflected in the pages of his spiritual diary. Prayer was his recourse: "Prayers enjoined on the whole Society concerning this matter of profession of the ordinands,"[72] as he wrote on that same day, June 26, 1567 (the word "ordinands" does not appear in its entirety in the manuscript because of a tear in the paper). Similar feelings of dismay spread among the rest of the Society. In a reply to the general on August 14 of that year, Nadal proposed a preliminary solution: For a certain length of time no Jesuits would be ordained; meanwhile, a large number of Masses would be offered that the Lord would have the pope retract his decree. Meanwhile, the pope should be given the assurance that no priest who had to leave the Society would be reduced to the state of begging for his subsistence. If the pope would not change his mind, provision could be made for the ordinands to make the solemn profession of the three vows and then carry on as scholastics or as spiritual coadjutors, something that Julius III had permitted.[73]

The decree that Pius V had framed in broad terms on October 14, 1568, did not leave much room for doubt. Even so, Borgia appealed to the commission of cardinals in charge of implementing this decision and asked if the pope's legislation also applied to the Society. The commission replied that the Society could keep its norms of procedure; in compliance with the papal resolution, however, it must guarantee the welfare of priests who were required to leave the order. But such an interpretation pleased neither the pope nor the Society.

Ultimately, as we gather from contemporary correspondence, candidates for ordination in the Society had to make the profession of the three vows before receiving holy orders. For example, in accord with this policy Father Claudio Acquaviva, a future general of the Society, made his solemn profession of the three vows before being ordained.

This legislation gave rise to serious consequences; for example, there were fewer priests in the Society than there would have been had the pope's order not existed. Also, this new state of affairs caused chagrin among those who had pronounced the simple vows of the spiritual coadjutors. It is not surprising, then, that among the postulates sent to Rome by the provincial congregations of 1571 was a petition that all coadjutors make the solemn profession of the three vows.

Fortunately, on February 28, 1573, Pius V's successor, Pope Gregory XIII, restored to the Society its own modus operandi in this matter. Borgia, however, did not survive to behold his labors and desires bear fruit as the

Institute regained its pristine form.

Pius V and bullfighting – On November 1, 1567, Pius V published an instruction forbidding bullfights. Borgia supported this repressive measure, recommending it to the pope in deference to the wishes of Pietro Camaiani, bishop of Ascoli, who in 1566 had carried out an extraordinary commission in Spain and who had gathered support for his project to outlaw the *corrida*. On the 19th of that same month, Borgia communicated to Father Polanco what he had done: "The Lord Bishop [of Ascoli] is a very dear friend of Ours, and I wish to be of service to him. Indeed I have done so in the matter of the *motu proprio* about bullfighting, which has come out quite nicely, has been published, and will shortly be on its way to Spain."[74] In 1585 Pope Gregory XIII lifted his predecessor's prohibition.

11. Expansion of the Society

A detailed presentation of the Society's expansion lies, strictly speaking, within the purview of the historian of the Jesuit order; the biographer of Francis Borgia, however, cannot avoid giving a cursory description of this expansion since it was the general who was its principal architect. The topic of new foundations appears over and over again in his correspondence. In our treatment of the matter we shall make a distinction between countries on the European continent and those which during his lifetime were considered mission territory.

I. EUROPE

Rome

Ever since the time of St. Ignatius, Rome had been headquarters for the Society. Being, as the Constitutions ([668]) specify, the ordinary place of residence for the general, it was where "the universal is attended to."[1] Rome was important because so many houses of the Society had been established there, and also because of the large number of Jesuits residing there and exercising their apostolates. A center for recruiting new members to the Society, it was at the same time a point of departure for many Jesuits missioned to the various provinces throughout the order.

Houses of the Society — In 1565 the Society had four houses in Rome: the professed house with the novitiate attached, the Roman and German colleges, and the diocesan seminary, entrusted to the order in 1564 and opened in 1565. Added to this list in 1566 was the novitiate of Sant'Andrea al Quirinale and the House of Catechumens; this latter was under the supervision of the Society even though no Jesuit actually lived there. Finally in 1570, members of the Society became penitentiaries of the basilica of St. Peter and took up residence near the Vatican.

Number and deployment of personnel – The combined number of Jesuits residing in these houses was ever on the increase. In 1565 there was a total of 280, of whom 68 were priests; in 1567 there were 300; in 1568, 304; in December of 1571 there were 337, 74 of them priests. The 13 Jesuits residing at the college in Tivoli and the 6 stationed at Frascati did not enter into these totals; the college of Tivoli was a house of rest and recreation, and Frascati depended on the novitiate of Sant'Andrea.

The number of candidates admitted into the Society from different nations was extraordinary. In 1567 there were fifty admitted, excluding those who were already in their first probation. In 1568 there were forty-seven, fewer than in the previous year because other provinces were already beginning to open their own novitiates. Another forty-seven were in their first probation; in 1569 this number was forty-four. Some novices were assigned to the professed house and others to the new novitiate of Sant'Andrea.

If Rome was the main recruitment center, it was also the Society's principal embarkation point. In 1565 forty men were dispatched from Rome to different parts of the world; in 1566 there were more than one hundred; in 1568 the number was again about one hundred; in 1570 there were more than eighty; in 1571, some sixty. On January 3, 1570, someone wrote that "we do not normally send men to Spain because there are plenty there already."

The students at the colleges – It might be of interest to record the number of students educated in the colleges of the Society during these years.

At the end of 1567 the Roman College counted more than 1,000 students enrolled in its classes; 300 of these were theologians, 150 were philosophers or liberal-arts students, and the rest were studying literature. There would have been even more had there been room for them. Except for minor variations, this number remained constant during the ensuing years.

In the German College there were anywhere from 230 to 260 students, depending on the particular year, despite the fact that the maximum number admitted was supposed to be 220. But more often than not administrators had to yield to the forceful importunings of prelates or persons of influence.

The Roman Seminary numbered 150 students, including some 20 Jesuits.

Apostolic ministries – Besides the daily work of teaching, the Society committed itself to ministries proper to its Institute, such as administering the sacraments, preaching, giving the Exercises, teaching catechism, and helping the poor and sick.

Worthy of note here is the progress made in converting Jews. In 1570 thirteen of them were baptized; and there were some twenty persons living in the House of Catechumens, some of these recently baptized and others still taking instructions. The director of this center resided in the professed house.

In his capacity as general, the superior of Jesuits working in Rome, Borgia encouraged all and was second to none in giving example of devotion, humility, and apostolic zeal. In 1566 and in 1570 he personally visited the Roman houses, listening to what his subjects had to say, hearing the confessions of those who came to him, delivering spiritual conferences to his men, and serving them in lowly offices in the kitchen and refectory. In 1569 he directed that each Wednesday a consultation be held at which matters of greater importance for the government of the Society could be discussed; he presided over these gatherings in person.

The church of the Gesù — It soon became evident that there was a desperate need for a spacious church, since the existing church of Santa Maria della Strada had become altogether inadequate. From the very beginning the Fathers wanted a church dedicated to the Holy Name of Jesus, in Italian "Gesù." This structure, whose architecture is so much admired today, took shape thanks to the munificence of Cardinal Alessandro Farnese, grandson of Paul III. He assumed responsibility for the construction, although the Society had to purchase the property for an anticipated price of more than ten thousand ducats. Borgia had to use every bit of his influence to raise this sum of money. On October 12, 1568, he sent Father Diego de Avellaneda letters addressed to a number of Spanish gentry, requesting contributions for what was to be "the best and largest church of the Society, where people [could] come from every nation."[2] Contributions began to arrive. The marquis and marquise of Alcañices sent a donation, acknowledged by Borgia on May 3, 1569; among a good many others, the viceroy of Catalonia, Diego Hurtado de Mendoza, appeared on the list of contributors. While the Fathers awaited gifts from the prince of Portugal and other notables, Borgia offered prayers and Masses for this project and had others do the same.

The first stone of the new church was to be laid on May 25, 1568, but the ceremony had to be postponed until June 26.[3] The following August 30 Borgia was able to inform Father Bustamante that "we have already begun tearing down the houses and laying the foundations for our house's church, which will be, the Lord willing, one of the best in Rome."[4] Borgia's predictions were not illusory, although he himself was not to behold the completion of this Farnesean temple and its consecration in 1584.

Italy

When Borgia was elected general in 1565, the Society had four provinces in Italy: Tuscany or Etruria, Sicily, Naples, and Insubria or Lombardy. Rome had always been under the immediate jurisdiction of the general. In 1567, however, Borgia set up the Roman province, which comprised all the houses in Rome except the professed house, the general's residence, and the colleges of Tuscany or Etruria. "The province[, which] will take the name of Rome, will be designated the Roman province; Your Reverence [Father Cristóbal Rodriguez] will be its provincial,"[5] as Father Polanco wrote on March 8, 1567. Ribadeneira was named superintendent of the houses in Rome while the provincial made his visitations to places at a greater distance from the city.

Borgia did not found many new colleges in Italy, but not for lack of requests. During the course of a single year, 1569, six cities in Sicily alone petitioned that colleges be opened; he turned down requests from Ancona (1565), Montepulciano (1568), Atri, Oristano, and Spoleto (1569), Chieti and Cosenza (1570). The colleges at Amelia and Caltabellota ceased operations during the course of 1567.

New colleges that came into existence in Italy included the one in Turin, the request for which had been approved in 1565 but not implemented until 1567; that of Catanzaro, in 1568; and of Teramo in 1570. This same year saw the beginning of classes in the college of Brescia, which had been in the planning stages ever since 1567. Finally, in 1570 a college in Caltagirone was approved and classes got under way there the following year.

New novitiates were created too. Besides Sant'Andrea al Quirinale in Rome, in 1568 a novitiate opened its doors at Città Sant'Angelo in the province of Teramo, only to close them shortly thereafter; also in 1568 another began receiving novices at Nola, and a third at Novellara, founded in 1570 by Count Camillo Gonzaga and opened in 1571. This novitiate was blessed with an excellent master of novices, Father Antonio Valentino. And finally, we can list the house at Arona, which was opened in 1572.

Special mention should be made of Milan, where since 1564 the Society had operated the seminary and a college annexed to it. In 1567 St. Charles Borromeo, the archbishop who had arranged to bring the Jesuits into his diocese, gave them the church of San Fedele as their residence and college. In 1569 the Fathers laid the cornerstone for a new church, an architectural jewel in the sixteenth-century style. Later on, Borromeo gave the Society the house and church of Santa Maria di Brera so that the college could have its separate building. This church and house had belonged to the order of the Humiliati, which had been suppressed in 1571. The Jesuits, however, continued to reside at San Fedele. Finally, Borromeo expressed his wish for the Society to open a novitiate in his city of Arona. It was inaugurated in 1572, the same year classes began at Brera. The Brera college's new building, erected in 1686, is today the seat of the famous art museum, library, academy, and observatory which bear its name.

Spain and Portugal

During Borgia's tenure as general nine colleges came into existence in Spain; requests for several others were turned down. The general continually bore in mind decree 8 of the Second General Congregation, which had curbed the proliferation of colleges. When Cardinal Espinosa asked for a new college in Sigüenza, Borgia reminded him that the Society "has held back from accepting new foundations, intending to bolster those already begun rather than laying the foundations for new ones."[6] But requests kept coming in and it was not easy to resist them. When John de Ribera was bishop of Badajoz, he asked the Society to erect a college in the town of Fregenal de la Sierra, so that there would be at least one Jesuit college in his diocese. He affirmed that "Your Lordship has no one in Spain nor anywhere else who loves you and who wishes to serve you more than I."[7] When he was installed in his new diocese of Valencia in 1569, he was particularly happy that there was already a college of the Society established there.

The Society had to take stock of its own resources, assuring that there were adequate personnel and financial support. As we have seen above, in addition to providing a residence and church, founders had to guarantee sufficient endowment to support at least twenty men before the Society would consider accepting a college. If an established endowment was not forthcoming, then a pledge had to be secured ensuring enough contributions to meet all requirements.

When he could not honor a petition for a new college, Borgia would offer the city whose request he had declined one or two priests to preach a mission in the general vicinity.

Here is a list of colleges established in Spain during Borgia's generalate. The colleges of Marchena (1567) and Baeza (1571) were begun in the province of Andalucía; in the Toledo province there were colleges founded in Navalcarnero (1565), Sigüenza and Segura de la Sierra (1569), Caravaca, Huete, and Oropesa (1570). The sources are not always perfectly consistent regarding the founding year of a number of these colleges. In the years we have given above the Jesuit communities began to function and to hold classes.

An effort was made to consolidate colleges already in existence. Such a policy made it possible to keep afloat the college at Burgos, founded by the constable Iñigo Fernández de Velasco, who had turned over to it an endowment left by Cardinal Mendoza. Endowments at the college of Córdoba provided forty ducats per man per year for the support of thirty-four Jesuits. In 1570 there were 560 students enrolled in this college, 60 of them inscribed in the theology course. The college of Belén was built in Barcelona thanks to the generosity of Doña María Manrique de Lara, who had to be wheedled into accepting the title of "Foundress" of this, "her college"; however, the catalogue of 1571 informs us that the college of Barcelona lived on donations as opposed to an endowment. Naturally, Borgia continued his interest in the college at Gandía because, "when I have in view the good of the college of Gandía, I am attending to the good of our own native parts."[8]

Borgia likewise showed an interest in opening professed houses, establishing three in Spain during his generalate: one at Toledo, which became operational in 1566 after being in the planning stage since 1558; one at Valladolid, founded in 1567; and one at Burgos, in 1571.

Germany, Austria, and Flanders

Ever since the time of St. Ignatius, countries in central and northern Europe exercised a particular attraction to the Society. Already in 1556 houses and colleges founded in these parts of the continent were combined into the Jesuit provinces of Upper Germany and Lower Germany. In 1564 Austria was the first province to be cut off from Lower Germany, and then in 1574 Poland was separated from Austria. In 1563 the province of Lower Germany was also divided into the provinces of the Rhine and of Flanders, which sometimes was referred to as Lower Germany.

After the first division in 1556, the colleges of Ingolstadt, Munich, Innsbruck, and Dillingen belonged to the province of Upper Germany, whose provincial was Peter Canisius until 1569, when he was succeeded by Father Paulus Hoffaeus. The colleges of Vienna, Prague, and Tyrnau were put under the jurisdiction of the Austrian province, whose provincial, Belgian Father Nicolas Lanoy, was succeeded by Italian Father Lorenzo Maggio in 1566. The province of the Rhine numbered within its territory the colleges of Cologne, Trier, and Mainz; its first provincial was Belgian Father Anton Vinck, followed in 1571 by Father Hermann Thyraeus. The Belgian Everard Mercurian governed the province of Flanders with colleges established at Louvain, Tournai, and Cambrai, as well as the newly founded colleges in Antwerp and Dinant.

Such was the state of affairs in the north when Father Francis Borgia was elected general in 1565. Even while commissary general in Spain, Borgia had shown that he was fully aware of Germany's serious needs. In 1557 he wrote, "Ever since it first began forty years ago, heresy has made such constant progress in Germany that today this nation is all but totally lost, and it has contaminated many other nations."[9] Two remedies were tried: The German College was founded in Rome and other colleges were established throughout Germany, with the result that "many Germans enter and seek admission into the Society." These men the Society could not support without the help and charity of Catholics; so it appealed for assistance in this noble enterprise, "so that helped by their charity and alms, the Society will be able to educate Germans in their religion for the purpose of aiding that nation, seeing the need is so crucial and the work so essential."[10]

During his term as general new colleges were founded in Germany, "established by the secular princes and the prelates," as he wrote to John of Avila on April 16, 1567.[11] In Germany, too, they tried to consolidate existing colleges rather than found new ones, following regulations laid down by the Second General Congregation; nonetheless, new colleges were inaugurated at Speyer, Würzburg, and Fulda. Moreover, the college begun at Hall in the Tyrol also belonged to the Upper German province.

Since 1566 negotiations to found a college in Speyer had been going on at the request of its bishop and cathedral chapter, but the final decision was not taken until 1569. This college was assigned to the province of the Rhine.

The plans to found a college in Würzburg in 1566 came to fruition with the beginning of classes on November 17, 1567.

The college in Fulda was begun in 1571.

Discussions about establishing a college in Augsburg were carried on during the whole of Borgia's generalate, but nothing was settled until 1582. Prince Cardinal Otto von Truchsess gave impetus to this undertaking; under his administration a great part of the city turned to Catholicism, thanks also to the zeal of Peter Canisius, who took time from his duties as provincial of the order to preach in Augsburg's cathedral. The Fuggers and the emperor Maximilian II himself also supported plans to found this college, in the face of stern opposition from the city and the cathedral chapter.

A college with a long history was located at Hall (now Solbad Hall), a Tyrolean town near Innsbruck. Here three of Ferdinand I's daughters, Magdalena, Margareta, and Helena, had retreated to dedicate their lives to God without formal religious vows. Now they wanted the Fathers of the

Society who had been their confessors to follow them to Hall, offering as an incentive the promise to found a college there. After an initial negative reply from Borgia, Ferdinand, archduke of Tyrol and brother of the princesses (or "the queens," as they were usually called), fired off a peremptory letter to the general on March 30, 1569. Borgia had no alternative but to yield, and thus in this same year of 1569 the college at Hall came into being. Father Jerome Nadal, who as early as 1566 was already lamenting "all the trouble these three princesses have caused,"[12] retired to this college toward the end of his life, from 1574 to 1577; here, in the midst of other apostolic endeavors, he wrote his famous meditations on the Gospels, first published in his illustrated edition of 1593.

In Flanders the colleges of Saint Omer's and Douai were founded in 1567 and 1568 respectively.

During Borgia's term of office the Austrian province opened the novitiate of Brno in Moravia (1572), as well as colleges in Pultusk, Poznan, Olomouc, and Vilna. The first two are in modern-day Poland; the third was built in Moravia and the fourth in Lithuania. We shall say a few words about each of these.

Poland, Lithuania, and Czechoslovakia

To a great extent the Jesuits came to Poland because of the interest shown by Cardinal Stanislaus Hosius, bishop of Warmia or Ermland in East Prussia, a concern he shared with the papal nuncio, Giovanni Francesco Commendone. On August 30, 1564, the first Jesuits left Rome for Poland, intent on founding a college in Braunsburg, today Braniewo, in Prussia. In September 1565 Father Stanislaus Rosdrazovius and his companions were sent to found a college at Pultusk. First appointed superintendent of the college of Braunsberg, Father Baltasar Hostovinus was shortly afterwards transferred to Austria. His replacement was the rector of the college, Father Francisco Sunyer, a native of Barcelona, who in 1574 was named the first provincial of the new Polish province, only recently separated from Austria; he remained in this office until his death in 1580.

In 1570 a novitiate was opened at Braunsberg, in a part of the building separated from the scholastics' quarters.

After it was agreed that the church and residence at Poznan were to be handed over to the Society, a college was founded there toward the end of 1571.

A request from the diocesan bishop of Lithuania's capital city of Vilna won a favorable response in 1570, and the Jesuits went to take over the college the following July. They opened a novitiate there as well, which at first was attached to the college but later had its own separate facilities.

Bishop Wilhelm Prussinov of Olmütz (today Olomouc in Czechoslovakia) invited the Society to found a college in that Moravian city. This college opened its doors in 1566, with Father Hurtado Pérez appointed as the first rector. He was a native of Mula, a town in the Spanish province of Murcia. In 1569 the Fathers moved into a new residence.

Founded in 1561, the college of Tyrnau (Trnava in present-day Czechoslovakia) was destroyed by fire and had to close in 1567; but, after the efforts to reopen this college proved successful, it began anew in 1615.

France

Instead of seeing its efforts greeted by the usual success, the Society met with serious roadblocks in France. First, there was the opposition from the University of Paris, already hostile during St. Ignatius's lifetime; then there were the civil wars with the Huguenots which had left in their wake a divided country, morally and materially bankrupt. Bound as they were by a special vow of obedience to the pope, the Jesuits were viewed as enemies of the special liberties of the church in France at a time when the university and the Paris parlement regarded themselves as the committed trustees of the Gallican liberties. By the beginning of Borgia's term, echos of the passionate diatribes against the Society delivered in the parlement by the university's counselor, Etienne Pasquier, were ringing throughout the land.[13] On April 5, 1565, the Parlement postponed a decision *sine die* until it could further investigate the case against the Society. Despite these setbacks, the Jesuits made headway not only in Paris but in the rest of France as well. The Society relied on the support of Charles IX, who in July 1565 granted a patent authorizing the order to found houses and colleges throughout the land.

In 1564, shortly before his death, Father Laínez divided the Society in France into two provinces, France properly so-called and Aquitaine. Father Olivier Mannaerts was appointed provincial in the former and Father Edmond Auger in the latter. The province of France counted among its colleges those of Paris, Billom, Mauriac, and Verdun, whereas the colleges at Avignon, Chambéry, Lyons, Rodez, Toulouse, and Tournon fell within the confines of the Aquitaine province.

High-powered negotiations preceded the creation of other colleges. In 1569 the general agreed to conditions authorizing the foundation of the college of Rouen, so earnestly sponsored by Cardinal de Bourbon. Its actual opening was put off, however, because of the opposition shown by the cathedral canons and the civil authorities of Rouen.

At the insistence of the archbishop of Bordeaux, plans were made to establish a Jesuit presence in that city. Borgia became personally involved in the negotiations when he passed through Bordeaux during his trip to France in 1572. On August 18 of this year he signed the contract to open a college there. Classes were held for the first time on the following October 1, literally just a few hours after the general's death. On June 3 of that year he also signed a contract providing for the establishment of a college in Nevers. Contemporary correspondence indicates that other cities were considered as possible sites for colleges, such as Metz and Poitiers.

The membership of the Society in France was also increasing. Two novitiates cared for the formation of novices, one at Billom for the province of France and another at Tournon for the province of Aquitaine.

Among eminent men of this period we should single out Fathers Mannaerts and Auger, who distinguished themselves as superiors; the same Father Auger and Father Antonio Possevino proved themselves outstanding preachers; and Fathers Juan de Maldonado, Juan Mariano, and Pierre-Jean Perpinien earned fame as professors. Father Perpinien, or Juan Perpinyà, as he was baptized in his native town of Elche in the ancient kingdom of Valencia, was a Spanish humanist of renown who died in 1566 in Paris at the early age of thirty-six, disappointing the high hopes for his future that many had entertained.

II. THE AMERICAS

Florida

One of the great glories of the third general of the Society was having founded the missions in Spanish American territories. Writing on March 20, 1571, to Pedro Menéndez de Avilés, *adelantando* and governor of Florida, he informed him that

> the Institute and purpose of this our Society . . . [is] to go to the assistance of people who have the greatest need and who are in the greatest danger of perishing, because it is our vocation to do so. . . . This is why Ours go with such dispatch throughout the world and why the few presently now in Florida have gone there.[14]

Florida was in fact the Society's first mission in Spanish America.

Even as early as St. Ignatius's time, many attempts were made to send Jesuits to these mission fields; other obstacles, however, stood in the way, especially the policy regulations of the Council of the Indies that accepted missionaries exclusively from four older religious orders, the Augustinians, Dominicans, Franciscans, and Mercedarians.

The one who brought about a change in policy was the governor referred to above, namely, Menéndez de Avilés. In March 1565 he petitioned Philip II to have a few Jesuits sent to Florida, and the king acceded to his request. On March 3, 1566, the king wrote to Borgia, asking him to send twenty-four Jesuits to "the Indies of the Ocean Sea."[15] This was the letter that opened up to the Society the missions of Spanish America.

Borgia complied with King Philip's wishes, assigning the first three Jesuits to the Florida mission, Fathers Pedro Martínez and Juan Rogel and Brother Francisco Villarreal. They set sail on June 28, 1566, and, after a series of sudden and unexpected adventures, landed at last on Florida's coast. From the very first days it became quite evident that this mission was off to an ominous start. On one of his first apostolic ventures Father Martínez was brutally cut down by the local natives on October 6 of that year, 1566. Two more groups of Jesuits were sent to Florida. The first, composed of Fathers Juan Bautista Segura, who was vice-provincial, Gonzalo del Alamo and Antonio Sedeño, in addition to three Brothers, arrived in 1568. One priest and two brothers constituted the second of these expeditions, which arrived in 1570. But this noble beginning did not lead to the hoped-for success. Several factors doomed the Florida mission: the opposition of the natives toward the Spaniards and in particular toward the missionaries; the nomadic life to which these natives were accustomed; and, finally, their cruelty. The Jesuits met an Indian named after his sponsor, the viceroy of New Spain, Don Luis de Velasco. Telling them about Ajacán, a friendlier country to the north, he offered to guide them there. In the first part of February 1571, the apostate Don Luis and his henchmen murdered Father Segura and his seven companions at a spot a few miles from the historic U.S. cities of Yorktown and Williamsburg, in the state of Virginia. Over a period of time some consideration was given to the feasibility of establishing a college in Havana. Since this city was the gateway to America, a college there seemed promising, but the final decision was to give preference to the mission of New Spain. So Fathers Rogel and Sedeño joined the expedition sent to Mexico in 1572.

Mexico

In 1572 the first Jesuits arrived in Mexico. The City of Mexico had petitioned Philip II in 1570 to have members of the Society sent there. In a letter of March 1571 to Father Manuel López, provincial of Toledo, the king expressed his desire that twelve Jesuits be assigned to New Spain, a request he repeated in a letter of May 4 to Borgia. The king's wish was implemented without delay; by June a number of priests and brothers had been selected to go to this mission. Father Pedro Sánchez, rector of the college of Alcalá, was appointed superior of the new province; and Borgia dispatched letters to the Spanish provincials, indicating the names of those he was sending to Mexico. It was providential that the general arrived in Madrid toward the end of September 1571, accompanying Cardinal Alessandrino, because he was thus able to organize this expedition. After conferring in Spain with Father Pedro Sánchez, he decided that the number of those to be sent should be increased to fifteen. In October, without further ado, he drew up the "Memoranda to Father Don Pedro Sánchez and to those who are going with him to New Spain."[16] In this instruction he assigned each missionary his particular office and outlined norms for carrying out his apostolic mission. Until they were well established in the country, he wrote, they were not to accept any college besides the one in Mexico City. They should undertake only ministries proper to the Society and should eschew the responsibility associated with being pastor of a parish church. All should be very conscious of religious poverty, not accepting stipends for their ministries and avoiding all types of avarice.

As was almost always the case in those days, a number of complications held up their departure. There was also a change in the assignment of personnel to the mission. Finally, however, on June 15, 1572, Father Sánchez and his fourteen companions embarked from the port of Sanlúcar de Barrameda, arriving in Mexico City on September 28, two days before Borgia's death. As already indicated, the survivors of the ill-fated Florida mission, Fathers Juan Rogel and Antonio Sedeño and four lay Brothers, came from Havana to join the expedition.

Borgia was not able to do more than to set in motion the glorious Mexican mission and to dictate the first regulations guiding its development; nevertheless, this Jesuit province justifiably considers him its founder and has chosen him as its special patron.

Peru

The Spanish viceroyalty of Peru, founded in 1543, took in the whole of South America except Brazil. Once this vast territory had been conquered, after Francisco Pizarro had founded the City of Kings (Lima) in 1535, and after the Inca emperor Sayri-Tupac had submitted to Pizarro's rule in 1558, the period of colonization got under way. As far as religious matters were concerned, it was the Augustinians, Dominicans, Franciscans, and Mercedarians who labored in this territory alongside the secular clergy.

The remote origins of the Jesuit mission go back to an initiative of the bishop of Popayán, a city in present-day Colombia. In 1565 this Augustinian prelate wrote to Francis Borgia, at the time vicar-general of the Society, requesting that Jesuits be sent to his diocese. Borgia deferred the decision to whoever would be elected general; since he himself was the one chosen, it fell to him to launch the Jesuit mission in Peru. But everything depended on the Council of the Indies, whose policy, as we have already seen, was to select missionaries for the Americas exclusively from the four older orders. On March 3, 1566, however, the Council of the Indies finally opened its territories to the Society. Philip II likewise was favorable to this initiative and addressed a "prayer and petition" to Borgia that he send twenty-four Jesuits to the Americas, twelve to Mexico and the same number to Peru.[17] Borgia complied with his request.

But a difficulty arose because of the shortage of available personnel. The chief reason for this lack was Pius V's order that no one was to be ordained until he had first made his religious profession. Not even the expedient of admitting ordinands to the profession of the three vows could increase the number of men ordained because one had to be in the Society seven years from the date of entrance before ordination. This explains why we find a large number of nonpriests, both scholastics and coadjutor brothers, among those sent to the Americas. There was certainly no lack of volunteers. Many generously offered themselves to this apostolate, and Borgia's fixed policy was to send only volunteers to the missions.

There were three different parties of missionaries sent to Peru during Borgia's term as general. The first, made up of eight Jesuits, disembarked from the customary port of Sanlúcar de Barrameda on November 2, 1567; they arrived at Cartegena in present-day Colombia on December 24; then on January 19 they were in Panamá; on March 28 they set sail from the port of Callao and entered the city of Lima on April 1. Heading this expedition was Father Jerónimo Ruiz de Portillo (c. 1532-89), who in 1567 was named provincial of all Jesuits missioned to Spanish America. Besides being a preacher of great renown, he was an excellent superior; he deserves credit for a good part of the success of this enterprise.

In 1568 a new viceroy was appointed to the viceroyalty of Peru. He was Francisco de Toledo, brother of Fernando Alvarez de Toledo, count of Oropesa, a great friend of the Jesuits, who persuaded the Society to found a college in his city in 1570. This new viceroy played an active role in organizing the second party of Jesuits assigned to Peru; for he was eager to have missionaries there, to such an extent that he wished to choose personally those who were to be sent and proposed that Father Martín Gutiérrez be appointed commissary. He had to be told that selecting men destined for the missions was the prerogative of the general and that, because there was already a provincial in Peru at the time, the office of commissary would be redundant.

Twelve Jesuits constituted this second party sent to Peru, one of whom, Father Juan García, died en route to Panamá. The Fathers and Brothers in this group set sail March 19, 1569, in one of four ships which made up the new viceroy's fleet, bound for the Panamanian port of Nombre de Dios. Because they were held up in Panamá for three months, they did not arrive in Callao until November 8 of that year.

The third expedition departed for Peru on April 27, 1572, including in its number the well-known theologian, missiologist, and humanist, Father José de Acosta. As soon as he arrived in Peru he added courses in theology to the arts and philosophy courses already being taught.

The apostolic endeavors of the Peru mission were to be in conformity with regulations handed down by the general. The first of these directives was contained in an instruction to Father Portillo in March 1567. Given the small number of men in the field, Jesuits were not to scatter to various places; instead, they were to have a fixed place of operation, with a residence and church of their own. They should give priority to the care of those already baptized and only afterwards work for the conversion of non-Christians. They should not bite off more than they could chew. In conformity with the pope's directives, they should not baptize people before they had undergone a suitable period of catechetical training. They should try to convert the native leaders, for the others would easily follow the example of their chiefs. No doubt recalling the bitter Florida experience, Borgia recommended that the missionaries be slow to put their lives in jeopardy because, even though to give up one's life in this undertaking would be a personal gain the common good demanded that they be cautious with their lives, given the small number of those spreading the Gospel message. Missionaries should confine themselves to activities proper to their missionary vocation and give satisfaction both to those in charge of governing the land and to the community at large.

In a letter of the following year, 1568, Borgia discussed the policy the Fathers should adopt in dealing with the *encomenderos* question. This was a delicate matter because these owners who had carved out large estates (*encomiendas*) acted as if they were feudal lords and the subjected Indians serfs. "I have already advised you about this matter," he wrote, "and again I commend it to you because it is of the utmost importance: [Jesuits] should not make it their policy to absolve or to condemn either the *conquistadores* of the Indies or the heirs of their great wealth and the like."[18] If other religious orders which have already spent so much time in the territory find it difficult to make a decision on this thorny question, Jesuits, who have only recently entered the country, should not step in with a judgment. They ought to show themselves "indifferent until, as it is hoped, the universities and scholars who have been commissioned by His Majesty come up with an agreement on this matter."[19] On this particular point, we should briefly note here that the Jesuits were faced with the problem of passing judgment on those Spaniards who had come to Peru and become rich. One Jesuit in particular, Father Bartolomé Hernández, one of the most distinguished Fathers who had come in the second expedition, and who had been appointed vice-provincial, remembered what he had heard in the lecture halls of Salamanca about this problem: "My teachers were Fra Domingo de Soto and Fra Pedro de Sotomayor and many other learned scholars, and I heard from them that the first arrivals used unconscionable methods and that those who had acquired lands there through these means were in much danger from their consciences."[20] It was for this reason that the good Father had serious misgivings about acting as confessor to the viceroy; he did not want to have to tackle problems touching on matters such as these.

As soon as they arrived in Peru the Jesuits put into practice the directives given them by the general. First, they set up a solid base in Lima, founding a college on a piece of property given to them. Valued in excess of fifteen thousand ducats, it was located in the heart of the city. In 1570 the college of Cuzco was founded; and toward the end of Borgia's generalate Juan de Ribas, a wealthy citizen of La Paz, offered to found a college for the Jesuits in what today is the capital of Bolivia. Father Portillo recommended that the general accept his offer.

Besides teaching, the Jesuits undertook ministries proper to the Society: "preaching, confessing, visiting hospitals and prisons, operating schools for small children, teaching Christian doctrine in the streets, aiding the dying, and directing individuals."[21] In undertaking excursions to catechize the Indians, they did so under safe conditions and were careful not to put too much distance between themselves and headquarters. Apart from this, life proceeded in an ordinary way, "just as at a college in Spain," as Father Diego de Bracamonte wrote in 1569.[22] The result of these ministries was by no means meager. People came from every quarter to the Fathers of the Society and were so generous in giving alms that the colleges of Lima and Cuzco were able to get along on these alone without having to depend on a fixed endowment. The Jesuits also enjoyed the goodwill of the authorities both civil and ecclesiastical, in particular, that of the Dominican archbishop of Lima, Jerónimo de Loaysa.

In no time excellent candidates began entering the Society. The treasurer of the audiencia, the dean of the Lima cathedral, and a canon of the Cuzco cathedral were among those who entered the Society in 1569. On the other hand, there was some objection to admitting Indians and candidates of mixed blood because of the fear that these were unstable; so they had to be over twenty years of age before they would be considered. As he did everywhere, Borgia endeavored to erect a novitiate with its own master of novices in Peru; for the time being this novitiate was established in a separate section of the college of Lima.

In selecting apostolates, he tried to follow what was prescribed by the Society's Institute, resisting pressures from the viceroy, who wanted the Jesuits to take on every type of ministry. The source of most of the problems in this area were the so-called *doctrinas* or parishes. The Constitutions of the Society explicitly rule out the "curacy of souls" ([588]). The Fathers explained to the viceroy the reasons their apostolates should not include pastoral care of parishes, but they failed to convince him or lessen his chagrin. His argument was that they had been brought out precisely for this work; in his judgment, if they did not accept parishes, they would be of little use to him in what he considered an essential ministry. He sent Father Bracamonte to Europe to resolve the problem before the superiors of the Society. The Jesuits replied that they could be "coadjutors to the parish priest," exercising all ministries except that of pastor. But despite all these objections, they did accept two *doctrinas*, one in Huarochirí and the other at Santiago del Cercado, an Indian town near Lima. The first one had to be given up when it became clear that it was not really necessary.

If the multiplication of houses was deliberately curtailed, the number of personnel was always on the increase, thanks to reinforcements coming from Spain and vocations recruited in the field. According to the 1569 catalogue there were thirty Jesuits in the country, of whom five were priests and the rest divided between scholastics and coadjutor brothers. The annual letter of 1570 lists forty-four Jesuits in Lima, twelve of whom were priests. The 1572 catalogue, the last issued during Borgia's tenure of office, shows ten priests among the thirty-five Jesuits at the college of Lima and eight men at Cuzco, two of whom were priests.

In Peru the Society did not experience the misfortunes that had so bedeviled its early days in Florida. Here the problems came from a lack of understanding on the part of a few. Faithful to the mind of Ignatius, Borgia advised Jesuits not to fear persecutions, for persecution "is a gift of God our Lord to the Society, which will never lack for persons to put it into effect."[23]

Borgia looked on the Peru mission with particularly sympathetic eyes. In a letter to Father Portillo in 1570, he declared that at the present time there was an opportunity to open up a mission in New Spain; however, with the scarcity of men, "it would be better for the time being to go ahead with the mission in Peru."[24] Still, as we have shown in the previous section, this predilection for Peru did not prevent him from dispatching missionaries to Mexico in 1572.

Brazil

St. Ignatius had founded the Jesuit province of Brazil in 1553. In 1566 there were 33 Jesuits there. In 1568 this total had gone up to 61, counting the novices, and in 1571 it had reached 101.

Among the institutional endowments set up during Borgia's term as general, we should single out the gift King Sebastian of Portugal gave to the college of Rio de Janeiro in 1568. This was a guaranteed endowment covering expenses for sixty religious at the college. However, the most impressive incident of this period and the one that stands out in Borgia's correspondence was the visitation and martyrdom of Father Ignatius de Azevedo and his companions.

Ignatius de Azevedo, an outstanding example of the saintly religious and fervent apostle, was appointed visitor to Brazil on February 24, 1566. On that same day the general addressed an instruction to the visitor describing how he was to carry out his office. Azevedo began his visitation after he arrived back in Brazil that August, but two years later he was elected a delegate by his province to the congregation of procurators. He arrived in Rome toward the end of May 1569, where he had the opportunity to discuss with Borgia the matter of recruiting men for Brazil, a territory greatly in need of reinforcements. Borgia generously welcomed the requests of the visitor, and arranged that the Spanish provinces should also offer a levy of missionaries to supplement recruits from the province of Portugal. Borgia wrote to the Spanish provincials about this. Armed with the general's authority, Azevedo visited several colleges of the Society in Spain and enlisted ten companions (one of whom, Francisco Pérez de Godoy, was a relative of St. Teresa). The expedition assembled in Portugal, eighty-seven persons in all, bound for Brazil; seventy-three of these were Jesuits and the others secular officials.

After they divided into three groups, Azevedo embarked on the *Santiago*, sailing from Lisbon on June 5, 1570. On June 12, they put in at the harbor of Funchal on the island of Madeira, and on the 30th they steered toward the Canaries. During this crossing, the ship was attacked on July 15 by French Huguenots under the command of Jacques Sore. Azevedo and his thirty-nine companions were cruelly martyred. Azevedo faced his final torture openly professing his faith and clutching in his hands the painting of the Blessed Virgin presented to him by Francis Borgia as he left Rome. Nearly all his companions who had remained in Madeira hoping to continue their journey to Brazil also suffered martyrdom.

III. INDIA AND EAST ASIA

During Borgia's generalate the vast territories that extended from India to Japan, including the islands in between, continued to constitute the Jesuit province of India. Its provincial was Portuguese Father Antonio de Quadros, with headquarters in Goa. Since 1567 Borgia had considered sending a visitor to these territories, just as he had done for the other provinces of the Society. After a series of consultations he chose Father Gonçalo Alvares, superior of the residence of San Roque in Lisbon, who eventually began his eastward voyage in 1568. Even before the visitor had been appointed, however, Borgia wrote out an instruction dated January 10, 1567, outlining what he wanted done in those lands. He supplemented this with another instruction dated October 1 of that year.

The Jesuit province took in India properly so-called, Malacca, China, Japan, and the Moluccas or Spice Islands. Ethiopia and Mozambique, where there were some Jesuits, were also considered parts of this province.

Naturally, India played the preponderant role because of the large number of houses and personnel located there. The main college was still functioning in Goa; in 1569 it housed 107 Jesuits. Besides being involved in the ordinary ministries of the Society, the Fathers at this college offered one course in the arts or philosophy and three in grammar or the humanities. Also in operation there was a novitiate, which in 1569 accommodated twelve novices; in 1572 this number had increased to eighteen. There was also a college at Bassein, near modern-day Bombay, and another at Cochin in Kerala, in addition to residences in a number of cities in the south of India.

Jesuits had served in Japan ever since St. Francis Xavier arrived there in August 1549. Upon leaving Japan in November 1551 he left behind his companion, Father Cosme de Torres, a native of Valencia, who died in the city of Shiki on October 2, 1570. Borgia demonstrated that he was aware of the importance of the Japanese mission; for instance, on December 20, 1565, he wrote a letter to Father Provincial Antonio Quadros in which he recommended this mission to him in a special way.

> Your Reverence should take particular care of that part of your province, because the wonderful success that God our Lord gives in respect to the conversion and the constancy and the spiritual progress of these people seems to us here a sign of His divine will for us to cooperate where He labors so much, and where we enter through the door that He opens to the Gospel for the welfare of these provinces.[25]

In the 1565/66 catalogue we find the names of thirteen Jesuits laboring in Japan, seven of whom were priests and six brothers. The catalogue of 1572 lists fifteen Jesuits, ten Fathers and five brothers. Among these were such distinguished names as Father Nicolão Organtino, as Father Gnecchi Soldo was called. This native of Brescia in northern Italy also acquired the epithet Apostle of Miyako, a city in the prefecture of Kyoto. Also listed in this catalogue was Portuguese Father Luis Fróis, who wrote the history of the mission from 1549 to 1594. Borgia had recommended to the visitor, Father Alvares, that if at all possible he should be sure to visit Jesuits residing in Malacca, the Moluccas, Japan, and China. Father Alvares did visit Malacca in 1572; from there he made his way to Macao, and then in 1573 sailed for Japan. En route he was lost in a shipwreck at sea on July 21.

As we have said, Borgia also concerned himself with the Molucca Islands. Ever since 1546, when St. Francis Xavier had stopped over in the islands of Ambon, Ternate, and Morotai, Jesuits had been at work in the Moluccas. The catalogue of 1571 lists fourteen names, although in reality only ten were actively engaged in that apostolate. The mind of the general is clearly reflected in a letter he wrote to the provincial, Antonio de Quadros, on November 29, 1569. He said that missionaries should be sent to these faraway islands, cautioning, though, that volunteers would not be equal to the demands "unless they were strongly grounded in the desire to suffer."[26] On another occasion, he showed his apostolic zeal when he confessed that seeing such "a small number [of missionaries] for so great a harvest arouses great compassion in us."[27]

As we have already indicated, the province of India also embraced

China, where a small number of Jesuits worked. The Society maintained a house and school at Macao.

As far as Ethiopia was concerned, the catalogue of 1572 listed the name of the heroic patriarch Andrés de Oviedo, who succeeded in penetrating that empire in 1557; and it also gave the names of three other priests and one brother.

Moreover, there were two priests and one brother laboring in Mozambique. This same catalogue of 1572, the year of Borgia's death, recorded the grand total of 185 Jesuits belonging to the province of India.

12.   Borgia's Interior Life

A biography of St. Francis Borgia would be incomplete if made no attempt to penetrate the secrets of his interior life, even though the mass of details we have assembled so far would alone suffice to prove Borgia a man totally consecrated to God. The administrative activities and preoccupations of his office did not hinder the development of his interior life or the rhythm of his life of prayer.

Let us focus on the final period of his life, his period of full maturity. His spiritual diary, which has fortunately survived in his own handwriting, will serve as our guide. Such a document of course lends itself to a variety interpretations. As a biographer I shall present my own.

Other first-generation Jesuits also kept spiritual journals. It is enough to recall merely two examples among many, those of St. Ignatius and Father Nadal. As we read these diaries we can clearly perceive that, although living under the same rule and within the framework of the same animating principles proper to the same religious order, each individual has his particular way of finding God and is led by God along his own particular path. St. Ignatius maintained that "it seemed to him that there was no greater mistake in spiritual things than to want to direct others by the criterion of oneself." He said this "referring to the long hours he had spent in prayer," but the principle applies to all aspects of an individual's spiritual life.[1]

When we compare Borgia's spiritual diary with Ignatius's, we are struck by the differences. First, they vary in length. Ignatius's journal, or at least that part of it which survives, covers a brief period, little more than one year; Borgia's begins on February 1, 1564, and continues until the beginning of 1570 (all of 1569 was written in a "new book" which is no longer extant). Ignatius's spiritual diary focuses on his deliberations about a single dominant theme—how the poverty to be observed by churches of the Society should be defined in the Society's Constitutions; Borgia's follows the train of the most heterogeneous events. Ignatius's diary discloses his mystical ascents, with a certain monotony; Borgia is more diversified, inspired by the changing circumstances of everyday life. A characteristic of Ignatius's journal is the mention of tears; Borgia does not speak of tears but continually refers to something equivalent—consolation, almost always mentioned in connection with hope.

Borgia's spiritual diary is a journal of prayer. We must therefore examine the nature of his prayer.

Prayer of petition

On the first page we find this note: "1564; reviewed; a year of petitions."[2] Indeed, it is. The entire spiritual diary records on paper the petitions Borgia made to God daily and hourly. His prayer was a prayer of supplication. We do not find here long considerations or protracted colloquies.

We do not know how much time Borgia dedicated to personal prayer during this period of his life. We do know that he made his prayer during the early morning hours. On March 20, 1565, he wrote, "Decided to make my prayer on arising and then say Mass" (780).[3] At times his Mass apparently preceded his prayer: "Mass very early in the morning, and prayer after Mass" (849). On June 13, 1568, he proposed: "This week: (1) going to bed, arising, Mass, reading at table, and rest, in prayer as the center " (881). On one occasion he noted: "read something from Scripture before prayer" (858). He tells us that he goes to prayer "to do the Lord's will and to so that He may build up the soul and repair what is out of order" (796).

Besides the time he set aside for mental and vocal prayer, he also practiced what he many times called continuous prayer. This consisted in directing to God one or several intentions, distributing them over the various hours of the day and night. This calls to mind exercises the practice of other saints. Speaking of the prayer of desire, St. Augustine wrote, "Your very desire is prayer, and continuous desire is continuous prayer."[4] Borgia would divide the day into equal blocks of several hours, for example, seven or eight.

An example: on February 1, 1566, he offered "continuous prayer for seven intentions: (1) the Church, (2) the sovereign pontiff, (3) Germany, (4) Francis, (5) persons devoted to me, relatives, benefactors, (6) scruples, (7) other matters" (815).

Sometimes he prayed for his personal intentions. Thus, on May 11, 1567:

> Asked again the 24 graces of each day. (1) To be an oblation
> and sacrifice through Christ to the Father. (2) To be dying
> for Him. (3) To be food for the sheep, with the senses, etc.,

giving myself out of love. (4) To continuously praise the works of the Lord in the soul. (5) To receive the favors ordained from eternity. (6) To feel shame "in every place of his dominion" [Ps. 102:22], for I am unworthy, etc., to stand. (7) To ask pardon for the bitterness I have given Him by the gall at the cross. (8) To say "I thirst," experiencing the pains of the cross. (850)

He begs for the twenty-four hours of the day the intercession of Christ, Mary, and a number of saints (734). Each hour he asks to put into practice one of Christ's virtues (740). He desires that each hour mean the beginning of a new life for him: "To offer each hour as if my life for Christ were beginning" (742). On May 28, 1564, feast of the Most Holy Trinity, he asked for a number of graces, divided up among the twenty-four hours of the day "for myself and for everyone" (746).

He often dedicated each of the hours of the day to praying for the various provinces and houses of the Society or for particular persons. For example, he prayed for a specific intention in 1566 when Pope Pius V assigned some of the Fathers to the Diet of Augsburg, and in 1564/65, when the Turks laid siege to Malta.

Anniversaries

He recalled the anniversaries of the most important events of his life: October 28, his birthday; May 1, the anniversary of the death of the empress Isabel; the eve of the Ascension, the day he of his first vows in the Society; February 1, the day of his solemn profession; October 31, the day of his "exodus from Egypt," his flight to Portugal after his spiritual writings were proscribed by the Inquisition; July 2, the anniversary of "the day of my cross," when he was elected general. He also recalled the anniversary dates of the deaths of Father Laínez and St. Ignatius.

Confusion

The graces he asks the Lord to grant him reveal to us the salient themes of his prayer. In the spiritual diary these are mingled helter-skelter. To lay bare the character of Borgia's spiritual life, we may arrange these themes in a certain order. Borgia did not spin out theories; he lets his soul speak at the impulse of grace. However, let us let him to speak for himself; rather than much commentary, the reader will prefer to see his exact words.

Let us begin with the spirit of "confusion" which is so characteristic of Borgia's spirituality. In the last stages of his life he expresses this idea with special nuances. It is no longer it the fruit of self-knowledge, which he had stressed at the beginning of his conversion. "I will ask for the spirit of confounding myself in every respect and for the spirit of confusion" (742). He still feels himself a sinner. On Carnival Sunday of 1564, the Sunday before Ash Wednesday, "he felt grief at what he had done on this day of Quinquagesima in days gone by" (779). "To ask that the heart that offended may enjoy nothing" (732). Confusion "because, even while snatching me from hell, He also let me know that there is no place that is not more than I deserve" (749). He wants to live like a man being led from prison and through the streets to the scaffold: he would have no interest in looking at anything (866). He feels like "chestnut wood, which never catches fire no matter how much one blows on it" (850). Confusion was with him in all that he did, "praying, eating."

What confounds him the most is contemplating the sufferings of Christ during his passion and seeing himself without these sufferings. Like a refrain, the Latin exclamation "et ego sine vulnere" constantly recurs. "You humiliated, and I honored" (863) "You with insults, I with honors. You dead, I alive. To see His wounds, and myself without wounds. He died for me, and still I have not died for Him" (804). "Confusion for not having given my life" (777).

He feels unworthy of his vocation. "How my enemies scoff at me: 'Is *he* a member of the Society?'" (886).

Detachment from the things of the world

The spiritual diary shows that Borgia attained total detachment from the things of this world and from himself. He succeeded in bringing self-love and disordered affections into subjection. He asked for love of God "so as to forget the things of this world and live in the Lord as if seeing nothing else but Him" (794). "Asked for grace to live for God alone, looking only at Him, as if at the hour of death." "To live as one about to die" (796). "Asked forgetfulness of all creatures so as to dwell in Him and taste His attributes in everything ordained by His Divine Providence" (742).

To achieve this goal, he resolved to keep his senses and faculties under control. "Today I must pay particular attention to my eyes, and throughout the week to the senses and faculties and entire soul, so as to please the Lord" (882). "To put ashes on the faculties and senses, and reduce the old man to ashes" (847). He strove "to reset the clock of the soul" (884). He wanted "a reformation in the senses and faculties" (870). "Asked for joy in his own will's being persecuted" (847). He used the comparison of a mirror: "As a slight vapor takes away its power to reflect, so does a slight sensual movement to the soul. I asked to cleanse the mirror frequently, etc." (791).

If he wanted to be detached from the world, it was so that he could live for God alone. "Asked the Holy Spirit for the love that would remove the love of all other things so as to place it in Him, and to love with the love with which we have been loved" (730). "Forgetfulness of all creatures in my memory so as to keep it in the Creator" (746). "Thanksgiving for the goodness with which He removes the love of creatures with the sweetness of His own love" (750). "To have a heart which longs for nothing but God" (772).

He tries to see God in creatures, but insists more on seeing them all in Him. "All creatures in Him" (751). "To love Him in Himself and to love creatures in the Lord because He loves them" (775). "Asked to look at all creatures in Him" (794). "To see things in the Lord, and for His sake to forget them all" (810).

Like St. Paul he wanted to die so as to live completely for the Lord. He felt "the desire to die for Him" (767). "Hope that He will bear me, or hold me by the hand" (767). "To make myself ready to die for Him, if necessary, once every hour" (769). "To die and be dying" (776). "Lord, rescue me from the waters of this wretched world" (807). "Let me live like a person about to die" (796).

Trinitarian devotion

The spirituality of Borgia is clearly Trinitarian. He addresses his petitions to one or another of the three Divine Persons. He considers and ponders their attributes—the power of the Father, the wisdom of the Son, the goodness of the Holy Spirit. "To consider with thanksgiving during the day the Father's power, the Son's wisdom, the Holy Spirit's goodness, beholding it in all things and particularly in myself; for if I am able to do anything it is with that power, if I understand it is by participating in that wisdom, if I love well I do so with that goodness" (768).

In the Father he admires the work of creation, in the Son the mystery of the Incarnation, in the Holy Spirit the work of sanctification.

He dedicated his faculties to the three Divine Persons—his memory to the Father, his intellect to the Son, his will to the Holy Spirit. He begged "to purify my faculties for the three Divine Persons" (810).

He consecrated the days of the week to them. Thus, on April 28, 1566, "Consolation. Hope. *Item*: Thursday to the Father, Friday to the Son, Saturday to the Holy Spirit, Sunday to the three Persons. Monday, Father; Tuesday, Son; Wednesday, Holy Spirit; for my faculties" (819).

"During Mass I shall ask the Father for power to annihilate every evil from my soul, the Son for light to remove darkness, the Holy Spirit for fire to burn" (838).

He wanted an interchange to be established between himself and God. "To Him for me, and to me for Him, and all my actions in Him" (814). He wanted to live "to Him, for Him, in Him" (824).

He meditated on the roles taken by God in his soul. "Consider how I have a father, a shepherd, and a medicine" (838).

He offered Masses to the Trinity for the intentions in his heart. Thus, before the inauguration of the novitiate of Sant'Andrea al Quirinale on St. Andrew's Day, November 30, 1566: "*Item*, to say three Masses to the Holy Trinity these three days before Saint Andrew, for the new foundation of the house of probation" (841).

He asked the Trinity to grant him seven requests: "faith, hope, poverty, dedication, feeling, solitude, dying" (841).

He offered the Roman houses to the Trinity: the professed house to the Father, the college to the Son, the novitiate to the Holy Spirit.

His meditation on the Godhead inspired in him sentiments of fear and love, with a clear preponderance of love. He asked each of the Persons for fear and love (737). "I asked to have measureless love, a participation in the love that is infinite" (748). He desired to participate in "the love with which the Father gives the Son, with which the latter came, and with which the Holy Spirit gave Himself. To ask for this love so as to forget the things of this world and to live in the Lord as if I saw nothing but Him" (794).

Carried away by his strong love, he is led to such moving formulations as: " 'I will love you to death.' O Lord! I first unloved you to death, and you love to death in order to give life" (797). He asks the Son "to die with him 'so that those who loved with a single love might be struck with a single sword'" (737). "Asked for the fire of love" (810). "Wood put into the fireplace becomes fire; similarly with the love and fire of the Holy Spirit."

With love went hope. We have already noted how often he experienced hope joined with consolation. Sometimes he added, "Hope always" or "Hope forever." "Hope which will not leave me." "If He did not leave me when I was intent on putting Him to death, how will He leave me now that He gives me the desire to die for Him?" (766). "If, at the inflicting of spiritual wounds He had mercy on me, will he leave me now when I make an offering of blood" (866). God echoes his sentiment: "If, when you persecuted me, I called you and offered you My mercy, will I desert you now?" (842).

Love for Christ

Borgia's sentiments toward the Incarnate Word were particularly tender. "I asked that He write His name in my heart." "Let me be wholly Jesus's, blood and all" (785). "May Francis be Jesus's forever" (788). "My life in and for Christ" (842). "Asked for union of charity with Christ, a share in His poverty, obedience, humility, innocence, and justice; and to go against my own will, to be pleasing to the Eternal Father" (815). In contemplating the mysteries of Christ's life he asked "to feel what Jesus felt in each of them" (821).

It was natural that so contemplative a soul would be particularly inflamed by Christ's passion. "Asked for love, experience of the passion" of Christ (849). He wanted "to feel sorrow in seeing the image of the Crucified." He resolved "to visit during each day of Holy Week one of Christ's seven wounds" (851).

In his spiritual treatises he had already recommended contemplation of Christ's seven sheddings of His blood: "circumcision, bloody sweat, scourging, crowning with thorns, hands, feet, piercing of the side."[5] In treatise 30 he suggested another formulation: the circumcision, the bloody sweat, the scourging, the crowning of thorns, the stripping off of His garments, the nailing to the cross, the piercing of the side. He recommended dedicating a day of the week to each of these bloodsheddings.[6] "To visit these wounds, one each day of the week" (847).

Following his practice of asking twenty-four graces for each of the twenty-four hours of the day, he petitioned "24 things from Christ crucified" (771). On Good Friday he meditated on the "24 points from the Passion account of the Gospel" (822).

The cross

Together with devotion to Christ's passion went love of the cross. Borgia felt desires to suffer with Christ, even to give his life for Him, with longings for martyrdom. "Asked to experience Christ's cross" (742). He asked "to suffer for Christ all his life" (765). "To be bound fast to the cross" (769). "To ask whenever I see the Crucified something of what the Mother of God felt when she saw the Crucified" (769). "To live at the foot of the cross. That not to suffer be a dagger; to love to suffer" (776).

> Whoever wishes to accomplish these spiritual works of the Society needs to be on the cross, that is, on the mortification of the cross. (1) To feel the cross of Christ. (2) To grieve at not suffering. (3) A cross when there is no cross. (4) To feel

the cross with my life, for not having given it for Christ. It is madness to believe that without the cross, without hardship, without suffering, we can accomplish the type of spiritual works our Society aims at (803).

He felt longings to die for Christ. "The life He gave for me I want to give for him" (770). "To ask to die for Christ, ... to desire only to die and to rejoice in whatever is a cross and a torture to this heart that has rebelled against its God" (774). "To stand at the foot of the cross offering my life to the most Holy Trinity for Christ and for His Church" (815). "Asked to stand always at the foot of the cross, dying" (856). "To open the wound of the heart wider every day, until it becomes mortal" (769).

Eucharistic devotion

His devotion to the Eucharist began early in life. As duke of Gandía, he would accompany the Blessed Sacrament being taken as viaticum to the sick. In his spiritual treatises he gave norms for worthy reception of Holy Communion. During the final phase of his life his devotion to the Eucharist intensified.

As we have seen, he celebrated Mass early each morning. "Resolved not to let business matters distract him before Mass" (805). Like St. Ignatius, although with less frequency, he noted his sentiments before, during, and after Mass. He asked the Blessed Virgin to be his advocate at each of these three periods (792). Particularly tender are his sentiments at the moment of touching the sacred Host. "Asked the touch of the Lord's hand when touching the Host" (731). "During Mass asked to feel, when touching the Host to lift up the Lord, the pain He felt when they lifted Him up on the cross" (732). He desired to experience "during Mass, at the three times that I take the Host in my hand, what the Mother of God felt when she held her Son at His birth, His circumcision, and His burial" (743). He felt respect for the hands of priests "for they must take Christ into themselves" (781).

While celebrating Mass he felt spiritual consolation. One day "looking at the picture in our chapel with the child Jesus in it, it was as if I asked the Mother why she reared Him, and I reflected that it was for me: His blood for me; His life for me" (861). He apparently means the picture of the Holy Family that is still venerated in the chapel where St. Ignatius also celebrated Mass.

Mass afforded Borgia with the most favorable opportunity to offer himself and his life as a pleasing sacrifice to the Divine Majesty. "Asked grace to offer myself in sacrifice during Mass, preparing myself for this and to be received during Mass in virtue of Christ's self-offering, and for every-thing else that I have offered and petitioned" (828). "Consolation at Mass: I offered my blood and the whole Society, with devotion, as I elevated the chalice" (862). "Asked to have the experience of offering Christ our Lord in the Mass, as the apostles offered Him" (871). "During Mass, at the thought and sight of the chalice, I long to shed my blood" (811).

He yearns to receive the Body of the Lord. "Asked to feel hunger for the bread of angels" (800). He wishes to receive Communion on the day of his death. "While receiving at Mass, offered once more (how I do not know) the final moment of my life; I offered myself to the Lord to depart this life at that moment. The way somehow who departs cares not for what he leaves behind but for where he is going" (802), "Asked every hour that the Lord give me the grace of receiving viaticum in the hour, or at least day, of my death; and that at the moment I may at least be able to make a spiritual communion" (815).

One devotion was to make visits or, as he used to say, visitations to the Blessed Sacrament. He prepared the petitions that he would present to the Lord on each of these visits. On one occasion he determined to "make a spiritual communion, offering, petition" on each of these visits (872). Another day he resolved to make seven visits with seven petitions "for myself and for the Society and for others who asked prayers" (841).

The Sacred Heart of Jesus

Borgia deserves to be numbered among those devoted to the Sacred Heart. He saw in the Heart of Jesus the symbol of His love for man and the place of refuge where souls could find rest. What he had written long before in his spiritual treatises, he repeated in more intimate accents in his spiritual diary. On August 20, 1565: "At every hour Christ's heart and what He felt there is presented, to bring me to have a feeling of His passion, His love, and the fulfillment of His holy will" (792). He centered his attention on the wound in the side and said that Christ "did not let His side be opened right away, so that He could suffer more. We must do the same, so that we can suffer more. *Item*, His side was opened after His death to show us that after his death the love of his Heart was to be given" (844).

He stresses the idea of finding his abode in Christ's side, and asks "to abide in the heart of Jesus by conformity to Him" (743). "That I may merit to live in His heart" (787). On June 11, 1565, he hoped for "whatever would be most pleasing to Him so as to abide in Him more intimately" (788). In turn, he wanted "to be worthy to have my side opened for Christ" (746).

Devotion to Mary

He had recourse to the Blessed Virgin as his mother and advocate: "The Mother as advocate" (842). "Asked many things of the Mother of God with devotion" (839). He commended himself to her before Mass (849). His devotion was intensified on Mary's feasts. On the Immaculate Conception, 1567: "Asked purity to keep the vows. *Item*, Chastity. *Item*, I took her as my advocate during my visitations by what occurred in her holy conception." (870). During Holy Week the same year he resolved "to go to the Mother of God and tell her what they are doing to her Son this week, and to weep with her" (851). After Mass he experienced devotion "offering Christ in his soul as His mother had offered Him in her arms" (810). He directed to the Lord the Blessed Virgin's petitions in the Magnificat (841).

He had always had a devotion to the Rosary. In his spiritual treatises he suggested ways of reciting it fruitfully. He retained this devotion to the end of his life. He prayed the Rosary meditating on the fifteen mysteries. He prepared himself for the coming of the Holy Spirit by meditating on fifteen days each of the mysteries (827).

He had a special veneration the picture at St. Mary Major in Rome, attributed to St. Luke and called "Salus populi Romani." He was the first person to get permission to have reproductions of this picture made, to send to those closest to him. He gave one to Father Ignatius de Azevedo as he was preparing to leave Rome for Brazil, and entrusted to him another for Queen Mother Catherine of Portugal, to whom he wrote:

> The picture he brings Your Highness is, I believe, one of the finest things that a queen devoted to the Mother of God could possess. It is the same portrait as that painted by St. Luke and so profoundly venerated at St. Mary Major. . . . Father Ignatius will explain to you how it came into my hands, and the rest.[7]

The prayer of the Society's general

Naturally, Borgia brought to his prayer the problems he faced each day in his office as general. We have already seen how reluctant he was to accept it. From day of his election his constant prayer to the Lord was that God would either take him from this world, release him from the office, or give him the grace to fulfill it for His greater glory. The formulas varied. One reads, "Let him either take me, or remove the cross of the office, or give me the grace to bear it according to His will" (806). "Let the Lord grant me His spirit for governance, or take it from me, or take me out of this life"

(826). While still vicar general he asked the Lord on February 23, 1565, "If it can be done, free me completely from this office" (778). On the following March 27: "Let this chalice of governance pass from me" (781).

The Lord did not take him from this life so soon, and he had to carry his cross for another seven years. His plan of resigning at the congregation of procurators of 1568 could not be carried out. He could only dedicate himself with fresh determination to the task of governing. How he did so we have seen in the foregoing chapters.

He frequently goaded himself to begin anew. He wanted to govern in imitation of Christ, the good shepherd of souls. This image of the good shepherd is the one which most frequently appears in the pages of his spiritual diary in reference to his office. To him, who saw himself as a wolf or lion, the Lord had entrusted the care of His flock. His first duty was to his sheep. "Asked for love to feed his sheep" (830). He wanted to sacrifice himself like a good shepherd. "The shepherd's responsibility . . . at each each of these [eight] hours to offer my blood, soul, and life for the sheep, as Christ teaches" (799).

> To ask for: (1) Eyes to watch them and to weep for them, seeing that I have no fodder to give them; eyes to espy the wolves that run after them, and so to rescue them; (2) Ears to hear them; (3) Hands to serve them; (4) Sense of smell to track out the way on which to guide them; (5) Tongue to console, to teach; (6) Memory to keep them present, individually, etc.; (7) understanding to know how to love them according to their different dispositions; (8) love, to love them and carry them gently, and to give my life for them. (799f)

He resolved to draw out of the Gospel everything related with the ministry of a good shepherd. He begged for "a shepherd's zeal to feel, remedy, help, suffer" (796).

Fidelity to the Society

Reading the spiritual diary one is struck by Borgia's commitment to promote the good of the Society in fidelity to the norms of its Institute. This underlies one of his constant petitions in prayer. "The manner of our Father Ignatius must be preserved," he resolved on August 10, 1566 (833). He prayed for the "founder's spirit of proceeding" (796). "I asked for the spirit of our Father Ignatius and of Laínez" (849). Another time he asked the Lord for "the gentleness of Father Laínez and the prudence and light of our Father Ignatius, both together, for His glory" (884). The qualities he admired in his predecessors were those that had struck his contemporaries. In Laínez they noted great goodness and discretion. Ignatius was distinguished by his prudence and intelligence in governing. "I asked that I may do everything for His greater glory, as was the aim of the founder of holy memory, Master Ignatius, and as we, his sons, must follow" (748).

He constantly asked in his prayer to govern the Society in total conformity with the norms of its Institute. He asked for "the purpose of the Society which is to do everything for the greater glory of the Lord" (781). "Asked for keeping of the rules" (784). "That the Lord may give strength and light in keeping the constitutions" (790). "Obedience to the constitutions and decrees" (796). "For what the congregation entrusted and ordered me me" (796). "The general congregation must be observed first and foremost" (870). We have already seen that Borgia's administrative policy consisted practically in implementing with concrete measures the decrees of the Second General Congregation which had elected him. He asked for "the virtues of the Constitutions. *Item,* the twelve means for preserving the Society" (825).

Borgia's commitment to the Society was total. "To die in the Society, or may he take me before letting me leave it, or whatever is for His greater glory (779). He offered his life "for His Roman Church and for the Society." "I offer myself for the Society, blood and life" (790).

In his prayers he constantly prayed to the Lord for each province and house of the Society. He also prayed the persons he knew to be most in need of his prayers. "To ask blessing for the Society many times a day" (802). "I prayed for the members of the Society, to Jesus, for Jesus, and in Jesus" (826). "Began continuous prayer for all the provinces, for the Institute and for the Society" (862).

Among all the graces he asked for the Society, one stands out as particularly dear to him—unity of minds and hearts (790).*

---

* For a full-scale treatment of Borgia's complex spiritual personality, see Juan M. García-Lomas, S.J., 'Con Temor y Amor': La fisionomía espiritual de San Francisco Borja (Rome: Centrum Ignatianum Spiritualitatis, 1979).

13. Journey to Spain, Portugal, and France; Death

Especially after the siege of Malta in 1565, Pius V was preoccupied by the Turks, seeing a threat in their growing power. Fortunately, this persistent military operation was repulsed. After 1566 he urged the European powers to form a league against the Turks; in particular, he invited the king of Spain and the Republic of Venice to cooperate in this enterprise. But all the while he realized that his objective would not be easily achieved, because each state looked after its own particular interests while regarding the other states with suspicion. Meanwhile, the Turks decided to occupy Cyprus, Christendom's last bastion in the Levant. The danger was now nearing the coasts of the Adriatic. So at last, after lengthy and complicated negotiations, Spain and Venice agreed to form a league with the Holy See. In St. Peter's Basilica on May 25, 1571, the pope solemnly proclaimed the formation of this league.

Mission from Pius V

To ratify this pact and to put it into operation, Pius V decided to send a legation to Spain under the leadership of his grandnephew Cardinal Michele Bonelli, who, as we have already mentioned, was usually called Alessandrino because he was a native of Bosco, a town near Alessandria in Piedmont. The pope wanted Francis Borgia, the general of the Jesuits, whom some considered the cardinal's chief adviser, to be a part of this legation. In addition to appearing at the court of Spain on this diplomatic mission, the deputies were also to visit the court of Portugal in the hope of getting that country to join the league. An additional motive for this visit was to attempt to arrange a marriage between King Sebastian and Marguerite of Valois, sister of Charles IX of France; but above all else they hoped to set up obstacles to a marriage between Princess Marguerite and Henry of Navarre, known in history as Henry IV, who had embraced the cause of the Protestant reformers.

No doubt Borgia's prestige in the courts of Spain and Portugal added weight to this delegation. As far as Portugal was concerned, his influence on the most important people at court was considerable, especially the queen mother, Catherine, sister of Charles V, and Catherine's daughter, Princess Juana, mother of King Sebastian. Moreover, we should recall that at this time the Spanish ambassador to Portugal was Juan de Borja, Francis's second son, and that the king's confessor was another Jesuit, Father Luis Gonçalves da Câmara. Juan de Zúñiga, Spanish ambassador in Rome, wrote to Philip II that "the affairs of Portugal had been the main reason why His Holiness had set his eyes on him [Borgia]."[1]

On June 1, 1571, the pope summoned Borgia to an audience to tell him his wishes. Father Polanco, who accompanied the general to this meeting, laid before the pope some serious consequences that his decision would entail: regarding the Society, its congregation of procurators was soon to convene; indeed, some of the delegates had already arrived in Rome. As far as Borgia was personally concerned, his advanced age and many infirmities presented grave problems. Setting aside all these arguments, the pope "judged that this journey could not and should not be put off, and so, in virtue of holy obedience, I am getting ready for this mission, placing my trust in the Lord, who directs His vicar, that He will draw fruit for His holy service from this undertaking."[2] So Borgia wrote to the provincials in a letter dated June 4, communicating to them the news of his forthcoming trip.

In obedience to the pope Borgia had moved from Spain to Rome in 1561, and now ten years later, in obedience he prepared to make the same journey in the opposite direction. But this time the sacrifice was much greater, not only because the trip did not bring any special benefit to him personally, but especially because of the innumerable hardships that such an adventure would bring to a man so racked with infirmities. Polanco went so far as to say that this trip "seemed to us little less than impossible." The fact is that it spelled death for Borgia, a death, we can be assured, he faced in heroic fulfillment of the fourth vow of special obedience to the pope made by the professed of the Society. It was not for nothing that Borgia spoke of this venture as a "mission."

Since he did not have to leave until the end of the month, he had the whole of June at his disposal. He took advantage of this delay and received the procurators who had arrived in Rome, discussing with each of them the affairs of his province. He appointed six new provincials, and dispatched twelve Jesuits to Mexico, naming Father Pedro Sánchez their provincial. He appointed as vicar-general during his absence Father Jerome Nadal, delegating him to look after non-Spanish affairs. He himself could attend to the affairs of Spain on the spot.

Cardinal Alessandrino's party set out on June 30. Accompanying Borgia were the secretary, Father Polanco, and Father Diego Miró, as well as the Spanish procurators, Fathers Baltasar Alvarez, Juan Manuel de León, Francisco Vázquez, and Francisco Boldó, who were returning home to their provinces. Forming a kind of community, they resolved to keep up continuous prayer along the journey, using the milestones to divide up each one's time for prayer.

One member of the cardinal's entourage, his master of ceremonies, was Cornelio Firmano; we are indebted to him for the detailed diary he kept along the journey. We shall fill out his account with Borgia's letters, for Father Francis and his companions followed the same itinerary as the cardinal, although there were some variations in the dates.

Their route led them through Viterbo, Siena, and Florence, bringing them to Bologna on July 14. From there, through Modena, Parma, and Piacenza, they made their way to Alessandria and Turin, where they rested from July 27 to August 3. On the 13th of that month they found themselves at Avignon; on the 21st in Narbonne; on the 27th, in Gerona; finally on the 29th they entered Barcelona.

On August 15 Philip II wrote to Borgia expressing his joy at Borgia's coming to Spain.[3] Bringing this missive was Father Francis's son, Fernando de Borja, whom the king had sent to travel with his father throughout the entire trip. On August 31, Borgia answered the king from Barcelona, thanking him for his kindness and adding, "I come with more strength than I had when I left Rome." So we see that on this first stage of the journey his health had not suffered. He answered Philip that he was completely at the king's service, adding, "My desire, more sure and more ready to serve, all the more since I see myself at the end of my life, is to die in this service [of the king] to which I am so devoted and which I carry on with so much pleasure."[4]

On September 3 the legate wanted to ascend the mountain of Montserrat. Borgia accompanied him.

On September 6 the party arrived in Tarragona and on the 15th, at Valencia. Here the patriarch, Juan de Ribera, and the duke of Gandía, Carlos de Borja, had come out to receive the travelers. On Sunday the 16th, at the insistence of the patriarch, Borgia preached a sermon at Valencia's cathedral before the legate and a great number of the faithful, who had come to hear the man whom they had known as the duke of Gandía and whom they now saw humbly dressed in the cassock of a religious. The theme of the sermon was the Gospel of that Sunday, the fifteenth after Pentecost; taken from Luke's Gospel, chapter seven, the text dealt with the restoration to life of the widow of Naim's son.

On September 29 the legate made his entry into Madrid. Borgia had taken a detour because he wanted to avoid the receptions, but especially because he wanted to visit the novitiate at Villarejo de Fuentes in the province of Cuenca. The legate's stay in Madrid was protracted for a month and a half. It would be out of place here to treat at length the story of this meeting. We shall restrict ourselves to saying that the negotiations bore meager results. As far as the league with the pope and Venice was concerned, Philip II had already sent a document of ratification to Rome before the legate arrived. On October 31 Madrid received from unofficial sources the news of the naval victory which had taken place at Lepanto on the 7th of that month.

Borgia took advantage of his stay in Madrid to attend to Society business. He completed the plans for dispatching the first Jesuits to Mexico, deciding to send fifteen men to that mission rather than twelve as had originally been proposed. He also had the opportunity to talk with the new provincial of this province, Father Pedro Sánchez. Moreover, he received the provincials of Castile and Toledo, with whom he discussed matters pertaining to their respective provinces. He also wrote to the provincial of Andalucía, expressing his hopes that before leaving Spain he would be able to finalize plans to establish the college of Madrid.

While in Madrid he could hardly fail to visit the convent of Poor Clares which he and Princess Juana had founded. The abbess here was his half sister, Ana de Borja y Castro-Pinós, who in religion had taken the name Sor Juana de la Cruz. She was the first to hold this office, serving from 1559 until her death on April 28, 1601. Another of the nuns there was Borgia's granddaughter Francisca, daughter of the lord and lady of Loyola, Juan de Borja and Lorenza de Oñaz, the latter of whom was the grandniece of St. Ignatius. In a deposition at her grandfather's beatification process, Francisca testified that she "had seen him and knew him in the city of Madrid, and that she had spoken with him many times during the year 1571, at the time he came with the lord cardinal Alessandrino, and it was at that time that the servant of God came to talk with and see the witness, inasmuch as she was his granddaughter, and that sometimes she was in the company of another and sometimes alone."[5]

On November 14 Borgia wrote to Father Nadal that the members of the legation "are already finished with the affairs of this court, and I have taken leave of Their Majesties."[6] Within a few days they were to leave for Lisbon. On this leg of the journey Borgia went ahead of the legate to prepare the way for him. He trusted his mission would soon be completed, even before the anticipated date, and that by January, or at least during the first part of

February, they would be back in Rome. They planned to make the return trip by sea, setting sail from the port of Tortosa. Indeed, with this in mind the legate sent his baggage ahead to that city.

Before leaving, Borgia gave Philip II a fragment of the true Cross as a present. During these days the king had shown his kindness and admiration; the deadly strain of 1559-61 had been forgotten. It is not difficult for us to imagine the feelings of these two great men as they met again under such different circumstances.

Borgia left Madrid on either the 16th of November or the day after. The legate followed on the 18th. After sixteen days on the road Francis arrived in the Portuguese capital on December 3, remaining there for ten days. The outcome of the legate's negotiations was disappointing, particularly in regard to the projected marriage of King Sebastian with Marguerite of Valois. At Lisbon Borgia had the opportunity to embrace his son Juan, who, as we have already indicated, was Spanish ambassador at the Portuguese court, a position he retained until 1575. Leonor, daughter of Juan and of Lorenza de Oñaz and future mistress of Loyola as well, testified at the time of her grandfather's beatification process that she became acquainted with him in Lisbon on the occasion of this visit.

Meanwhile, Cardinal Alessandrino's plans to return immediately to Rome had to be modified when new orders arrived. He was to go to France and try to persuade that court to join the league; also he was to negotiate the marriage of Princess Marguerite.

The trip, on which Borgia's son Fernando accompanied him, meant crossing Spain once again. They left Lisbon on December 13, 1571. During their brief layover in Madrid, Philip II requested that Borgia assist at the baptism of his new son by his fourth wife, Anne of Austria. The child had been born on the 5th of that month and was given the name Fernando. Even though at the time Borgia was in good health, he faced this new stage in his travel with trepidation, especially because of the hardship of the winter and the length of the journey. "From today on," he wrote to Nadal on January 3, 1572, "all our business is walking."[7] The king ordered Fernando de Borja once more to accompany his father, this time as far as Bayonne. The legate had arrived at Bordeaux on January 26, and on February 7 he reached Blois, where the French court was residing at that time. Borgia joined him there two days later. The results of Cardinal Alessandrino's mission to France amounted to nothing, both his attempts to persuade France to join the league against the Turks and his efforts to negotiate Princess Marguerite's marriage. Queen Mother Catherine of Portugal and Philip II had both personally given Borgia letters urging him to do everything possible to prevent the marriage of Marguerite with Henry of Navarre. Borgia fulfilled this mission on February 10 in an audience with Marguerite's mother, Queen Catherine de' Medici. Borgia wrote saying that he and the legate were between hope and fear, "although fear rather exceeds hope."[8] The legate also intervened in this affair, but "he worked in vain." The fact is that two months later, on April 5, 1572, a settlement was arrived at for the much-dreaded marriage of Marguerite with Henry of Navarre.

Return to Rome and death

Borgia quit Blois on February 24. With the legate's permission he left Lyons on March 6, a half day's march ahead of Alessandrino. His brother Tomás met him here in Lyons and stayed with him all the way to Rome. From this point on in the journey, Borgia's health markedly deteriorated. He was forced to halt at Saint-Jean-de-Maurienne in Savoy, and again for five days in Modane. The weather was good but the ground was covered with snow. Moreover, they had to cross the pass of Mont Cenis on their way to Turin. That obstacle was surmounted only with enormous difficulties; Borgia was seated in a very comfortable and well-covered chair that had been placed on a litter and was carried on the shoulders of porters. Father Achille Gagliardi, rector of the college of Turin, came out to meet him with a doctor sent by the duke of Savoy. From Turin he continued his journey, sailing down the Po to Ferrara in a boat sent by Duke Alfonso II d'Este.

The invalid's condition forced him to stay on in Ferrara for more than four months, from his arrival on April 19 until September 3. It was here at Ferrara that he heard the news of Pius V's death on May 1, and of the election on May 13 of his successor, Gregory XIII.

Administrative matters resulting from the transition from one pontificate to another increased the work of the vicar, Father Nadal, who was obliged to ask Borgia to send Father Polanco, the secretary, to Rome, at least temporarily. Borgia wrote to the new sovereign pontiff on May 7, greeting him, offering him his prayers, and sending him Father Polanco so that he, in Borgia's name, could kiss his foot. Moreover, he reminded the pope of the fourth vow of the professed of the Society and begged for his blessing. At the end of that month of May, the decision was made to have Polanco return to Ferrara to be at the services of the general. On August 6, the secretary informed Nadal that Borgia was feeling better and was thinking about continuing his journey, even though the duke of Ferrara wanted a medical consultation to be held first.

For a description of this last stage of Borgia's journey to Rome and of his holy death, we will rely on his brother Tomás, future archbishop of Zaragoza. On October 2, two days after Borgia's death, Tomás wrote a letter to the duke of Gandía describing in detail everything about these events. Here are his words:[9]

> Most illustrious Lord: It would give me the greatest pleasure to spare Your Lordship the news, so painful for us who remain here below, of the death of my lord Father Francis, whom it pleased the Lord to call to Himself, after the long illness about which I have given an account to Your Lordship in another letter. Being in Ferrara—with the intention of not leaving there until his convalescence permitted or the doctors ordered it—I learned by letter from His Paternity September 2 that he was leaving on the 3rd for Loreto, and from there to Rome. He stated that it was better to leave in such a hurry, although his health was of no assistance at all because he was so weak.
>
> Though the duke made every possible objection to his departure, he left Ferrara on September 3. In the end his determination had won out. He arrived in Loreto middling well; at least it seemed to the doctors that during the journey to Loreto to his health had neither augmented or worsened. He stopped over for eight days at the Holy House. Then he set out for Rome with the all imaginable haste.
>
> His pulse began to weaken by the time he got to Macerata, so that we wanted to hold him there, but no one was able to succeed in dissuading His Most Reverend Paternity. He insisted that he had to get to Rome; and so he proceeded from there, getting continuously worse and weakening so rapidly that I very much feared he would die on us along the way. Toward the end we had to rush on faster. Despite the great suffering which every movement caused him, he was so anxious to get to Rome that we could not hold him back.
>
> We arrived Sunday afternoon, Michaelmas eve. From the moment he entered the city he said he thanked God that the journey of his life was ending together with his journey of obedience. Finally, My Lord, as soon as he entered his house, he had but one wish only: to prepare for what he had so long prepared. He told the members of the Society that their

prayers should henceforth be no longer for his corporeal health but indifferent, because he wanted their prayers' support.

It pleased our Lord that his agony should last until the stroke of midnight of St. Jerome's day. He remained completely conscious until the moment he expired, in continuous and profound prayer, not responding except when questioned, then again fixing his eyes on the crucifix with the same admirable serenity he manifested throughout his life. I asked his blessing for Your Lordship and for all, each one in particular. He gave it, saying in the end that he recommended to all the path of salvation, and that from now on he he would be beseeching our Lord to give us His grace. Seeing me weep, he told me not to, saying that he had firm hope in our Lord there was no reason for doing so.

This was vouched for by both the holiness of his life and his exemplary death. The people of Rome learned of it, and it was wonderful seeing them coming in droves to kiss his hand, and not only the people but prelates too. His Holiness sent someone to visit him and bestow on him his blessing *cum plenitudine clavium*, which was no small consolation for His Most Reverend Paternity.

We ought not to lament his decease; our Father has obtained what he strove for so strenuously throughout his life. What we ought to lament is our own having lost forever such a jewel as my lord Father Francis. It has been a tremendous blow to me. Blessed be our Lord for it, both for the consolation that it was to serve him and for the special kindness showed to me without my deserving it. I do not know which is greater—the good fortune of having known and served him or the misfortune of having lost him.

I tried to have his portrait painted before he died, since it was not just that such a great man's memory should fade away, for the holiness of his soul appeared in his very countenance. I had him embalmed and placed between the two generals. Since I intend writing Your Lordship later about my thoughts on his funeral, I shall say no more here. I shall merely add that during his whole life his illness was never understood. He was always treated for his liver and spleen, which were found as to be healthy as those of a kid; whereas in the lungs he had an enormous abscess from which a gallon of pus was drained. It had never given any sign during his whole illness that could have indicated it.

Thus, it pleased our Lord to fulfill his desires at the time when he most desired it. He was able to escape what he had always fled and from which nothing else would have succeeded in delivering him, according to what is understood of the present pope's intentions. Blessed be our Lord, who sends us so many afflictions at this time. One of the worst, no matter how bad the others may be, is in my opinion the departing of the good.

May the Lord give us strength to conform ourselves to His will. And may He preserve Your most illustrious Lordship, as we and all your servants desire and need. From Rome, October 2, 1572.

[Signature:] Your most illustrious Lordship's servant, who kisses Your Lordship's hands, Tomás de Borja.

We can supplement Tomás's information in this letter with the fuller detail he gave in the Zaragoza process of his brother's beatification. We shall select the principal items.

In Ferrara Borgia altogether declined the duke's invitation to stay in his palace, preferring instead to be taken to the college; on the other hand, he ordered Tomás to accept the hospitality of Cardinal Ippolito d'Este.

Cardinal Ippolito asked Tomás to go on ahead to Rome. When he reached Bologna, the archbishop of that city, Cardinal Gabriele Paleotto, asked him to do everything in his power to get Father Francis to the conclave, because he had learned that many of his fellow cardinals "adhered to His Paternity with a view to occupying him in the service of their Church." Tomás said these words in Latin. The implication was that in the cardinal's opinion Borgia could have received votes for the papacy. When Tomás replied that the Father was not a cardinal, Paleotto replied that the cardinals could do what they liked. Obviously Paleotto did not realize the state of Borgia's health.

They entered Rome through the Porta Flaminia, also known as the Porta del Popolo. Here in the church of the Blessed Virgin (presumably the church of Santa Maria del Popolo near the gate of the same name), Borgia remained for a half hour in prayer, thanking the Lord for the grace of reaching Rome as he had so strongly desired.

In Rome, Tomás continues, Francis was visited by all the cardinals, not once but on several occasions. In particular Cardinal Giovanni Aldobrandini came in the name of Pope Gregory XIII to see him. As we have already noted, Tomás had implied in his letter that the new pope seemed disposed to allow Francis to resign from his office as general of the Society.

But Francis lingered on for two days after arriving in Rome. When they asked him to appoint a vicar, he smiled and answered, "It will be enough for me to give an account of myself to God." He received viaticum, tried to give an exhortation to those present, and then asked to be alone. The faithful Brother Marcos asked the vicar to let him remain at Francis's side until his death.

Father Pedro Hernández asked the saint to allow them to have his portrait painted "for the consolation of the Fathers." He would not allow it. Notwithstanding, they summoned a painter, who began to paint his portrait while hiding behind one of the Fathers. When Borgia noticed him, he turned his face away, showing that this displeased him. They had to remove the painter.

The general spent two hours in prayer, after which he said, "Fathers and brothers, for the love of God, forgive me." He told Tomás to be a good minister of the Church.[10] When Tomás asked for his blessing for the family, Borgia wanted him to name them one by one. As he came to the name of a certain Juan, the saint asked if this was his son or one of his cousins—a moving detail which shows that he maintained love for his family until the end. So far the information found in the deposition of Tomás de Borja at the Zaragoza process.[11]

When Brother Marcos asked him if he wanted anything, Borgia answered that it was Jesus alone he wanted. These were perhaps his last words.

His agony continued until midnight, at which hour he delivered his soul to God. Did he die on September 30 or, as some believe, on October 1? At the process Tomás testified that he died around midnight of September 30; and in the letter to the duke of Gandía quoted above he specified that he died "at the stroke of midnight." Documents from the beatification process declare that he died "a little before midnight." We can conclude from all this that Borgia died on September 30. Brother Marcos, who was with him at the time, confirms this fact clearly in a letter of October 2 to the duke of Gandía: ". . . for Whom [God] he departed the day before yesterday at night, which was St. Jerome's day."[12]

As Tomás has informed us, an autopsy was performed before the interment, and, as was done in the case of St. Ignatius, a death mask was made of his features.

Beatification and canonization

The history of Father Francis's canonization and the transferral of his mortal remains to Madrid would fill a long chapter, but would require more space than is available. However, we could not conclude this biography without presenting a rough sketch of the essential facts.

The main promoter in the process of Borgia's canonization was his grandson, Francisco de Sandoval y Rojas, duke of Lerma and favorite minister of Philip III. At his request, Decio Carafa, papal nuncio to Spain, ordered the ordinary process to begin in the dioceses of Madrid, Valencia, Barcelona, and Zaragoza. These processes were completed in a two-year period, 1610/11, and the results sent on to Rome in 1615. In this same year the Congregation of Rites ordered the so-called remissorial processes to be conducted with apostolic authority. Once these processes were completed, their results were submitted to the decision of the judges of the Roman Rota, who in 1623 handed up a favorable opinion to Pope Gregory XV. Gregory's successor, Urban VIII, submitted the relation to the judges of the Sacred Congregation of Rites, which gave a positive vote with respect to both the beatification and the canonization. Urban VIII then proceeded to the beatification on November 23, 1624.

After some years had passed, two miracles among those attributed to the Blessed were selected for presentation at the canonization process. The Congregation of Rites gave a favorable decision on June 21, 1670. Pope Clement X canonized Francis along with Philip Benizi, Cajetan of Thiene, Louis Beltran, and Rose of Lima.

The transference of the remains of Father Francis took place as a result of the initiative of the duke of Lerma. With authorization from Pope Paul V, Father Muzio Vitelleschi, then general of the Society, granted the duke's request; and on April 22, 1617, he turned the body over to Cardinal Antonio Zapata for its transference to Madrid. An arm bone was kept behind and can still be seen among the relics in the church of the Gesù in Rome. In Madrid Borgia's remains were handed over to the provincial of Toledo, Luis de la Palma, on December 17, 1617.

After the completion of the church the duke of Lerma had built for the professed house on Madrid's Calle del Prado, the body of Borgia was brought there. On March 9, 1627, it was transferred to the new church of the professed house on the Plazuela de Herradores. We cannot delay to describe the vicissitudes and upheavals that resulted when the Jesuits were expelled from Spain in 1767 or when the Napoleonic forces occupied the capital. On July 30, 1901, the relics were taken to the church serving the professed house in the Calle de la Flor. On May 11, during the popular disturbances of 1931, this church went up in flames and Borgia's remains were incinerated. The fragments that could be salvaged are today venerated in the Society's new church in Madrid, on the Calle de Serrano.

Notes

Notes to Chapter 1

1. In drawing up the genealogy of St. Francis Borgia, we have followed the detailed documented studies of Father Miguel Batllori and Luis Cerveró y Gomis. Miguel Batllori, "La stirpe di san Francesco Borgia," *Archivum Historicum Societatis Iesu* 51 (1972):5-47; id., *Enaltiment de la familia Borja*, vol. 3 of *A Través de la historia i la cultura* (Montserrat: Abbey Press, 1 979), 155-209.

2. Postulation documents for the cause of St. Francis Borgia, ms. 38, f. 637-48 and ms. 42, f. 177ff, Archives of the Postulator General of the Society of Jesus, Rome, Italy. Here after, these documents will be cited as Postulation documents.

3. Francisco de Borja, *Tratados espirituales*, edited with an introduction by Cándido de Dalmases, S.J., vol. 15 of Espirituales españoles, series A: Texts (Barcelona: Juan Flors, 1964; Madrid: Universidad pontificia de Salamanca y Fundación Universitaria española), 360-68. Hereafter this book will be cited as Borja, *Tratados*.

4. *Franciscus Borgia*, 5 vols., Monumenta Historica Societatis Iesu (Rome: Historical Institute of the Society of Jesus), 1:388. Hereafter these books will be referred to as *F. Borgia*. The series Monumenta Historica Societatis Iesu will be abbreviated MHSI.

5. Pedro de Ribadeneira, "Vida del P. Francisco de Borja," ed. Eusebio Rey, S.J., *Historias de la Contrarreforma* (Madrid: Biblioteca de Autores Cristianos normal 5), 635. Hereafter this work will be referred to as Ribadeneira, *Vida*.

6. *F. Borgia* 1:265f. References to this ork indicate volume and page.

7. Postulation Documents, ms. 38, f. 644.

8. *F. Borgia* 1:267.

9. For relationships between St. Francis Borgia's family and those of St. Ignatius and the marquises of Alcañices, see *Fontes documentales de S. Ignatio*, MHSI, 805-9 and Genealogical Tree No. 2, attached to p. 816.

10. Ribadeneira, *Vida*, 646f.

11. On the obsequies of Empress Isabel see J. F. Rodríguez Molero, "Dos santos, Avila y Borja, en Granada," *Manresa* 42 (1970):253-78.

12. *F. Borgia* 5:741.

13. Ibid. 5:824.

14. Ibid. 5:854.

15. Ribadeneira, *Vida*, 647.

Notes to Chapter 2

1. *Boletín de la Real Academia de la Historia* 10 (Madrid, 1887):247. Hereafter this periodical will be cited as *Boletín*.

2. Ibid. 10:248.

3. Registro de la Cancillería, 4182, f. 96v-100v, Archivo de la Corona de Aragón, Barcelona. Henceforth this documentation will be cited as Registro.

4. *Boletín* 10 (1887):164.

5. Ibid. 10:248-50.

6. *F. Borgia* 2:582-98.

7. Ibid. 2:560.

8. Registro 4182, f. 100v-103v. See *Boletín* 10 (1887):250.

9. *F. Borgia* 2:6^2. The text of the oath is in Registro 4182, f. 103v-7r.

10. *Dietari* vol. 4, p. 81. See *Boletín* 10 (1887):252.

11. *F. Borgia* 2:615.

12. Francés de Beaumont was St. Ignatius's commanding officer at the battle of Pamplona. See *Fontes Narrativi de S. Ignatio*, 4 vols., MHSI, 1:155. The lord of Asparrós sur-

rendered to him at the battle of Noaín (June 30, 1521), which ended the French occupation of Navarre. See an unfinished biography of his life in L. Fernández Martín, "En torno a la batalla de Noaín," *Príncipe de Viana* (Pamplona, 1979), nos. 156f, pp. 375-422.

13. For the viceregal institution in Catalonia see Jesús Lalinde Abadía, *La institución virreinal en Cataluña (1479-1716)* (Barcelona: Universidad de Barcelona, 1958). On the viceregency of St. Francis Borgia, see Joan Reglà, *Els virreis de Catalunya*, Biografies catalanes, Historical Series 9 (Barcelona: Editorial Teide); P. Blanco Trías, *El virreinato de San Francisco de Borja en Cataluña* (Barcelona: El Apostolado de la Buena Prensa, 1921); L. Batlle y Prats and R. García Cárcel, "Gerona y el virrey D. Francisco de Borja," *Anales del Instituto de Estudios Gerundenses* 23 (1976/77):1-30.

14. Osuna file 1041, no. 37, preserved in the Archivo Histórico Nacional, Madrid.

15. F. *Borgia* 2:109.

16. Ibid. 2:12.

17. Ibid. 2:617.

18. A. Navagero, *Il viaggio fatto in Spagna* (Venice, 1536), 3.

19. "Contribución al estudio del bandolerismo en Cataluña," *Estudios de Historia moderna* 3 (Barcelona: A. Borrás, 1953):157-80.

20. F. *Borgia* 2:90.

21. Ibid. 2:9[2].

22. Ibid. 2:593, no. 40.

23. Ibid. 2:9.

24. Process of St. Francis Borgia, f. 23, documents found in the Diocesan Archives of Barcelona.

25. Ibid., f. 15v.

26. Osuna file 1037, no. 63.

27. F. *Borgia* 2:229.

28. Ibid. 2:278.

29. Ibid. 2:657.

30. Ibid. 2:658.

31. Ibid. 2:340-42.

32. Ibid. 2:7.

33. Ibid. 2:127f.

34. Ibid. 2:178.

35. Ibid. 2:196.

36. Ibid. 2:199-205.

37. Ibid. 2:196-99.

38. Ibid. 2:629.

39. Ibid. 2:33f.

40. Ibid. 2:636.

41. Ibid. 2:69.

42. Ibid. 2:91.

43. Osuna file 1037, no. 76.

44. F. *Borgia* 2:596, no. 51.

45. Ibid. 2:22.

46. Ibid. 2:516-21.

47. *Boletín* 10 (1887):249.

48. F. *Borgia* 2:617.

49. Ibid. 2:86f.

50. Ibid. 2:97.

51. Ibid. 5:742.

52. F. *Borgia* 2:392f.

53. Ibid. 2:599.

54. Ibid. 2:299.

55. Ibid. 2:305.

56. Ibid. 2:655.

57. Ibid. 2:312.

58. Ibid. 2:316f.

59. Ibid. 2:353.

60. Osuna file 1041, no. 115.

61. Registro 3900, f. 46v.

62. Beatification documents in the Diocesan Archives of Barcelona.

63. Ribadeneira, *Vida*, 654.

64. Dionisio Vázquez, manuscript life, *Vitae* 80, bk. 1, chap. 19, Archives of the Society of Jesus, Rome.

65. Ibid.

66. The "Seis tratados" cited here can be found in Borgia, *Tratados*, 43-148.

67. The original parchment is in the Osuna file, folder 13, no. 19[2].

68. F. *Borgia* 2:415.

69. *Fabri Monumenta*, MHSI, p. 154.

70. F. *Borgia* 2:560.

Notes to Chapter 3

1. F. *Borgia* 2:437.

2. Ibid. 3:5

3. Osuna file, folder 13, no. 28; Postulation documents, ms. 40, f. 400

4. Osuna file, folder 13, no. 14.

5. F. *Borgia* 2:455.

6. Ibid. 2:668.

7. Ibid. 2:443.

8. Ibid. 5:739.

9. Ibid, 2:674-76.

10. Charles V's 1543 instruction to his son Philip was published by Karl Brandi in *The Emperor Charles V: The Growth and Destiny of a Man and of a World-Empire*, trans. C. V. Wedgewood (London: J. Cape, 1971), 485-89.

11. So he wrote to Cobos on November 17, 1544 (*F. Borgia* 2:490).

12. Ibid. 2:457.

13. Text written in Valencian (*F. Borgia* 1:7f); for Castilian translation see ibid. 1:69. On the duchy of Gandía see ibid. 1:362-65.

14. *F. Borgia* 2:459.

15. This information is found in P. Sanz y Forés, *Colegio y Universidad de Gandía*, 4, and is cited in *F. Borgia* 2:505¹.

16. See León Amorós, O.F.M., "El Monasterio de Santa Clara de Gandía y la familia ducal de los Borjas," *Archivo Ibero-Americano* 20 (1960):441-86; 21 (1961):227-82, 399-458.

17. Georg Schurhammer, *Francis Xavier: His Life and Times*, trans. M. Joseph Costelloe, S.J., 4 vols. (Rome: Jesuit Historical Institute, 1973-82), 1:172-75.

18. Borja, *Tratados*, 234.

19. *F. Borgia* 3:9.

20. *Epistolae Mixtae*, 5 vols., MHSI, 1:355. Hereafter, references to this source indicate volume and page.

21. Borja, *Tratados*, 43-148.

22. Published for the first time in Valencia in 1550 and included in Borgia's *Opera omnia* (Brussels, 1675), 396-420. Cándido de Dalmases and J. F. Gilmont, "Las Obras de San Francisco de Borja," *Archivum Historicum S. I.* 30 (1961): 129, no. 10; 155, no. 104; 162, no. 130. Hereafter the *Archivum Historicum* will be cited as *AHSI* and this particular article as Borja, *Obras*.

23. *F. Borgia* 2:445.

24. Ibid., 1:279f.

25. Ibid., 2:528.

26. *S. Ignatii Epistolae*, 12 vols, MHSI, 1:444. Hereafter this source will be referred to as Ignatius, *Epistolae* and references to it will indicate volume and page.

27. *F. Borgia* 1:598.

28. Postulation documents, ms. 38, f. 93r.

29. *F. Borgia* 2:514.

30. Ibid. 2:522.

31. See M. Ruiz Jurado, "La entrada del duque de Gandía en la Compañía de Jesús," *Manresa* 44 (1972):122-44. Oviedo informed St. Ignatius about Borgia's vocation in a letter dated September 22, 1546 (*F. Borgia* 2:691f).

32. *F. Borgia* 3:15. Borgia recorded this vow in his spiritual diary in 1564 and 1566 (*F. Borgia* 5:743, 828).

33. Ignatius, *Epistolae* 1:422-44. The Monumenta editors of St. Ignatius's letters give October 9, 1546, as the probable date of this letter. If Borgia's request to be admitted to the Society was brought to St. Ignatius by Blessed Peter Faber, this would be the date, or any date later than July 17.

34. See M. Ruiz Jurado, "El impacto ignaciano en el alma de San Francisco de Borja," *Manresa* 46 (1974):105-22.

35. Postulation documents, ms. 38, f. 292.

36. Juan de Polanco, *Chronicon Patris Joannis A. de Polanco*, 6 vols., MHSI, 1:250. Hereafter this work will be referred to as Polanco, *Chronicon*, and its citations will indicate volume and page.

37. *Epistolae Mixtae*, MHSI, 1:385.

38. *F. Borgia* 2:536.

39. Ibid. 2:545.

40. Ibid. 3:663.

41. Published in Borja, *Tratados*, 149-52.

42. *Fabri Monumenta*, 424.

43. Ignatius, *Epistolae* 2:29f; *Monumenta Paedagogica*² 1:373-75.

44. *Epistolae Mixtae* 2:67; see also ibid. 2:28f.

45. *Monumenta Paedagogica*² 1:50-63.

46. For this case see M. Ruiz Jurado, "Un caso de profetismo en la Compañía de Jesús: Gandía 1547-1549," *AHSI* 43 (1974):217-66.

47. *Epistolae Mixtae* 1:467-74

48. Ignatius, *Epistolae* 2:56.

49. Ibid. 2:42-44.

50. Ibid. 2:43.

51. *F. Borgia* 2:546.

52. Ignatius, *Epistolae* 2:65-67.

53. *F. Borgia* 2:548.

54. Ignatius, *Epistolae* 12:648.

55. Ibid. 12:632-54.

56. Ibid., 2:495.

57. *F. Borgia* 2:563.

58. Ibid. 2:566; Ps. 101:8.

59. Ibid. 2:568.

60. Letter from Borgia to Ignatius in *F. Borgia* 2:514f.

61. *Exercitia*[2], series 2, *Monumenta Ignatiana*, MHSI, 71-74.

62. *F. Borgia* 3:24f.

63. *Exercitia*[2], 416f and Plates 5 and 6.

64. Ibid., 74-78.

65. Jerome Nadal, *Epistolae Hieronymi Nadal*, 5 vols., MHSI, 5:787f. Hereafter this source will be referred to as Nadal, *Epistolae*, and its citations will indicate volume and page.

Notes to Chapter 4

1. Ignatius, *Epistolae* 3:303f.

2. Ibid. 2:634f.

3. *F. Borgia* 1:537-63.

4. So Borgia recorded in his spiritual diary on August 30, 1564 (*F. Borgia* 5:764.)

5. *F. Borgia* 2:576f.

6. *F. Borgia* 1:560.

7. Ibid. 3:69f.

8. Ibid. 3:63.

9. Ibid. 3:78.

10. Ibid. 3:79.

11. Ibid. 3:76.

Notes to Chapter 5

1. Polanco, *Chronicon* 2:162.

2. Ignatius, *Epistolae* 4:67.

3. Ibid. 5:319.

4. *F. Borgia* 5:731.

5. *Epistolae Mixtae* 2:777.

6. *F. Borgia* 3:81.

7. Published in Borja, *Tratados*, no. 10, pp. 164-225.

8. *F. Borgia* 3:137.

9. Ibid. 3:78; 1:309.

10. *Epistolae Mixtae* 2:554.

11. Ignatius, *Epistolae* 3:429; Polanco, *Chronicon* 2:303.

12. *Epistolae Mistae* 2:652; *F. Borgia* 3:108.

13. Ibid. 3:104-7.

14. *Epistolae Mixtae* 2:644-46.

15. Ibid. 2:641-43.

16. *Litterae Quadrimestres*, 7 vols., MHSI, 1:493f. Hereafter, references to this source

will indicate volume and page.

17. Ignatius of Loyola, *The Autobiography of St Ignatius Loyola, with Related Documents*, ed. with introduction and notes by John C. Olin, trans. Joseph F. O'Callaghan, Harper Torchbooks (New York: Harper and Row, 1974), no. 87.

18. *F. Borgia* 2:562.

19. *Literae Quadrimestres* 1:583; Ignatius, *Epistolae* 4:428f.

20. *F. Borgia* 3:122-24.

21. *Epistolae Mixtae* 3:492.

22. Ibid. 3:499. Borgia's account differs from Bustamante's; the latter wrote that Borgia arrived at Coimbra on August 31 and remained there for five days (*F. Borgia* 3:155).

23. *Epistolae Mixtae* 3:502.

24. Bustamante wrote to Ignatius about this card game in his letter of September 20, 1553 (*Epistolae Mixtae* 3:502-5) and in his letter of October 20 (ibid., 546-48). See also the "Amonestación para la sagrada comunión" which Borgia wrote for the benefit of Princess Juana (Borja, *Tratados*, no. 12, pp. 272-74).

25. Nadal, *Epistolae* 1:196f.

26. Ibid. 1:277; see also ibid. 1:167.

27. Borja, *Tratados*, no. 35, pp. 438-539.

28. *Epistolae Mixtae* 3:283.

29. Polanco, *Chronicon* 2:612, no. 451.

30. Ignatius, *Epistolae* 4:283-85.

31. Ibid. 4:255-58.

32. Ibid. 4:256.

33. Ibid.

34. *Epistolae Mixtae* 2:847.

35. Ribadeneira, *Vida*, 700-702.

36. Ignatius, *Epistolae* 6:713.

37. Nadal, *Epistolae* 1:265-68.

38. *F. Borgia* 3:174f.

39. Ignatius, *Epistolae* 8:87.

40. Ribadeneira, *Vida*, 702. Regarding Borgia's cardinalate, see also Polanco, *Chronicon* 2:424-26 and 4:494f.

41. *F. Borgia* 4:265.

Notes to Chapter 6

1. Ignatius, *Epistolae* 6:122f, 151-53.

2. Nadal, *Epistolae* 1:248.

3. Ibid.

4. Ibid. 1:227, no. 16.

5. Ibid. 1:253, no. 13.

6. *F. Borgia* 3:233.

7. Ignatius, *Epistolae* 10:110f; see also ibid. 9:133.

8. Ibid. 11:262, 278.

9. *F. Borgia* 3:412.

10. Ibid. 3:496f.

11. Ibid. 3:317.

12. Ibid. 3:173.

13. Nadal, *Epistolae* 1:254.

14. *F. Borgia* 3:303.

15. Ignatius, *Epistolae* 9:130.

16. *Litterae Quadrimestres* 5:78.

17. Nadal, *Epistolae* 1:253.

18. Ignatius, *Epistolae* 8:193.

19. *F. Borgia* 3:315.

20. Ibid. 3:330.

21. Ignatius, *Epistolae* 6:440.

22. Ibid. 9:83.

23. Ibid. 9:365.

24. Polanco, *Chronicon* 5:521; 4:443.

25. *Litterae Quadrimestres* 3:21, 66.

26. *F. Borgia* 3:407f.

27. Ignatius, *Epistolae* 8:215, 233.

28. *F. Borgia* 3:205, 220.

29. Ignatius, *Epistolae* 8:333.

30. *F. Borgia* 3:338, 352.

31. Ibid. 3:218, 230, 240.

32. *F. Borgia* 3:79, 281. See also ibid., 69, 83, 113, 181, 244, 409.

33. Ricardo García Villoslada, *Storia del Collegio romano dal suo inizio (1551) alla soppressione della Compagnia di Gesù (1773)*, vol. 66 of Analecta Gregoriana, series published by the Faculty of Church History (Rome: Gregorian University, 1954), 133.

34. Ignatius, *Epistolae* 9:66.

35. *Obras de Sta. Teresa de Jesús*, ed. and annotated by Father Silverio de Santa Teresa, C.D., 8 vols. (Burgos: Tipografia de El Monte Carmel, 1915). From this work the following are cited: "Relaciones," 2:32; "Camino de Perfección," 3:145; "Vida," 1:186f. Reference is made to but the translation not taken from *The Collected Works of St. Teresa of Avila*, trans. Kiernan Kavanaugh, O.C.D., and Otilio Rodríguez, O.C.D., 3 vols. (Washington, D.C.: Institute of Carmelite Studies, 1976). Of particular relevance are the themes "Spiritual Relations" from 1:328, "Life" from 1:154, and the "Way of Perfection" from 2:129. Cándido de Dalmases, "Santa Teresa de Jesús y los jesuitas," *AHSI* 35 (1966):359f.

36. *Litterae Quadrimestres* 3:23.

37. *F. Borgia* 5:747.

38. Ignatius, *Epistolae* 9:80.

39. *Litterae Quadrimestres* 3:65.

40. Ignatius, *Epistolae* 8:219; see also ibid. 7:685-87.

41. Ibid. 8:220.

42. *Litterae Quadrimestres* 3:387; *F. Borgia* 3:226.

43. *F. Borgia* 3:259.

44. Ibid. 3:415, 418.

45. Ibid. 3:475.

46. *Litterae Quadrimestres* 3:120; see also ibid., 124.

47. Antonio Rodríguez Villa, *La Reina doña Juana la Loca: Estudio histórico* (Madrid: M. Murillo, 1892), 506.

48. *F. Borgia* 3:210.

49. *Epistolae Mixtae* 5:560.

50. *F. Borgia* 3:271f.

51. Louis Prosper Gachard, *Retraite et mort de Charles-Quint au monastère de Yuste*, 3 vols. (Brussels: C. Muquard, 1854/55), 1:74.

52. See M. Fernández Alvarez, "Las 'Memorias' de Charles V," *Hispania* 18 (1958): 690-718.

53. *F. Borgia* 3:301f.

54. Ibid. 3:303f.

55. Ibid. 3:304^3.

56. Ibid. 3:306, 308. For the plan of Charles V see also Karl Brandi, *The Emperor Charles V*, p. 641 and P. and M. Morán Mariño, *Tratados internacionales de España: Charlos V*, 3 vols. (Madrid: Consejo superior de investigaciones científicas, 1978-present), 1:l.

57. *F. Borgia* 3:321.

58. Ibid. 3:404.

59. Published by Cardinal Alvaro Cienfuegos, "La heroica vida . . . del grande S. Francisco de Borja," bk. 5, chap. 2, as reproduced in *F. Borgia* 3:475-83.

60. *F. Borgia* 3:266.

61. Ibid. 3:283.

62. Ibid. 3:280, 288.

63. Ibid. 3:341f.

64. The text of the memorial is found in *F.*

Borgia 3:342-53.

65. Ibid. 3:353-59.

66. Ibid. 3:412.

67. *Lainii Monumenta*, MHSI, 4:666. Hereafter, references to this source will indicate volume and page.

68. *F. Borgia* 3:588.

Notes to Chapter 7

1. Borja, *Tratados*. In addition to the title of each of Borgia's opuscules, in this chapter we shall indicate the number that refers to the *Tratados* edition. This number will appear in parentheses after the quotation.

2. Borja, *Obras* 125-79. A description is given in this presentation of Borgia's known works, both published and unpublished, and divided into three sections: works, editions, and manuscripts.

3. Juan Eusebio Nieremberg, *Vida del Santo Padre y gran siervo de Dios el B. Francisco de Borja: Van añadidas sus obras, que no estavan impressas antes* (Madrid, 1664). See Borja, *Obras* no. 126.

4. Francis Borgia, *Opera omnia quae nunc extant aut inveniri potuerunt*. See also Borja, *Obras*, no. 130.

5. The complete modernized re-edition is found in Borja, *Tratados*, 43-148.

6. *Litterae Quadrimestres*, ed. Bertrand de Margerie, S.J., new ed., Studi Tomistici 22 (Città del Vaticano, 1983), 1:192.

7. Borja, *Obras*, no. 43.

8. Ibid., no. 59. M. Ruiz Jurado, S.J., "San Francisco de Borja y el Instituto de la Compañía de Jesús," *AHSI* 41 (1972):176-206.

9. Borja, *Obras*, no. 2.

10. Nieremberg, *Vida*, 475-78, note 3; see also Borja, *Obras*, no. 70.

11. These sermons are listed in Borja, *Obras*, nos. 27 and 207.

12. *Epistolae Mixtae* 3:283.

13. See Borja, *Obras*, nos. 46, 48, and 207. The meditations for Sundays and feast days were published by Federico Cervós, S.J., ed., "El Evangelio meditado," unpublished works from the hand of St Francis Borgia, corrected by the editor from the original manuscript (Madrid: Razón y fe, 1912). See *Obras*, no.

147. Borgia's meditations for the feast days of the saints were published by José María March in *Meditaciones sobre las fiestas de los santos* (Barcelona, 1925). See Borgia, *Obras* no. 149.

14. See fn. 13 above.

15. Nadal, *Epistolae* 2:172.

16. *F. Borgia* 5:859.

17. Ibid. 5:855.

18. Joseph de Guibert, S.J., *The Jesuits: Their Spiritual Doctrine and Practice: A Historical Study*, trans. W. J. Young, S.J. (Chicago, 1964; reprinted by St. Louis: Institute of Jesuit Sources, 1972), 197.

19. See fn. 13 above.

20. *F. Borgia* 5:77.

21. Ibid. 5:86.

22. "Ejercicios para el propio conocimiento" (treatise 17) from Borja, *Tratados*, 296f. See also ibid., 120-33; 291-96.

23. Manuscript "Historia de la vida del Padre Francisco de Borja," bk. 4, chap. 1.

24. Borja, *Tratados*, 104.

25. Ibid., 154. [It is impossible to render into English the original text, "Si deseas, alma mía, de andar mucho en Dios, trabaja primero de andar mucho en tí," without sacrificing the poetry and the subtle beauty and force of the Spanish.—Translator's note]

26. Ibid., 287.

27. Ibid., 154f.

28. See Rufino José Cuervo, *Diccionario de construcción y régimen de la lengua castellana* (Colombia: Instituto Caro y Cuervo, c. 1953), s.v. "confundir." Cándido de Dalmases, "El sentimiento de confusión en San Francisco de Borja," *Manresa* 34 (1962):99-118.

29. Santa Teresa, *Vida*, chap. 40.

30. Borja, *Tratados*, 99.

31. The Latin expression reads, "Nolo, Domine, sine vulnere vivere, quia Te video vulneratum." "Meditatio D. Francisci super illa verba: Quis es Tu, et quis sum ego?" *AHSI*, vol. 29, f. 145. The expression which we have cited here comes from the *Stimulus amoris*, pt. 2, chap. 2, an opuscule which was attributed to St. Bonaventure. See Borja, *Tratados*, 19, 26.

32. Borja, *Tratados*, 409.

33. Ibid., 403.

34. Ibid., 475-79.
35. Ibid., 327.
36. Ibid., 235f.
37. Ibid., 247.
38. Ibid., 101f.
39. Ibid., 426-30.
40. Ibid., 432.
41. Ibid., 304.
42. Ibid., 112.
43. Ibid., 327.
44. Ibid., 355.
45. Ibid., 329f.
46. Ibid., 339.
47. Ibid., 358.
48. Ibid., 370.
49. Ibid., 40.

Notes to Chapter 8

1. *F. Borgia* 3:549. For the episode with the Inquisition in which Borgia found himself enmeshed, see Cándido de Dalmases, "San Francisco de Borja y la Inquisición española (1559-1561)," *AHSI* 41 (1972):48-135.
2. *F. Borgia* 3:369.
3. *Lainii Monumenta* 3:297.
4. See the account of the auto-da-fe which F. Borgia sent to Laínez on June 16, 1559, in *F. Borgia* 3:508-12.
5. Ibid. 3:512f.
6. José Luis González Novalín, *Historia de la Iglesia en España*, directed by Ricardo García Villoslada, 5 vols. (Madrid: EDICA, 1979-82) 3:187.
7. Ibid. 3:191.
8. *F. Borgia* 3:555.
9. *Lainii Monumenta* 4:513.
10. *Litterae Quadrimestres* 6:354.
11. For the clandestine volumes of Borgia's works see Borja, *Obras*, 154f.
12. Borja, *Tratados*, 153-63.
13. *F. Borgia* 3:564, 550; *Epistolae Salmerón*, MHSI, 1:351. References to these sources indicate volume and page.
14. *F. Borgia* 3:550.
15. Ibid. 3:554.
16. Ibid.
17. See the actual text in *F. Borgia* 3:556-76.
18. *F. Borgia* 3:554.
19. Ibid. 3:854.

20. Ibid.
21. Ibid. 3:851-53, 856.
22. *Lainii Monumenta* 4:521f.
23. The letter of the Cardinal Infante is in *F. Borgia* 3:578f.
24. Dalmases, "San Francisco y la Inquisición," 84.
25. *F. Borgia* 5:839; see also ibid., 775, 802.
26. Letter of February 9, 1560, in *F. Borgia* 3:588f.
27. Dalmases, "San Francisco y la Inquisición," 80.
28. Ibid., 79.
29. *F. Borgia* 3:612-14.
30. Dalmases, "San Francisco y la Inquisición," 84.
31. Ibid., 89, 90.
32. Ibid., 93.
33. The text of this papal brief is found in *F. Borgia* 3:632f.
34. *Lainii Monumenta* 5:265-72.
35. Concerning Philip II's position in this affair with Borgia, see Dalmases, "San Francisco y la Inquisición," 130.
36. Nadal, *Epistolae* 1:780.
37. Dalmases, "San Francisco y la Inquisición," 96.
38. Ibid., 114. See Nadal, *Epistolae* 1:111-14.
39. The complete text of this letter is found in *F. Borgia* 3:635-38.
40. Ibid. 3:637, 638.
41. Dalmases, "San Francisco y la Inquisición," 115.
42. *F. Borgia* 3:666f.
43. Ibid. 3:667f.
44. The text of these documents is found in *F. Borgia* 3:663f; Nadal, *Epistolae* 1:486f.
45. Rom. 12:1.
46. *F. Borgia* 3:649.
47. Dalmases, "San Francisco y la Inquisición," 107.
48. The text of Nadal's declaration is found in Nadal, *Epistolae* 1:485f.
49. Ibid. 1:784.
50. *F. Borgia* 5:883.
51. Ibid. 3:673f.
52. Dalmases, "San Francisco y la Inquisición," 121.
53. Letter of October 1561 in Nadal, *Epistolae* 4:764-70.

54. Letter of October 28, 1561, in Nadal, *Epistolae* 1:539-42.

55. Letter of November 5, 1561, ibid. 1:549-51.

56. *Lainii Monumenta* 6:160-63.

57. F. *Borgia* 3:687f.

58. Nadal, *Epistolae* 1:672.

59. Ibid., 2:79.

60. Franz Heinrich Reusch, *Der Index der Verbotenen Bücher*, 2 vols. (Bonn: M. Cohen & Sohn, 1883-1885), 1:492.

61. Borja, *Obras*, 175, note 11.

Notes to Chapter 9

1. F. *Borgia* 3:734.

2. Text in *AHSI* 34 (1965):88-92.

3. F. *Borgia* 4:17f.

4. Ibid. 5:789.

5. Ibid. 5:790.

6. Ibid. 5:791.

7. Henceforth we shall cite the decrees and canons of the Second General Congregation according to the numeration found in the *Institutum Societatis Iesu*, 3 vols. (Florence: Immaculate Conception Press, 1892/93). We shall refer to this work as *Institutum S.I.*

8. Text in *AHSI* 34 (1965):93-95.

Notes to Chapter 10

1. Ignatius of Loyola, "Preamble to the Declarations," *The Constitutions of the Society of Jesus*, ed., trans., and commentary by George E. Ganss, S.J. (St Louis: Institute of Jesuit Sources, 1970), [136].

2. The rules written during St Ignatius's lifetime have been published in MHSI, *Regulae Societatis Iesu (1540-1556)* (Rome, 1948). We will refer to this work as *Regulae*. On the evolution of these rules see August Coemans, *Breves notitiae de Instituto, Historia, Bibliographia Societatis* (Brussels: Northern Belgian Province, 1937), 31-42. We will refer to this work as *Breves Notitiae*.

3. *Regulae*, 320-31.

4. See ibid., 545-55 for the text.

5. Ibid., 156-68, 332-34.

6. Ibid., 555f.

7. *Institutum S.I.*, decrees in 2:188-215,

canons in 2:530-37.

8. *Instit. 81*, f. 4; *Congr. 41*, f. 291. Both of these sources are found in the Archives of the Society of Jesus, Rome (ARSI).

9. Nadal, *Epistolae* 3:413.

10. F. *Borgia* 4:501, 523, 525, etc.

11. *Instit. 109*, f. 113v-14v, ARSI; Juan de Polanco, *Complementa*, eds. D. Restrepo and D. F. Zapico, 2 vols. (Madrid, 1916/17) 2:678, no. 40; Franciscus Sacchini, *Historiae Societatis Iesu Pars tertia sive Borgia* (Rome: Manelfi Manelfij Press, 1640), bk. 3, no. 96. Hereafter this work will be cited as *Historiae*.

12. Carlos Sommervogel, S.J., *Bibliothèque de la Compagnie de Jésus*: part 1, *Bibliography*, ed. Augustin and Aloys de Backer, S.J.; part 2, *History*, ed. A. Carayon, S.J., and *Tables*, ed. P. Bliard, S.J., 12 vols. (Brussels and Paris, 1890-1932; reprinted by Héverlé-Louvain, 1960), 5:99f. Coemans, *Breves notitiae*, 38-43; László Polgár, *AHSI* 33 (1940):93.

13. Sommervogel, *Bibliothèque* 5:99f. There is a copy of this edition in the library of the Historical Institute of the Society of Jesus in Rome. Spanish translation of the Rules in *Instit. 38*, f. 19-23, ARSI. Because one sheet in this copy is missing, the first five rules are not recorded.

14. Rules for the provincial are in the *Instit. 220*, f. 168-74, ARSI; those for the rector are found in f. 178-85. We shall deal with the rules for the visitor in section 5 of this chapter.

15. Ignatius, *Constitutions*, [582]. References to this source indicate bracketed paragraph numbers.

16. Ibid., [545], critical apparatus.

17. Ibid., [342].

18. Luis Gonçalves da Câmara, "Memoriale," nos. 195-98, 256, *Fontes Narrativi*, MHSI, 1:644-46, 676f.

19. Ignatius, *Constitutions*, [340]; see also [361]. Nadal spoke of this in his second address at Alcalá in 1561; see *Fontes Narrativi* 2:200 and Nadal, *Epistolae* 5:282.

20. St. Ignatius said this to Father Nadal in 1554 when the latter had returned from Spain. Nadal had shown himself to be inclined to allow more than one hour of prayer there. (Gonçalves da Câmara, *Memoriale*, no.

196, *Fontes Narrativi* 1:644.

21. *Lainii Monumenta* 5:357; *Monumenta Indica*, MHSI, 4:856.

22. Sacchini, *Historiae*, pt. 3, bk. 1, no. 46.

23. Otto Braunsberger, S.J., *Beati Petri Canisii Societatis Iesu Epistulae et Acta*, 8 vols. (Freiburg im Breisgau: Herder, 1896-1923), 5:357.

24. Pedro Leturia, "La hora matutina de oración," *Estudios ignacianos* 2 (1957):223.

25. *Institutum S.I.* 2:201f.

26. *Instit. 81*, f. 4v; Nadal, *Epistolae* 4:250.

27. *Hisp. 90*, vol. 1, f. 112, ARSI; Antonio Astráin, *De oratione matutina in Soc. Iesu* (Bilbao, 1923), 33[1].

28. *Regulae*, 221f; Leturia, "La hora," 202f, 224, 245.

29. Nadal, *Epistolae* 3:487; Ignacio Iparraguirre, "La oración en la Compañia naciente," *AHSI* 25 (1956):482[8].

30. Pierre Suau, *Histoire de S. François de Borgia, troisième général de la Compagnie de Jésus (1510-1572)* (Paris: Beauchesne, 1910), 392.

31. Nadal, *Epistolae* 4:253; see also ibid. 4:290, 318.

32. Ibid. 4:358f.

33. *Institutum S.I.* 2:248.

34. Giulio Negrone, *Regulae communes S. I. commentariis illustratae* (Milan, 1613), Rule 1, no. 16.

35. Francisco Suárez, S.J., *Tractatus de Religione S.I.*, vol. 16 *bis* of *Opera omnia*, editio nova a. d. M. Andre . . . juxta editionem venetianam, XXIII tomos in f° continentem, accurate recognita reverendissimo ill. domino Sergent . . . ab editore dicata (Paris: Louis Vives, 1856-76), 929.

36. Gil González Dávila, *Pláticas sobre las Regulas de la Compañía de Jesús*, introduction and notes by Camilo M. Abad (Barcelona: J. Flors, 1964), 292. The new distributor of this book is Fundación Universitaria Española, calle de Alcalá 93, 28009 Madrid, Spain.

37. *F. Borgia* 4:562.

38. Ibid., 5:75.

39. Ibid., 5:74.

40. Ignatius, *Epistolae* 8:215f; Manuel Ruiz Jurado, *Orígenes del noviciado en la Compañía de Jesús* (Rome: Historical Institute of the Society of Jesus, 1980), 44-47.

41. Ruiz Jorado, *Orígenes*, 192-95, 197-205.

42. *F. Borgia* 4:348.

43. Ibid., 4:408.

44. Ibid., 5:110; 4:460.

45. See L. Lukács, "De prima Societatis Ratione studiorum sancto Francisco Borgia praeposito generali constituta (1566-1569)," *AHSI* 27 (1958):209-32; id., ed., *Monumenta paedagogica* (Rome, 1965), 2:181-233.

ss 46. Lukács, *Monumenta Paedagogica* 3:382-85.

47. Ignatius, *Constitutions* [765].

48. G. Philippart, "Visiteurs, commissaires et inspecteurs dans la Compagnie de Jésus de 1540 à 1615": First Part: 1540-1572, *AHSI* 37 (1968):23f. For an extract of the text, see ibid., 61-66.

49. Nadal, *Epistolae* 5:364.

50. *Institutum S.I.* 2:196f.

51. *F. Borgia* 3:346., no. 8; 356, no. 7.

52. See above pp. 209f.

53. Philippard, "Visiteurs," 43f; for text see ibid., 103-25.

54. Nadal, *Epistolae* 3:413.

55. Philippard, "Visiteurs," 45f; for text see ibid., 103-25.

56. Here is a list of the visitors named by Borgia. In 1566 Bartolomé de Bustamante for Andalucía and Toledo; Miguel de Torres for Portugal; Jerome Nadal for Austria, Lower Germany, Upper Germany, and the Rhine; in December of that same year he sent him to the Provinces of Aquitaine and France; Juan de Vitoria to Sardinia, and Ignatius de Azevedo to Brazil. In 1567 Gil González Dávila to Aragón and Castile; Gonzalo Alvares to India; Benedetto Palmio to Naples; Juan de Montoya to Sicily. In 1569 Juan Bautista Suárez to Andalucía; Everard Mercurian to the provinces in France.

57. *F. Borgia* 4:144. In Spanish the text reads *escribir* (to write). Probably Borgia meant *prescribir* (to prescribe); so the text was probably written to read, "He should conduct his visitation with sincerity and simplicity in the way he prescribes and orders."

58. Sacchini, *Historiae*, pt. 3, bk. 4, no. 149.

59. "As if I had to relinquish it by Octo-

ber," he noted in his diary on January 21, 1568; see *F. Borgia* 5:875.

60. *Vida*, p. 794.

61. Ibid., 795.

62. *F. Borgia* 4:163.

63. Ibid. 4:167.

64. Polanco, *Complementa* 2:95, no. 46; 700, no. 18.

65. Ibid., 31f, no. 4.

66. Nadal, *Epistolae* 3:625f.

67. Polanco, *Complementa* 2:688, no. 27.

68. *F. Borgia* 4:576.

69. Polanco, *Complementa* 2:118; Nadal, *Epistolae* 3:652-54.

70. *Bullarium Romanum*, Turin ed., 7:923; *Institutum S.I.* 1:46-49.

71. Pius V's breviary was published July 9, 1568. Borgia began to implement its use on July 25 of the same year. See *F. Borgia* 5:883.

72. *F. Borgia* 5:857.

73. Nadal, *Epistolae* 3:523f; Estanislao Olivares, *Los votos de los escolares de la Compañía de Jesús* (Rome, Historical Institute of the Society of Jesus, 1961), 19:69f.

74. *F. Borgia* 4:551.

Notes to Chapter 11

1. Polanco, *Complementa* 2:30.

2. *F. Borgia* 4:660.

3. *F. Borgia* 5:882; Polanco, *Complementa* 2:42.

4. *F. Borgia* 4:638.

5. Ibid. 4:424.

6. *F. Borgia* 5:145.

7. *F. Borgia* 4:267.

8. *F. Borgia* 5:26.

9. Lucács, *Monumenta paedagogica* 3:255-57.

10. Ibid. 3:256f.

11. *F. Borgia* 4:457.

12. Nadal, *Epistolae* 3:196.

13. See a fragment of Pasquier's discourse in *Fontes Narrativi* 3:813-17.

14. *F. Borgia* 5:571f.

15. Antonio Astráin, S.J., *Historia de la Compañía del Jesús en la Asistencia de España*, 7 vols. (Madrid, 1902-25), 2:286.

16. Clifford M. Lewis, S.J., and Albert J. Loomie, S.J., *The First Spanish Mission in Virginia, 1570-1572* (Chapel Hill: University of North Carolina Press, 1953), 36, 62. *Monumenta Mexicana*, MHSI, 1:20-29.

17. *Monumenta Peruana*, MHSI, 1:34.

18. Ibid. 1:143.

19. Ibid. 1:144.

20. Ibid. 1:228f.

21. Ibid. 1:248.

22. Ibid. 1:255.

23. Ibid. 1:392.

24. Ibid. 1:394.

25. *F. Borgia* 4:153.

26. *Monumenta Malucensia*, MHSI, 1:477.

27. Ibid., 569.

Notes to Chapter 12

1. Gonçalves da Câmara, *Memoriale*, no. 256, *Fontes Narrativi*, 1:677.

2. *F. Borgia* 5:729.

3. To accommodate those who wish to verify our citations and put them in context, we have indicated the page number from Borgia's diary printed in *F. Borgia* 5:728-887.

4. "Ipsum enim desiderium tuum, oratio tua est; et si continuum desiderium, continua oratio. Non enim frustra dixit apostolus: 'Sine imtermissione orate'" (1 Thess. 5:17) (Saint Augustine, "Enarratio in Psalmum 37," *Enarrationes in Psalmos i-l*, Corpus Christianorum: Latin Series, 50 vols. [Turnhaut: Brepols, 1956], 38:392).

5. Borja, *Tratados*, no. 31, p. 432.

6. Ibid., 428-30.

7. *F. Borgia* 5:113; Sacchini, *Historiae*, pt. 3, bk. 5, no. 296.

Notes to Chapter 13

1. Luciano Serrano, *Correspondencia diplomática entre España y la Santa Sede durante el pontificado de San Pío V* (Madrid, 1914), 4:333.

2. *F. Borgia* 5:581.

3. Ibid., 5:619.

4. Ibid. 5:623.

5. Postulation documents, ms. 38, f. 92v.

6. *F. Borgia* 5:641.

7. Ibid., 5:657.

8. Ibid. 5:670.

9. Tomás de Borja's letter is kept in the Osuna file, folder 13, no. 6, preserved in the

Archivo Histórico Nacional in Madrid.

10. Tomás de Borja y de Castro-Pinós (1541-1610) was a canon of Toledo; from 1594 to 1596 he governed the Toledo diocese in the name of its titular, Archduke Albert of Austria. After 1599 he was bishop of Málaga. In 1603 he was transferred to the see of Zaragoza, which he governed until his death. Moreover, he was viceroy of Aragón.

11. Postulation documents, ms. 38, f. 637ff and ms. 42, f. 177v.

12. *F. Borgia* 5:710.

ABBREVIATED GENEALOGY

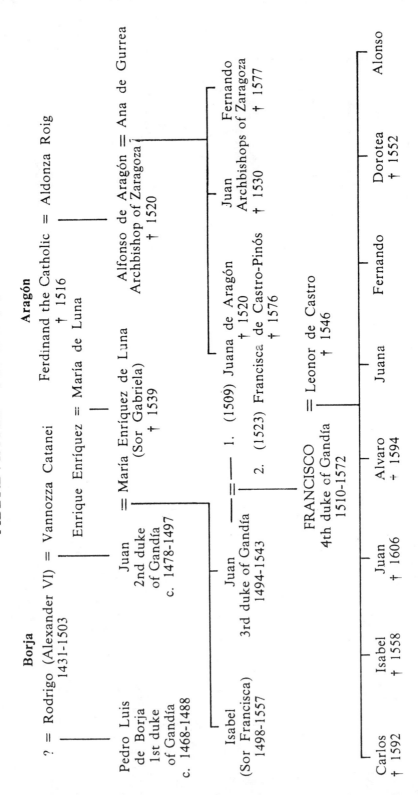

Borja

? = Rodrigo (Alexander VI) = Vannozza Catanei
1431-1503

Aragón

Ferdinand the Catholic = Aldonza Roig
† 1516

Enrique Enríquez = María de Luna

Juan
2nd duke
of Gandía
c. 1478-1497

= María Enríquez de Luna
(Sor Gabriela)
† 1539

Alfonso de Aragón = Ana de Gurrea
Archbishop of Zaragoza
† 1520

Pedro Luis
de Borja
1st duke
of Gandía
c. 1468-1488

Juan
3rd duke of Gandía
1494-1543

1. (1509) Juana de Aragón
† 1520

2. (1523) Francisca de Castro-Pinós
† 1576

Juan   Fernando
Archbishops of Zaragoza
† 1530   † 1577

Isabel
(Sor Francisca)
1498-1557

FRANCISCO
4th duke of Gandía
1510-1572

= Leonor de Castro
† 1546

Carlos   Isabel   Juan   Alvaro   Juana   Fernando   Dorotea   Alonso
† 1592   † 1558   † 1606   † 1594   † 1552

Glossary of Names*

ACOSTA, JOSÉ DE, S.J., (1539?-1600): one of five brothers who became Jesuits; sent to Lima, Peru, where he was provincial; wrote extensively on the history and nature of the South American Indians.

ALCÁNTARA, ST. PETER OF (1499-1562): son of the governor in Alcántara; became a Franciscan Observant at sixteen; ordained a priest 1524; reform-minded, he advised St. Teresa of Avila in her renewal of the Carmelites.

ALEXANDER VI (1431-1503): Cardinal Rodrigo Borgia; founder, by Vannozza Catanei, of the Borgia dynasty; great-grandfather of St. Francis Borgia; pope 1492-1503; patron of Raphael and Michelangelo.

ALFONSO V (1385-1458): "the Magnanimous"; son of Ferdinand I; king of Aragón, Naples, and Sicily 1416-58; patron of Renaissance culture.

ALFONSO DE ARAGÓN (1470-1520): son of Ferdinand the Catholic and maternal grandfather of Francis Borgia; archbishop of Zaragoza; preoccupied with reform; convoked regular diocesan synods.

ALVAREZ, BALTASAR, S.J. (1533-1580): early Jesuit writer on prayer; became a Jesuit in 1555; spiritual director of St. Teresa of Avila; assisted her in the reform of the Carmelites.

ALVAREZ, JUAN, DE TOLEDO (1488-1557): Dominican, named bishop of Córdoba 1537 and later a cardinal; assisted with the reforms of Trent.

ANNE OF AUSTRIA (1549-1580): daughter of Emperor Maximilian II; became fourth wife of Philip II of Spain 1570; mother of the heir Philip III.

AQUAVIVA, CLAUDIO, S.J. (1543-1615): entered Society 1567; fifth general of the Society 1581-1615, longest term of office as general; witnessed a time of expansion of the Society and a great demand for its services.

AQUINAS, ST. THOMAS, O.P (1225-1274): scholastic philosopher and theologian; known as the Angelic Doctor; author of system of Catholic theology and philosophy now known as Thomism.

---

*Prepared by Michael P. Caruso, S.J.

ARAOZ, ANTONIO, S.J. (1516-1573): one of the earliest Jesuits; relative of Ignatius; first provincial of Spain, and then of Castile.

ARCHINTO, FILIPPO (1500-1558): bishop; born in Milan; served Pope Paul III at Rome as governor; presiding officer at Trent; friend and loyal advocate of St. Ignatius; provided imprimatur for the first printing of the *Spiritual Exercises*.

AUGER, EDMOND, S.J. (1530-1591): born in Troyes, France; became a Jesuit; preached effectively against the Huguenots, converting thousands; founded college at Lyon; confessor and military chaplain to King Henry III; author and educator.

AZEVEDO, BL. IGNATIUS DE, S.J. (1539?-1600): born at Oporto, Portugal; became a Jesuit 1548; sent to Brazil as visitor of the missions; Borgia sent him back to Brazil as provincial; murdered, with thirty-nine missionaries, by Huguenot sailors.

AZPILCUETA, DR. MARTÍN (1492-1586): professor at the university of Coimbra; known for his piety and humility.

BACCIO, D'AGNOLO, byname of BARTOLOMEO D'AGNOLO BAGLIONI (1462-1543): Florentine woodcarver, sculptor, and architect who exerted an important influence on the Renaissance architecture of Florence; his studio was frequented by Michelangelo, Raphael, and other notable artists of the day.

BARBAROSSA II, KHAIR ED-DIN (1466?-1546): leader of the pirates who controlled the Mediterranean; evacuated thousands of Moors driven from Spain by the Inquisition; defeated by campaign of Charles V, under the leadership of Andrea Doria, 1535.

BELLARMINE, ST. ROBERT, S.J. (1542-1621): born in Tuscany; nephew of Pope Marcellus II; entered Jesuits 1560; notable theologian, author of polemical and spiritual works; aided the revision of the Vulgate 1591; rector of Roman College 1592; created cardinal 1599; involved in Galileo case; articulate champion of papal supremacy; canonized 1930; declared a Doctor of the Church 1931.

BOBADILLA, NICOLÁS DE, S.J. (1511-1590): born in Valencia; original member of the Society; he and Ignatius were constant thorns in one another's sides; chaplain in army of Charles V; wrote in defense of Trent.

BONELLI, CARDINAL MICHELE (1541-1598): entered the Dominicans 1560; made a cardinal by Pius V; his tomb is a magnificent work by Bernini.

BORGIA, CESARE (1476-1515): son of Alexander VI and Vannozza Catanei; notorious and treacherous leader favorably characterized by Machiavelli in his work *The Prince*.

BORGIA, JOFRÉ (1481/82-1506): last son born of Alexander VI and Vannozza Catanei.

BORGIA, LUCREZIA (1480-1519): daughter of Alexander VI and Vannozza Catanei; given in marriage three times by her father for dynastic reasons; third marriage to Alfonso d'Este, heir and duke of Ferrara; devoted later life to education and charity.

BORJA, ALFONSO DE: see Calixtus III.

BORJA, brothers and sisters of Francis Borgia: ALFONSO became the acclaimed abbot of Valldigna; ENRIQUE became cardinal in 1539; appointed bishop of Squillace; MARÍA, ANA, and ISABEL became Poor Clares; LUISA married Count Martín de Aragón y de Gurrea.

BORJA, JUAN (1478-1497): son of Alexander VI and Vannozza Catanei; second Duke of Gandía; grandfather of St. Francis Borgia; the circumstantial evidence of his unsolved murder pointed to his brother Cesare as the chief suspect.

BORJA, PEDRO LUIS (1468-1488): first Borgia to become Duke of Gandía; son of Alexander VI; mother unknown.

BORJA, RODRIGO: see Alexander VI.

BORJA Y DE CASTRO-PINÓS: half brothers of Francis Borgia from his father's second marriage to Francisca Castro de So y de Pinós): RODRIGO was baron of Navarres, and created cardinal in 1536; PEDRO LUIS GALCERÁN became grand master of the Montesa military order; DIEGO was executed by Philip II for the murder of Diego of Aragón; FELIPE was exiled from Spain as an accomplice of his brother Diego and became governor of Messina, Sicily.

BORROMEO, ST. CHARLES (1538-1584): son of Margaret de' Medici and Count Gilbert Borromeo; nephew of Pius IV; created cardinal and archbishop of Milan, 1560; towering figure of the Catholic Reformation; noted for his work on the catechism of Trent, revision of the missal and breviary, and reform of the clergy.

BOURBON, CARDINAL CHARLES DE (1523-1590): uncle of Henry IV; archbishop of Rouen and cardinal; Catholic leader; proclaimed king as Charles X by the Guises 1589; died soon after their defeat by Henry IV.

BROËT, PASCHASE, S.J. (1500-1562): born in France; one of the original Jesuits; sent on first papal mission to help reform a monastery of Benedictine nuns in Siena 1538; first provincial of France 1555.

BUSTAMANTE, BARTOLOMÉ, S.J. (?-1570): known as an unbending superior who created many problems by his severity; before becoming a Jesuit he served as secretary to Cardinal Tavera of Toledo.

CALVIN, JOHN (1509-1564): French theologian and convert to the tenets of the Protestant reformation; established a theocratic government in Geneva; organized body of doctrine known as Calvinism, presented in one of the most influential Protestant works, the *Institutes*.

CALIXTUS III (1378-1458): born Alfonso Borja; pope 1455-58; uncle of Alexander VI; launched unsuccessful crusade against the Turks; reopened the trial of Joan of Arc, clearing her name.

CANISIUS, ST. PETER, S.J. (1521-1597): born in Nijmegen, Holland; entered the Jesuits 1543; influential in re-establishing Roman Catholicism in parts of Germany and

Poland; prepared an influential catechism; canonized and declared a Doctor of the Church in 1925.

CANO, MELCHIOR, O.P. (1509-1560): theologian; became a Dominican 1524; attended the Council of Trent; indefatigable adversary of the Jesuits.

CARLOS, PRINCE DON (1545-1568): eldest son of Maria of Portugal and Philip II; his betrothal to Elizabeth of Valois, daughter of Henry II of France, was suddenly annulled, and Philip II married her himself; Don Carlos was imprisoned for plotting against his father's life.

CARRANZA, BARTOLOMÉ, O.P. (1503-1576): imperial theologian at Trent 1545-47; archbishop of Toledo 1558; imprisoned by Inquisition on suspicion of heresy; abjured questionable statements attributed to him.

CASTRO, LEONOR DE (d. 1546): wife of Francis Borgia.

CATANEI, VANNOZZA, (1442-1518): mistress of Cardinal Rodrigo Borgia (Alexander VI); mother of a disputed number of his children; legitimately married twice.

CATHERINE (1507-1562): daughter of Juana la Loca and Philip I; caretaker of her mother; married John III of Portugal.

CHABOT, PHILIPPE DE (1480-1543): led delegation to negotiate ratification of the Treaty of Cambrai by Charles V; commander of troops fighting the Duke of Savoy 1535.

CHARLES III (1716-1788): also known as Don Carlos of Bourbon; king of Spain 1759-1788; strengthened kingdom by reforming finances; aided agriculture and commerce; expelled Jesuits in 1767.

CHARLES V (1500-1558): son of Philip I of Spain; grandson of Ferdinand and Isabella; king of Spain, Holy Roman Emperor 1519-56; married Isabel of Portugal 1525; tolerant of Protestants in Germany; great friend and admirer of Francis Borgia; abdicated and retired to the monastery of Yuste in western Spain 1556.

CHARLES VII (1403-1461): began reign in 1422 with much of France in English possession; king at time of Joan of Arc; reign marked by reforms, recovery of lands, and increased royal authority in France.

CHARLES IX (1550-1574): second son of Henry II and Catherine de' Medici; king of France 1560-74; his reign was dominated by his mother and marked by fierce civil wars between Catholics and Huguenots.

CHRISTINE OF DENMARK (1521-1590): niece of Charles V; successively married Francesco Sforza, duke of Milan, and François, duke of Lorraine.

CLEMENT VII (1478-1534): born Giulio de' Medici; elected pope 1523-34; entered Holy League with France against Charles V; suffered sack of Rome in 1527; made peace with Charles and crowned him emperor in 1530; denied approval of divorce of Henry VIII from Catherine of Aragón 1534.

CLEMENT VIII (1536-1605): Ippolito Aldobrandini, born at Fano, Italy; pope 1592-1605; ordered revisions of the Vulgate, breviary, and other liturgical books; absorbed in dispute between the Dominicans and Jesuits on the question of grace.

CLEMENT X (1590-1676): Emilio Altieri, born in Rome of a noble family; became a cardinal in 1669; pope 1670; sought to preserve peace in Europe; canonized many saints, including Francis Borgia.

CLEMENT XIV (1705-1774): Giovanni Ganganelli, born at Sant'Angelo, Italy; became a Franciscan in 1724; pope 1769-1774; labored to pacify the crowned heads; capitulated to secular powers and issued the apostolic brief suppressing the Jesuits in 1773; his pontificate was afflicted with much bitterness and strife.

COGORDAN, PONCE, S.J. (1502-1582): loyal companion of Nicolás de Bobadilla, sharing the same sentiments and opinions about the Society of Jesus.

COLLETTE OF CORBIE, ST. (1381-1447): sought to restore the rule of the Poor Clares to its pristine austerity; met much opposition but was approved by the Avignon Pope Benedict XIII; she founded seventeen convents.

COLONNA, MARCANTONIO (1535-1584): duke of Paliano; exiled from Rome by Pius IV; entered Spanish military, defeating the Papal States 1556; was recalled and successfully commanded the papal fleet at Lepanto 1571.

CORDESES, ANTONIO, S.J. (1518-1601): spiritual writer; entered the Society 1545; assisted Borgia, Mercurian, and Aquaviva.

DOMÉNECH, JUAN JERÓNIMO, S.J. (1516-1592): born at Valencia, entered Society, where he held many high posts; founded the college at Valencia.

DORIA, ANDREA (1468-1560): successful admiral; commanded the French fleet against Charles V; transferred allegiance to Charles V in 1528; established safety in the Mediterranean from pirates and Turks.

ESTE II, ERCOLE D' (1508-1559): son of Lucrezia Borgia; patron of the arts; married Renée, daughter of Louis XII of France.

ESTE II, IPPOLITO D' (1509-1572): cardinal archbishop of Milan; built Villa d'Este at Tivoli.

ESTRADA, FRANCISCO, S.J. (1518-1584): entered Society under St. Ignatius 1538; contemporary of Francis Borgia; noted preacher.

FAVRE (FABER), BLESSED PIERRE, S.J. (1506-1546): born in Villaret, Savoy; met Ignatius Loyola and Francis Xavier in Paris; one of the original Jesuits; ordained priest in 1534; helped spread the early Jesuit order in northern Europe.

FARNESE, ALESSANDRO (1520-1589): born at Parma, Italy; named cardinal-deacon 1534; became bishop of Monreale, Sicily, 1536; solicitous of the poor; patron of the arts; patron of the Society; benefactor of the Gesù in Rome; vigorous in further-ing the Tridentine reforms.

FERDINAND I (1503-1564): younger brother of Charles V; elected king of the Germans 1531; Holy Roman Emperor 1556-64; failed to resolve religious strife.

FERDINAND II ("THE CATHOLIC") OF ARAGÓN (1452-1516): married Isabella of Castile 1469; joint sovereigns 1474-1504 uniting Aragón and Castile; expelled Jews 1492; assisted Christopher Columbus.

FERRER, ST. VINCENT (1350-1419): Spanish Dominican; renowned as a preacher and effective in motivating people to conversion; advisor to King John of Aragón; canonized in 1445.

FISHER, ST. JOHN, 1469-1535): born at Beverley, Yorkshire; distinguished scholar at Cambridge; ordained priest 1490; became chancellor and bishop 1504; defended the validity of Henry VIII's marriage to Catherine of Aragón; beheaded for high treason 1535; canonized by Pius XI 1935.

FRANCIS I (1494-1547): Born in Cognac, France; crushed power of nobles and bishops; fought four wars against Charles V; undermined the concept of Christendom; patron of arts and the humanist movement.

GAGLIARDI, ACHILLE, S.J. (1537-1607): born in Padua; became a Jesuit in 1559; pro-found spiritual theologian; wrote earliest commentary on the Spiritual Exercises.

GERMAINE DE FOIX (1488-1538): queen of Aragón and Naples; second wife of her great-uncle Ferdinand II; her only son died in infancy leaving Charles V as the only heir to the Spanish throne.

GHISLIERI, MICHELE: see: Pius V, St.

GONÇALVES DA CÂMARA, LUIS, S.J. (1520-1575): early Portuguese Jesuit; superior of the Roman house; it was to him that St. Ignatius of Loyola dictated his autobio-graphical memoirs; later tutor to the Portuguese prince, Don Sebastian.

GREGORY XIII (1502-1585): Ugo Buoncompagni, born at Bologna; held responsible positions under Paul III and Pius IV; pope 1572-1585; stabilized Catholicism in defecting areas; great benefactor of Gregorian University named after him; reformed the Julian calendar 1578.

GONZAGA, ERCOLE (1505-1563): born at Mantua, Italy; made cardinal 1527; estab-lished diocesan seminary at Mantua; zealous reformer; legate at the Council of Trent.

GONZÁLEZ DÁVILA, GIL, S.J. (1578-1658): born in Avila; provincial in Castile, Toledo, and Aragón.

GREGORY XV (1554-1623): Alessandro Ludovisi, born in Bologna; became cardinal in 1616; established current precepts of papal elections; founded the Congregation for the Propagation of the Faith; canonized St. Francis Xavier and St. Ignatius of Loyola.

GUZMÁN, TOMÁS DE, O.P.: Dominican provincial, resource to Francis Borgia.

HENRY II (1519-1559): king of France 1547-1559; of the house of Valois; second son of Francis I; died of a wound received in a tournament; three of his seven children became kings of France.

HENRY OF NAVARRE (1553-1610): first of the Bourbon line; king of France 1589-1610 as Henry IV; raised as a Calvinist; married Marguerite of Valois, the sister of Charles IX; embraced Catholicism 1593; assassinated.

HOFFAEUS, PAULUS, S.J. (1525-1608): born in Germany; one of the first students of German College in Rome; Jesuit in 1555; rector at Prague, Ingolstadt, and Munich; provincial of Upper Germany; German assistant.

HOSIUS, STANISLAUS (1504-1579): Polish prelate; made a cardinal 1561; tireless opponent of the Protestant Reformation; introduced Society of Jesus into Poland 1565; spent his last ten years in Rome as a papal advisor and then as the voice of Poland.

ISABEL, EMPRESS (1503-1539): born in Lisbon; daughter of Manuel, king of Portugal; married Holy Roman Emperor Charles V 1525; mother of Philip II of Spain; dear friend of Francis Borgia.

JAMES I (1208-1276): king of Aragon 1213; married Leonor of Castile, but divorced and remarried Yolande of Hungary; overcame national anarchy after his father's death, and became known as "the Conqueror."

JAY, CLAUDE, S.J. (1504-1552): one of the original Jesuits; friend of Pierre Favre; effective confessor; acclaimed professor at Ingolstadt; lobbied for education as the primary apostolate in Germany.

JOHN III (1502-1557): born at Lisbon; son of Manuel; married Catherine, sister of Charles V; king of Portugal 1521-1557; during his reign the power of Portugal began to decline.

JOHN OF AVILA, ST. (1500-1569): born in Spain; became a priest; renowned reforming preacher; supportive of early Society of Jesus in Spain; influence on Sts. Teresa of Avila, John of God, Francis Borgia.

JUAN DE ARAGÓN (1492-1530): archbishop of Zaragoza; temporary guardian of Francis and Luisa Borgia; he was their maternal uncle.

JUANA DE ARAGÓN (1502-1575): duchess of Tagliacozzo; wife of Ascanio Colonna and mother of Marcantonio Colonna.

JUANA "LA LOCA," QUEEN (1479-1555): daughter of Ferdinand II and Isabella; married Philip I of Spain, archduke of Austria; mother of Charles V; abandoned by Philip 1501-1503 and driven mad by his death 1506.

JUANA, PRINCESS ((1535-1573): daughter of Charles V; married João Manuel of Portugal; mother of King Sebastian; after husband's death pronounced vows as a Franciscan; vows commuted to vows as a scholastic in the Society under the alias "Mateo Sánchez."

JULIUS III (1487-1555): Giovanni Maria Ciocchi del Monte, born in Rome; became pope 1550; battled with Charles V; issued bull *Exposcit debitum*, containing the revised Formula of the Institute, which confirmed and expanded the purpose of the Society of Jesus 1550.

KOSTKA, ST. STANISLAUS (1550-1568): born in Rostkovo, Poland; attended the Jesuit college at Vienna; against his father's wishes but with the counsel of St. Peter Canisius, he entered the Jesuits in Rome in 1567; died less than a year later, but had impressed all by his innocence and humility; canonized 1726.

LAÍNEZ, DIEGO, S.J. (1512-1565): born in Castile; one of the original companions of Ignatius in Paris; indispensable theologian at Trent; second general of the Society.

LANOY, NICHOLAS, S.J. (1507-1581): entered the Society in Rome 1548; rector at Vienna and Ingolstadt; provincial of Austria.

LEDESMA, DIEGO, S.J. (1519-1575): prefect of studies at the Roman College, published a popular catechism entitled *Christian Doctrine*; Jesuit educational theorist; greatly responsible for work on Ratio Studiorum.

LEUNIS, JEAN, S.J. (1535-1584): founder, at the Roman College, of the first Marian congregation, or sodality.

LOUIS II OF HUNGARY (1506-1526): king 1516-1526; in 1522 married Mary of Hungary, also known as Mary of Burgundy, who later became regent of the Netherlands, 1531-1552; he died at the battle of Mohács, with Hungary then passing to the Hapsburgs.

LUTHER, MARTIN (1483-1546): father of the Protestant Reformation; Augustinian friar; ordained a priest 1507; his ninety-five theses of 1517 challenged the Catholic Church's teaching on salvation and indulgences; author of great German translation of Bible.

MADRID, CRISTÓBAL DE, S.J. (1503-1573): born in Spain; entered Jesuits in 1550; longtime superior at the Jesuit curia; proponent of frequent Communion.

MAFFEI, CARDINAL BERNARDINO (1514-1549): born in Bergamo, Italy; secretary to Cardinal Alessandro Farnese, who became Pope Paul III; composed commentary on Cicero's letters.

MAGGIO, LORENZO, S.J. (c. 1532-1605): member of the court of Pope Julius III; entered Society 1555; rector of several colleges; provincial of Austria; Italian assistant; visitor of France and Germany.

MALDONADO, JUAN DE, S.J. (1533-1583): Spanish Jesuit; theologian; entered Society 1562; taught at Paris; author of Gospel commentaries; commissioned by Gregory XIII to make a new edition of the Septuagint.

MANNAERTS, OLIVIER, S.J. (1523-1614): entered Society 1550; first rector of Roman College 1554; first provincial of France 1564; later assistant in Rome and provincial of Belgium; recovered apostates, and converted Huguenots in large numbers.

MARCELLUS II (1501-1555): Marcello Cervini, born in Tuscany; became bishop in 1538 and a cardinal in 1539; instituted sweeping reforms in two sees; elected pope April 9, 1555, and died three weeks later on May 1; Palestrina's *Missa Papae Marcelli* was dedicated to him.

MARGUERITE OF VALOIS (1553-1615): daughter of Henry II and Catherine de' Medici; noted for her beauty and learning; in 1572 married Henry of Navarre, later Henry IV of France.

MARTIN V (1368-1431): born Ottone Colonna; elected pope 1417-1431 at the Council of Constance, ending the Western Schism, and bringing peace to the Church.

MARY OF BURGUNDY (1505-1558): also known as Mary of Hungary; sister of Charles V; queen of Hungary 1522-1526; regent of the Netherlands, 1531-1552.

MASCARENHAS, LEONOR (1503-1584): lady in waiting to the empress Isabel; early benefactress of the Jesuits.

MAXIMILIAN I (1459-1519): son of Frederick III; Holy Roman Emperor 1493-1519; father of Philip I of Spain; authored a book on hunting and several volumes of an autobiography.

MAXIMILIAN II (1527-1576): archduke of Austria; king of Hungary and Bohemia; Holy Roman Emperor 1564-1576; son of Ferdinand I; tolerant of Protestants in Germany.

MEDICI CATHERINE DE' (1519-1589): born in Florence; married Henry II of France; meddled in the reigns of her sons Francis II, Charles IX, and Henry III; instigated conflicts between Catholics and Huguenots, siding with either at different times; architect of the St. Bartholomew's Day Massacre, 1572.

MEDICI, COSIMO I DE' (1519-1574): known as "Cosimo the Great"; Grand Duke of Tuscany; ally of Charles V; patron of arts and archaeology.

MENDOZA Y BOBADILLA, FRANCISCO (1508-1566): cardinal; friend of St. Ignatius and patron of the Society; wrote on Christology.

MERCURIAN, EVERARD, S.J. (1514-1580): born in Marcour, Luxembourg; became a Jesuit in 1548; fourth general of the Society, and first non-Spaniard to hold this post; completed a summary of the Constitutions; established Maronite and English missions; approximately 5000 Jesuits at the time of his death.

MONTMORENCY, HENRI I, DUC DE (1534-1614): leader of the moderate Catholic *politiques* during the French wars of religion; administered Languedoc independently of Paris; 1593 acknowledged Henry IV as king and was rewarded with the office of constable.

MORE, ST. THOMAS (1478-1535): English statesman; leader in humanist and Renaissance thought; succeeded Wolsey as chancellor; refused to recognize Henry VIII's supremacy over the Church in England or his divorce from Catherine of Aragón; executed 1535; canonized 1935.

MORO, ANTONIO (1512?-1576): Flemish portrait painter; invited to Madrid by Charles V; sent to England to paint a portrait of Mary Tudor for Philip II.

NADAL, JERÓNIMO, S.J. (1507-1580): native of Majorca; after theological studies at Paris and Avignon entered Society at Rome in 1545; close collaborator of St. Ignatius and commissioned by him to present the Society's newly written Constitutions to the Jesuits in Spain, Portugal, and Italy.

NICHOLAS V (1397-1455): born Tommaso Parentucelli; pope 1447-1455; removed last anti-pope; patron of Renaissance art; unsuccessfully tried to launch a crusade.

NIEREMBERG, JUAN EUSEBIO, S.J. (1595-1658): born in Madrid of German parents; joined the Jesuits 1614; author of fifty-six titles covering a wide range of subjects; naturalist, the genus *Nierembergia* is named for him.

OÑAZ Y LOYOLA, BELTRÁN DE (d. 1549): nephew of St. Ignatius; his daughter Lorenza signed a marriage contact with Juan Borja, son of Francis.

OVIEDO, ANDRÉS DE, S.J. (1518-1577): named coadjutor bishop in Ethiopia, 1555; unsuccessfully pursued the conversion of the Monophysites.

PACHECO, PEDRO (1488-1560): cardinal; involved in the affairs of Church and state; assisted with Trent.

PALMIO, BENEDETTO, S.J. (1523-1598): born at Parma; provincial of Lombardy; preached at the Mass before the election of Francis Borgia as the third general of the Society.

PASQUIER, ÉTIENNE (1529-1615): French jurist; advocate general at Paris Chambre des Comptes 1585; author; opponent of the Jesuits.

PHILIP I, "THE HANDSOME" (1478-1506): son of Emperor Maximilian I and Mary of Burgundy; married Juana la Loca; father of Charles V and Ferdinand I.

PHILIP II (1527-1598): son of Charles V and Isabel of Portugal; pious, sincere, and inflexible; he was consumed with the restoration of Catholicism in the Low Countries and England; patron of the arts; married four times: Maria of Portugal (1543), Mary I of England, daughter of Henry VIII (1554), Elizabeth of Valois, daughter of Henry II of France (1560), and Anna, daughter of Emperor Maximilian II (1570).

PHILIP III (1578-1621): son of Philip II; inherited a country of declining power; uninterested in government concerns, leaving them to the duke of Lerma; relished court festivities; issued the final expulsion of the Moriscos 1609.

PIUS IV (1499-1565): born Giovanni de' Medici (no relation to the famous Florentine family); elected pope 1559; appointed his nephew Charles Borromeo secretary of state; patron of the arts; under him the Council of Trent was reconvened and brought to a successful conclusion.

PIUS V, ST. (1504-1572): Michele Ghislieri was born in Switzerland; Dominican; elected pope 1566; zealously implemented the reforms of Trent; responsible for Tridentine missal, breviary, and catechism; canonized in 1712.

POLANCO, JUAN ALFONSO DE, S.J. (1516-1576): born in Burgos; entered the Society 1544; he was Ignatius of Loyola's indispensable secretary; first historian of the Society.

POSSEVINO, ANTONIO, S.J. (1534-1611): joined the Jesuits 1559; acclaimed preacher in France and Italy; prolific author; papal ambassador in Germany, Hungary, Sweden, Poland, and Russia.

PUENTE, LUIS DE LA, S.J. (1554-1624): entered the Society 1575; skilled theologian who combined piety and scholarly precision in his spiritual writings.

QUIROGA, CARDINAL GASPAR DE (1500 or 1512-1594): published 1583 edition of the Index of Forbidden Books; inquisitor general.

RECALDE, JUANA DE: widow of Ignatius's nephew Beltrán de Oñaz y Loyola; her daughter Lorenza married Juan Borgia.

RIBADENEIRA, PEDRO DE, S.J. (1526-1611): born in Toledo, Spain; became a Jesuit in 1540; wrote in defense of Mary Tudor; held several leadership positions within the Society; wrote a very popular biography of Ignatius.

RODRIGUES, SIMÃO, S.J. (1510-1579): early companion of Ignatius and original member of the Society; founder and provincial of the Society in Portugal.

ROSE OF LIMA, ST. (1586-1617): born in Lima, Peru; became a Dominican, recognized as a holy mystic; first American-born saint, patron of the New World; canonized in 1671 along with Francis Borgia.

ROSER, ISABEL (d. 1554): early benefactor of St. Ignatius; by order of the pope, Ignatius received her vows as a Jesuit in 1545, along with those of two other women; many problems necessitated their release from the vows; her stormy relationship with Ignatius was amicably resolved.

Sá, Manuel de, S.J. (1530-1596): born in Portugal; became a Jesuit 1545; taught Francis Borgia at Gandía; involved with preparation of the new edition of the Septuagint.

Sacchini, Francesco (1570-1625): historian of the Society.

Salmerón, Alfonso, S.J. (1515-1585): born at Toledo, Spain; one of the original companions of Ignatius in Paris; theologian of Paul III at Trent; helped Ignatius draft the Constitutions; first provincial of Naples; composed sixteen-volume Scripture commentary.

Sánchez, Mateo: see Juana, Princess.

Sebastian (1554-1578): king of Portugal 1557-1578; son of Don João Manuel and Princess Juana; educated by Jesuits; died on disastrous expedition in Morocco.

Soto, Domingo de (1494-1560): born in Segovia, Spain; a leader of the moderate realists in the dispute with nominalists; became a Dominican 1524; imperial theologian at Trent; confessor of Charles V, 1547; author.

Suleiman I (1496-1566): Turkish ruler known as "the Magnificent"; added to his territories Belgrade, Budapest, Algiers; organized the *ulema*, or clerical class in hierarchical order; improved administration of country; encouraged arts and sciences.

Tavera, Cardinal Juan de (d. 1545): born in Spain; served at court; founded the general hospital outside Toledo; archbishop of Toledo 1534.

Teresa of Avila, St. (1515-1582): made profession as a Carmelite in 1537; practical, known for her sense of humor; founded reformed (discalced) Carmelites; author of profound spiritual writings; canonized 1622; named "Doctor of the Church" by Paul VI in 1970.

Titian (Tiziano Vecelli, 1477-1576): chief master of Venetian school of painting; court painter to Charles V and Philip II; one of greatest portraitists and painters of religious and mythological themes.

Toledo, Fray Juan de: archbishop of Burgos; president of the entourage accompanying the body of Empress Isabel to her tomb.

Truchsess, Otto von Waldburg (1514-1573): born in Swabia; earned a doctorate in theology; made cardinal 1544; initiated sweeping reforms as archbishop of Augsburg; established a university and seminary at Dillingen; head of the Roman Inquisition 1555.

URBAN VIII (1568-1644): Maffeo Barberini; held many high offices in the Church; pope 1623-1644; patron of foreign missions; beatified Francis Borgia 1624.

VEGA, GARCILASO DE LA (1503-1536): Spanish poet and soldier; fought under Charles V; killed in battle.

VEGA, LOPE DE (1562-1635): Spanish poet; founder of the Spanish national drama; served in Spanish Armada 1588; ordained a priest after the death of his second wife 1614.

VELÁSQUEZ DE CUÉLLAR, COUNT JUAN (d. 1517): chief treasurer of the royal court; Ignatius of Loyola served and was educated in his household; fell from Ferdinand's favor.

VITELLESCHI, MUZIO, S.J. (1563-1645): born in Rome; joined Jesuits 1583; served as provincial at Rome and Naples; elected general 1615; extended missionary activities of the Society; established English mission as a province.

XAVIER, ST. FRANCIS, S.J. (1506-1552): born in the Basque area; one of the original companions of Ignatius in Paris; renowned for his missionary work in the Far East; proclaimed patron of the foreign missions; canonized with St. Ignatius in 1622.

R